C000154096

STRATEGY IN ACTION

STRATEGY IN ACTION

John L. Thompson

Head of Management Strategy

University of Huddersfield

UK

CHAPMAN & HALL
University and Professional Division

London · Glasgow · Weinheim · New York · Tokyo · Melbourne · Madras

Published by Chapman & Hall, 2–6 Boundary Row, London SE1 8HN, UK

Chapman & Hall, 2–6 Boundary Row, London SE1 8HN, UK

Blackie Academic & Professional, Wester Cleddens Road, Bishopbriggs, Glasgow G64 2NZ, UK

Chapman & Hall GmbH, Pappelallee 3, 69469 Weinheim, Germany

Chapman & Hall USA, One Penn Plaza, 41st Floor, New York NY 10119, USA

Chapman & Hall Japan, ITP-Japan, Kyowa Building, 3F, 2–2–1 Hirakawacho, Chiyoda-ku, Tokyo 102, Japan

Chapman & Hall Australia, Thomas Nelson Australia, 102 Dodds Street, South Melbourne, Victoria 3205, Australia

Chapman & Hall India, R. Seshadri, 32 Second Main Road, CIT East, Madras 600 035, India

First edition 1995

© 1995 John L. Thompson

Typeset in Usherwood and Eurostile by Fox Design, Bramley, Surrey
Printed in Great Britain by The Alden Press, Osney Mead, Oxford

ISBN 0 412 62340 4

Apart from any fair dealing for the purposes of research or private study, or criticism or review, as permitted under the UK Copyright Designs and Patents Act, 1988, this publication may not be reproduced, stored, or transmitted, in any form or by any means, without the prior permission in writing of the publishers, or in the case of reprographic reproduction only in accordance with the terms of the licences issued by the Copyright Licensing Agency in the UK, or in accordance with the terms of licences issued by the appropriate Reproduction Rights Organization outside the UK. Enquiries concerning reproduction outside the terms stated here should be sent to the publishers at the London address printed on this page.

The publisher makes no representation, express or implied, with regard to the accuracy of the information contained in this book and cannot accept any legal responsibility or liability for any errors or omissions that may be made.

A catalogue record for this book is available from the British Library

♾ Printed on permanent acid-free paper, manufactured in accordance with ANSI/NISO Z39.48-1992 and ANSI/NISO Z39.48-1984 (Permanence of Paper).

CONTENTS

FOREWORD

SIR COLIN MARSHALL

CHAIRMAN, BRITISH AIRWAYS

Before a British Airways aircraft departs Heathrow, or any other airport on the network, the flight crew will have been briefed on conditions en route – prevailing winds, areas of known turbulence – and on conditions for landing at the destination. In the light of this information, the Captain will select the most efficient routing and the optimum flight levels. Once airborne, programmed navigation systems will keep the aircraft on track. Radar and radio contact with the ground will warn of potential hazards. Sufficient fuel will have been loaded to cope effortlessly with diversions, should problems occur at the intended destination airport. Such strategic planning and action goes, as a matter of everyday course, into the almost 300 000 individual flights which British Airways operates in an average year. The running of air transport services seems, therefore, to form an obvious analogy with the commercial 'navigation' of business in general.

Business development is, on the face of it, a journey into the unknown. The crystal ball which tells us precisely how markets will react to new products, how competitors will respond, when economic cycles will dip and rise, how political effects might come to bear, has not yet been invented. We do, however, possess the means to draw a fairly accurate map and chart a safe, efficient course. Economic and marketing research facilities may not be inexpensive, but they are as essential to progressive business as meteorological forecasting and navigational aids are to aviation. So too are leaders, or commanders, competent and confident enough to take a firm grip on the corporate rudder to steer an organization firmly towards its strategic destination, and able to re-trim and change tack according to conditions encountered on the way.

There cannot, however, be any kind of journey without a destination. To travel aimlessly is simply to meander. Leadership's most important role is, therefore, to identify firmly the desired point of arrival or, in other words, the strategic objective. Those two words may flow easily from the pen, but they represent the very essence of commercial endeavour: the decisions on core product or service; the level of both quality and cost efficiency required for competitive production; marketing strategies; and the prescription for vital financial performance targets.

Contemporary changes taking place in the world trading economy, most notably the moves towards open markets and free commerce, are shifting the geography of trade. Cross-border trade is now growing faster than domestic commerce. New trade routes are becoming available and traditional ones obscured, as centres of manufacturing move from one part of the world to another and, in turn, the global consumer market takes on a different shape and scope. Above all, competition is becoming more and more intense. The successful companies of the 21st Century will be those that are able to interpret the long-term effect of change for their business, with carefully-honed strategic objectives and supporting programmes of action which identify and deliver the optimum benefits. They will also be the ones which recognize that the according adjustments to structures and processes they need to make are unlikely to be one-off arrangements. Change must be seen as a continuous process if the momentum of business development is to be at least maintained and at best accelerated.

With his book *Strategy in Action*, John Thompson articulates these lessons, by relating text-book theory to practical, market-place example through the fictional but, nevertheless, entirely plausible experience of the 'Special Components' company. The book, presented in a novel, documentary style, does not attempt to plot a universal strategic route. Rather, it provides a valuable demonstration of the art of navigating the course of change and development.

It is commended to working managers and students of management at every level.

PREFACE

David Marshall is a strategy maker with two important challenges. As marketing manager of Special Components – a small subsidiary of a diverse international conglomerate – he becomes involved in the implementation of a merger when the parent company, Universal Engineering, buys up a struggling competitor.

Meanwhile, a major German customer is complaining about the quality of a new product ... and the management team in Special Components does not function as a co-ordinated team. Under pressure from his managing director, Bob Langley, to produce results, David turns for help to an old friend ... Tony Anderson, a successful management consultant, helps David and Bob to understand better and deal with the important strategic issues which affect the competitive success of their business – and many others – in the 1990s.

With an original blend of this fictional storyline and text covering the major themes of strategic management, *Strategy in Action* provides a useful introduction to the subject for both practising managers – in any organization – and students of strategy.

The book explains:

- **corporate strategy** – how companies arrive at a particular portfolio of products and services, diversified or focused, national or international;
- **competitive strategy** – the search for sustainable competitive advantage;
- **strategic control** – the management of organizations; and
- **strategic change**

I believe the single most important contribution to competitiveness is the ability of managers and management to think strategically about the business or businesses they are in (Sir Trevor Holdsworth, when Group Chairman, Guest Keen and Nettlefolds (GKN) plc)

Strategy in Action shows how all managers can be strategy-makers through their contributions to both strategy creation and strategy implementation.

ORIGIN

This book is based on my observations of how companies make strategic decisions and attempt to deal with the various challenges they face. I have sought to piece together the important theories and concepts which underpin a study of strategic management with these observations and discussions with managers in a variety of different organizations. My intention has been to write a book which will help people understand more clearly how companies actually create and change their strategies, and gain greater awareness and insight into those strategic issues they must deal with if they are to become and remain successful.

I have avoided a standard textbook format in a deliberate attempt to make the subject more practical and hence more meaningful for both practising managers and students.

STRATEGIC MANAGEMENT

Strategic management is a complex and fascinating subject with straightforward underlying principles but no 'right answers'.

Companies succeed if their strategies are appropriate for the circumstances they face, feasible in respect of their resources, skills and capabilities, and desirable to their important stakeholders – those individuals and groups, both internal and external, who have a stake in, and an influence over, the business.

Companies fail when their strategies fail to meet the expectations of these stakeholders or produce outcomes which are undesirable to them.

To succeed long-term, companies must compete effectively and out-perform their rivals in a dynamic, and often turbulent, environment. To accomplish this they must find suitable ways for creating and adding value for their customers. A culture of internal co-operation and customer orientation, together with a willingness to learn, adapt and change, is ideal. Alliances and good working relationships with suppliers, distributors and customers are often critically important as well.

Strategy in Action looks at the various ways in which companies create and implement their strategies – and manage the demands of strategic change pressures.

Some changes are gradual and continuous – emergent in an environment of 'competitive chaos' and uncertainty. On other occasions, some companies must face the need for major discontinuous change – strategic regeneration, or simultaneous changes to strategies, structures and styles of management.

FRAMEWORK

The framework for the book is built around the essential strategic decisions that companies must take when creating and implementing strategies – the **process** of strategic management. These topics form the basic structure for most courses in business policy and strategic management.

Five key themes are introduced in Chapter 2, where it is argued that they comprise the crucial determinants for strategic success in the 1990s. They summarize the essential **content** of effective strategies and strategic management. These themes – adding value; core competencies and strategic capabilities; internal and external linkages (strategic architecture) and synergy; competitive advantage; and strategic regeneration – then permeate through the whole book. The matrix in Chart 1 illustrates how these theme strands are developed in particular chapters.

AUDIENCE FOR THE BOOK

Strategy in Action has been written to explain strategic management – and in particular the important issue of strategic decision-making (including both corporate and competitive strategies) – in an easy-to-read, easy-to-understand style in order to provide:

- an '**interesting read**' for people in business who want to know something about the subject, but who are not inclined to tackle a traditional textbook; and
- at the same time, act as an ideal **introductory text** on the subject for:
1. students whose course will be mainly case study based;
2. students on short duration executive programmes and limited treatment courses, for whom advanced texts are too detailed; and
3. students who are looking for a *taster* before they read a more detailed treatment.

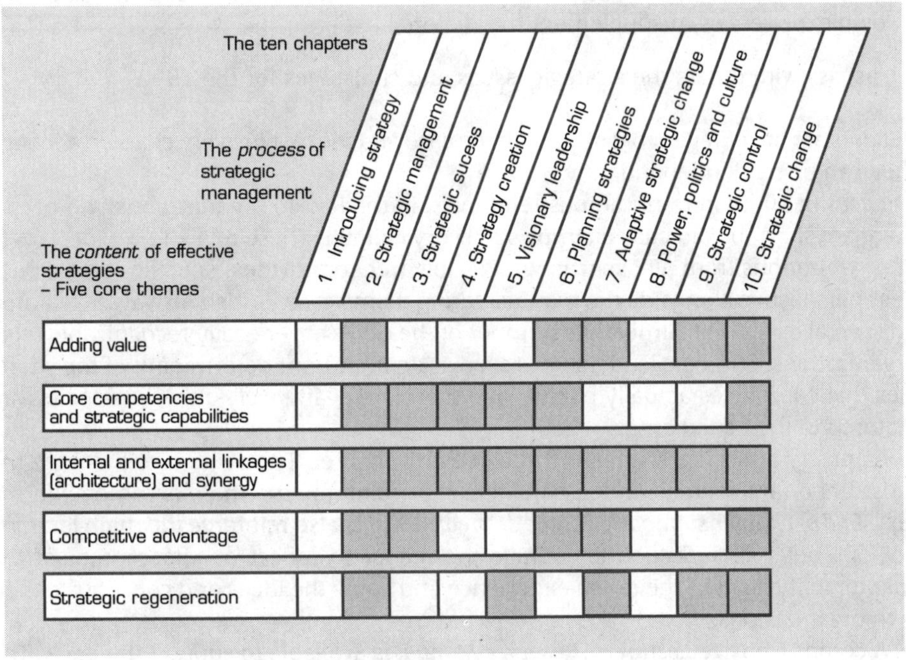

Chart 0.1 Strategy in action

KEY FEATURES

The theme case The Special Components case introduces every chapter; and sometimes there is a continuation of the case at the end of a chapter to lead on to the next one. The case describes an unfolding set of events as managers attempt to deal with two main strategic issues – one, a corporate strategy change in the form of an agreed acquisition, and two, the competitive difficulties arising from the poor quality of a new product. The story is fictional but realistic, and many readers will readily relate to the types of situation.

While the case is set in a small company, which is itself a subsidiary of a large manufacturing organization, the basic themes and issues are equally relevant for service businesses and public-sector organizations. The basic idea is that you, the reader, learn more about strategy alongside the main characters in the case as they increase their awareness and insight.

Organization charts for both the parent company and the subsidiary are included in chapter 1.

The text then develops the theories, concepts and ideas which are introduced in the case and relevant for a study of strategic management. The material is deliberately summarized at the expense of some of the detail which is to be found in longer textbooks on the subject.

The text provides a theoretical underpinning for the issues presented in the case, and together they provide an ideal introduction which will enable readers to:

- think about strategic management in their own organizations, and using their own experiences to supplement the material

- discuss with others the strategic issues and challenges for the 1990s.

Readers are encouraged to look at both the case and the text in every chapter, although they can be read independently.

Cases In addition to numerous references in the text to organizations and events there are short, boxed case examples in every chapter. These relate to a wide variety of organizations from all over the world. However, to provide a specific service business perspective alongside the manufacturing theme case, British Airways is featured on several occasions. Similarly a number of the cases cover easily recognizable retail organizations. Strategic leadership is seen as an important determinant of the strategies that companies actually pursue, and therefore again, well-known strategists are featured in the boxed cases.

Summary boxes are scattered through every chapter. Their role is to highlight the most important themes and lessons and thus reinforce the main arguments in the text. *End of chapter summaries of the strategic lessons* also reinforce the main learning points. *Points for reflection* encourage the reader to reflect on the content of the chapter in the light of their own experience and apply the ideas and concepts to their own organizations.

A comprehensive *Lecturers' Resource Manual* is available to support the book. The manual contains ideas on how to use *Strategy in Action*, cross-references to longer and more detailed texts on strategic management, a variety of full-length cases and OHP transparency masters for the key charts.

ACKNOWLEDGEMENTS

Finally I would like to acknowledge the many unnamed people – friends, colleagues and business contacts – whose experiences, struggles and reflections have been instrumental in the development of this book. I am particularly indebted to Mark Wellings, my editor at Chapman and Hall, for his ideas and support throughout the project, to Frank Martin for his constructive comments during the development of the text and to my wife, Hilary, for her persuasive encouragement.

John L. Thompson
University of Huddersfield

1 INTRODUCING STRATEGY AND STRATEGIC MANAGEMENT

This chapter defines the terms *strategy* and *strategic management* and introduces a number of important themes and ideas which are developed throughout the book.

A CHANGE OF CORPORATE STRATEGY

Universal Engineering is a large conglomerate which operates plants around the world, but is best known in Northern Europe. Most of Universal's products are related through either marketing or technology, but the business is generally described as diversified. Recent growth has mostly been organic (internally generated), and the company invests in research and development at a rate well above the average for British manufacturing industry. There have been several large acquisitions in the past, but Universal has always tended to avoid acrimonious and hostile takeover battles.

Bob Langley, Managing Director of Special Components (UK), a subsidiary of Universal Engineering, had arranged a meeting with five of his senior managers immediately after lunch. It was the first Tuesday in September. Present were Roger Ellis (operations), David Marshall (marketing), Susan Scott (sales), the personnel manager and the company accountant. Langley surprised his colleagues by announcing that Special Components was to acquire a leading competitor, Benson Engineering.

Chart 1.1 shows the organization structure of both Universal Engineering and Special Components.

GROWTH AND DECLINE

Benson's was a family business, but one where the remaining family members were essentially owners without active involvement in the day-to-day decisions. They were near retirement age, with no natural

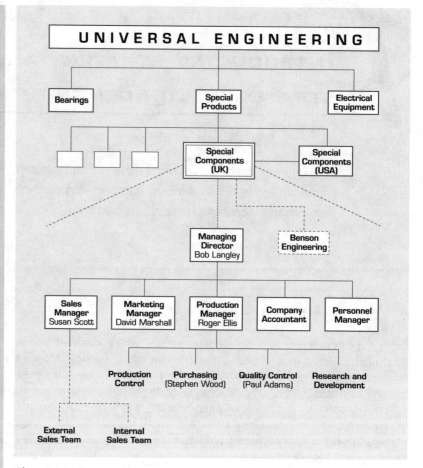

Chart 1.1. The Universal Engineering/Special Components organization structure

successors, and relied on a small team of managers. Benson's suffered badly in the economic recession and was trading at a loss.

Their problems developed gradually over a number of years. The company was started after the Second World War by Graham Benson, an energetic and entrepreneurial engineer. The growth and success derived from just one range of distinctive and high-quality components designed by him. Benson had systematically widened the single range and continually improved the technical specification and quality over a period of 25 years. Although never large, the company came to be recognized as a leading and distinctive competitor in its industry.

Graham's two sons inherited a sound business with an excellent reputation when he died suddenly in the early 1970s. The brothers' real interests were not in engineering, and consequently they were never very active in the company. In recent years their involvement had all but disappeared.

The Benson managers continued to run an efficient business, with sound cost control, which had ensured survival – and acceptable dividends – for a further 20 years. But the entrepreneurial flair of the founder had been lost and never replaced. Profits were not reinvested in the business, and the recent innovation record was poor. Now Benson's was barely solvent and in need of a radical turnaround strategy.

In the last two years, during the economic recession, Benson's had been heavily discounting their dated products. Their previously excellent reputation and competitive edge had been lost. This low price strategy had worked for a while, but eventually a number of their major customers switched to other suppliers, including Special Components, whose products were now technically superior.

Earlier in the Summer Benson's managing director had resigned, giving two months' notice. When, shortly afterwards, the financial director had announced he intended to retire early, matters had been brought to a head.

The family owners contacted Universal Engineering and offered their company for sale. The asking price was a bargain relative to the book value of the assets, and the Universal Board eventually agreed to the acquisition. Bob Langley had been involved in the negotiations, but he was instructed to keep the matter confidential until a final decision had been reached. Special Components' strategy for the forthcoming year had been agreed with Head Office in June, and the acquisition of a competitor had not been included in the plan.

THE CHALLENGE FOR SPECIAL COMPONENTS

Briefing the managers who would be involved in implementing the strategic change, Langley emphasized a number of points:

- If Benson's was to be rescued and returned to profit a new **competitive strategy** and direction was needed urgently.

- Rationalization would be necessary to cut costs, and, at the same time, it was essential to prevent any further deterioration in both customer confidence and the order book.

- The implementation aspects of the strategic change had not been thought through in detail, and there were several uncertainties. In particular the production systems and the culture and values of the two businesses were markedly different.

- The real qualities and abilities of Benson's remaining managers and workforce were unknown.

- Synergies (mutually beneficial improvements from linking the two businesses) must be sought when the most appropriate way of integrating the two companies was decided upon. It might be possible to combine the sales forces and some production facilities, for example. However, while Benson's and Special Components competed in the same industry, with basically similar products, their customer bases were known to be different.

Langley announced that he would take personal charge of the merger but that he intended to second David Marshall part-time to the project. Marshall had been selected because of his background and experience. He had an MBA and used his wide range of acquaintances and contacts to stay aware of new ideas, techniques and developments.

Langley intended to talk to the remaining Benson managers at the earliest opportunity and explain Special Components' strategies, values and management style to them. How decisions are reached and acted upon. The nature and contribution of Universal's corporate planning procedures, and how and why this is, are only a partial explanation of how changes are managed.

Bob Langley finished the meeting by commenting that he saw this as a golden opportunity for Special Components to reflect upon their own strategic position and management. The company had survived the recession by moving quickly, cutting costs and searching for new niche market opportunities around the world. The challenge was to maintain this momentum when the upturn came. This would need a group of hungry managers who operate as a team.

DAVID MARSHALL'S BACKGROUND

David Marshall had been Marketing Manager for just over a year, having spent the previous eighteen months as a member of the corporate planning team at Universal's head office. These posts had both represented a major change of career direction for him.

David first studied law and qualified as a solicitor. He joined the legal department of a small City council but grew more and more frustrated when policies and strategies were altered every year as the balance of political power changed. Marshall became less and less happy with the organization culture that resulted from this uncertainty and inconsistency, and began to look for a way out. He was introduced to an international engineering company, and joined their legal department. After five years he became the chief legal advisor to the largest division, which was responsible for civil engineering projects around the world, and for manufacturing exploration and drilling rigs for offshore oil and gas fields. The legal work included contract negotiations and a variety of other business development agreements, including strategic alliances and joint ventures. Marshall had to work closely with the group's corporate planning team, and found it very exciting and very challenging. Unfortunately the travelling demands grew, and eventually he found he was spending two or three weeks every month in America, Africa or the Far East. His marriage became increasingly fragile.

He requested a transfer to corporate planning, but was turned down. His lack of financial expertise was the major difficulty. After some considerable heart-searching and long discussions at home Marshall opted to leave the company and study full-time for an MBA. He joined Universal at the end of his course.

THE PRESENTATION

Marshall agreed to prepare a draft presentation which would help Bob Langley explain three major issues to the Benson managers:

1. what is meant by 'strategy' and 'strategic management';

2. how strategic success might be evaluated;

3. how strategies are formulated and implemented, and how the process of strategic change is managed and controlled – both in general and in Universal Engineering.

Preparing this presentation would also help them to think through the implementation issues arising from the merger.

INTRODUCING STRATEGY AND STRATEGIC MANAGEMENT

Strategy is a complex topic, as can be seen from the extended case study which introduces each chapter. However, the underlying principles are essentially simple. There is no 'one best way' of managing strategic change; and no single technique or model can provide either the right answer concerning what an organization should do, or superior and crystal-clear insight into a situation. Instead managers should utilize the range of theories and concepts which are available, adapting them to meet their own situation and circumstances.

At the same time, a study of strategic changes in a variety of different organizations is valuable. An examination of outcomes, followed by an analysis of the decisions which led to these relative successes and failures, is rich in learning potential. Examples should not be confined to just one sector. Manufacturing and service businesses, the private and public sectors and not-for-profit organizations are all relevant.

Everyone who can make or influence decisions which impact upon the strategic effectiveness of the business should have at least a basic understanding of the concepts and processes of strategy. The processes will often be informal, and the outcomes not documented clearly. But they still exist, and managing the processes effectively determines the organization's future.

Without this understanding people often fail to appreciate the impact of their decisions and actions for other people within the business. They are less likely to be able to learn from observing and reflecting upon the actions of others. They are also more likely to miss or misjudge new opportunities and growing threats in the organization's environment.

CHALLENGES

Many organizations must compete in uncertain, dynamic and turbulent environments where change pressures are continuous and changing. New opportunities and threats appear at short notice and require a speedy response. Strategies which were appropriate 'yesterday' are unlikely to be suitable 'today', let alone 'tomorrow'.

As a result there are a number of major challenges for organizations in the mid-1990s.

- The need for many businesses to develop a culture of change orientation without losing internal cohesion and stability. This implies an explicit and shared vision of where the organization is heading.

- The need to decentralize and give managers more delegated authority while not losing sight (at chief executive level) of the changes they are introducing.

- The trade-off between such empowerment (delegating real responsibility in order to make the business more effective in its relations with all its stakeholders) and the greater efficiencies often yielded by centralized control and systems which harness the latest information technology.

- The need to act quickly in response to opportunities and threats, but not at the expense of product and service quality – achieving high quality at the same time as cutting costs and improving efficiencies.

These challenges are all related.

- Finally the dilemma of the recession. Organizations must cut back, control their costs and accept lower margins when supply potential exceeds demand in an industry. Profits fall. Paradoxically those competitors which are able to consolidate and invest strategically during a recession will be best prepared for the economic upturn.

The strategic decisions which we look at in this book – **the process of strategic management** – reflect how organizations choose to deal with these and other challenges.

Part of the task Bob Langley had given David Marshall was a clarification of the role and contribution of planning, and the group corporate planning procedures. The term 'corporate planning' is often taken to mean a systematic, formal planning process, using models and techniques, which results in clear decisions about strategic change, decisions which are then implemented and monitored. Such systems were very popular in the 1960s and early 1970s when environments for many industries were more stable, and forecasting was more reliable. Environments are always changing, of course; the issues concern the speed of change and the extent of the uncertainty. Planning systems still exist, and used properly, make a significant contribution to the process of change. But they do not, and cannot, explain the overall process of strategic change. The option to purchase Benson Engineering had not been a consideration in Universal's annual strategic plan.

Organizations and managers must react quickly and behave opportunistically in rapidly changing environments. Consequently corporate chief executives must also plan how their managers can first be in a position to behave this way – issues which depend upon the structure of the organization and communication systems – and second be willing and able to accept responsibility, use their initiative and take the appropriate risks. These latter issues are an integral part of the organization's culture, and they are very dependent upon reward systems.

DEFINITIONS

Strategies are means to ends, and these ends concern the purpose and objectives of the organization. They are the things that businesses do, the paths they follow, and the decisions they take, in order to reach certain points and levels of success.

Strategic management is a process which needs to be understood more than it is a discipline which can be taught. It is the process by which organizations determine their purpose, objectives and desired levels of attainment; decide upon actions for achieving these objectives in an appropriate timescale, and frequently in a changing environment; implement the actions; and assess progress and results. Whenever and wherever necessary the actions may be changed or modified. The magnitude of these changes can be dramatic and revolutionary, or more gradual and evolutionary.

The three essential elements are:

- **Awareness**   understanding the strategic situation;
- **Formulation**   choosing suitable strategies;
- **Implementation**   making the chosen strategies happen.

On their own, good ideas are inadequate. They must be made to work and bring results. The three elements are shown together in Chart 1.2. Monitoring progress continuously is essential if the organization is to stay properly aware of the strategic situation.

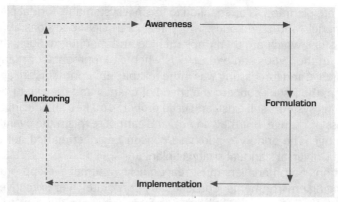

Chart. 1.2 Strategic management

LEVELS OF STRATEGY

There are three linked and interdependent levels of strategy. See Chart 1.3.

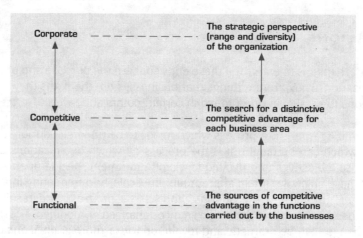

Chart 1.3 Levels of strategy

Competitive strategy is concerned with creating and maintaining a competitive advantage in each and every area of the business. It can be achieved through any one function, or a combination of several. For each functional area of the business, such as production, marketing and human resources the company will have a **functional strategy**. It is critical that these functional strategies are designed and managed in a co-ordinated way, such that they interrelate with each other and at the same time, collectively allow the competitive strategies to be implemented properly.

Successful functional and competitive strategies **add value** which is perceived as important by the company's stakeholders, especially its customers, and which helps distinguish the organization from its competitors. An individual functional area can add value. Internal linkages and co-operation between functions can also add value.

External networks which create **synergy** (definition 1) by linking a company closely with its suppliers, distributors and/or customers are also a source of added value, but these are an aspect of the corporate strategy.

Corporate strategy, essentially and simply, is deciding what businesses the organization should be in, and how the overall group of activities should be structured and managed. The term *strategic perspective* is often used to describe the range and diversity of activities; and then each activity should have a *distinctive competitive position*.

The acquisition of Benson Engineering represents a change in corporate strategy normally termed **horizontal integration** (definition 2). The challenge facing Special Components concerns an effective competitive strategy for the combined businesses.

Definitions

1. **Synergy** is the term used for the added value or additional benefits which ideally accrue from the linkage or fusion of two businesses, or from increased co-operation between either different parts of the same organization or between a company and its suppliers, distributors and customers. Internal co-operation may represent linkages between either different divisions or different functions.

2. **Horizontal integration** is the term used to describe the merger between firms at the same stage of the supply (or added value) chain. Such firms may be direct competitors or focus on different market segments or niches.

Where firms directly enter those parts of the added value chain served by their suppliers or distributors, the term used is **vertical integration**. To achieve the potential benefits of vertical integration (specifically synergy from co-operation) without acquiring a business which normally requires specialist and different skills firms will look to establish strong alliances and networks.

These two strategies are explained in greater detail later in the book.

Key Point

1.1 Strategies are means to ends. Normally these ends will be the objectives of the organization – either the broadly defined purpose or shorter term targets for achievement.

Strategic management is the process by which these strategies are created, implemented and changed. Strategies can be examined at three levels:

- corporate strategy – the scope of the whole business;

- competitive strategies for each business area;

- functional strategies which provide the competitiveness.

EXAMPLES

Cases and examples are useful for giving meaning to this subject and fostering an understanding of the ideas and concepts. Theories provide useful analytical frameworks, but understanding comes from examining what companies have actually done, and how successful their decisions have proved to be.

The examples included in Box 1.1 cover two aspects of strategy – major changes of direction, and smaller changes which have strengthened competitiveness.

 ## EXAMPLES OF CORPORATE AND COMPETITIVE STRATEGIES

Sony, the Japanese electronics company, is probably best known for the Walkman, and the range of personal audio products which have been spawned from the original idea. Sony has always been innovative and has, over the years, been at the forefront of developments in consumer electronic products. The Walkman, which is rumoured to have originated when a Sony executive wanted to be able to listen to classical music while playing golf, was really only a repackaging of existing technologies. Nevertheless, it needed a creative imagination to capitalize on the market opportunity for highly portable miniature audio products for people on the move and in situations where they need to listen quietly. Quite simply, Sony realized the potential ahead of its rivals. If one studies the culture of Sony, and its approach to marketing and product development, it is not difficult to imagine how the idea might have been fermented and exploited. Sony is an organization which constantly seeks such new opportunities, and encourages its managers to take risks, but among the many successes there have also been failures. The VHS video format, pioneered by JVC, a subsidiary of Sony's great rival, Matsushita, was preferred to Sony's Betamax system, for example.

A study of strategic change at Sony would also include an evaluation of the acquisition of CBS Records in 1987 and Columbia Pictures in 1988. Sony was buying a presence in the international entertainments industry, an industry traditionally dominated by American companies. The logic was based on the argument that benefits would accrue from the integration of electrical and electronics hardware products (such as radio, hi-fi and televisions) with their associated software products (compact discs, cassettes and videos).

Both of these events are examples of strategic change. The Walkman is an example of new product evolution and organic growth from the exploitation of existing businesses and technologies by Sony's managers; the American acquisitions represent major changes in the corporate strategy which could only happen if the most senior executives reached a deliberate agreement.

The decision by many leading **banks and building societies** to diversify and **buy estate agencies** in the 1980s is another example of corporate strategic change. The intention was to strengthen their control on the distribution of their mortgage funds. There have been difficulties. The housing market collapsed at the end of the 1980s and there were too many estate agencies for the level of activity. In addition the skills required to run a successful estate agency business are markedly different from those needed to manage a bank or building society. The anticipated benefits did not accrue, the banks and building societies lost money on their acquisitions, and many of them chose to close or divest the agencies.

Some changes are forced on organizations by powerful external forces. Several of **London's** leading **museums,** including the Victoria and Albert and the Natural History Museum, reluctantly introduced admission charges when the government reduced the real value of their annual subsidies. It is unlikely that most local authorities would have invited private sector tenders for providing many of their services unless they had been forced by legislation.

ICI grew to be one of Britain's largest companies. It operated plants throughout the world, and its products competed in the international chemical, petrochemical and pharmaceutical industries. Arguably it became too big and complex to exploit properly the true potential of all its businesses. In 1993 the company was split into two separate companies. Chemicals, paints (the Dulux brand) and explosives stayed as ICI; the drugs and agro-chemicals interests became Zeneca. Some years previously Courtaulds had similarly split its textiles and engineering businesses.

Rover Cars, itself a subsidiary of British Aerospace, agreed a series of strategic linkages with Honda throughout the 1980s. Before its sale to BMW in January 1994 Rover gained a number of benefits, including access to Honda's superior engine technology, help in achieving world quality standards, and support in new model design and development. Honda used the strategic alliance as a stepping stone to establishing their own assembly plant in the UK.

People typically perceive **W H Smith** as primarily a retailer of books, music and stationery products, and this view has remained largely unaltered in recent years. But changes have still taken place. The acquisitions of Waterstone's specialist bookshops and Our Price (music), supplemented by a number of music stores bought from Virgin, have complemented the traditional high-street multiple stores, which themselves have lost their travel agency businesses. Prerecorded videos have become an increasingly important product line.

Smith's Do It All DIY stores, which have been formed into a joint venture with Boots, represent greater diversity. The products and the retail concept are different from the other operations, and the stores are sited out-of-town rather than in high streets.

Virgin, as well as selling some of its music stores to W H Smith, has also divested its record business, its original core product, and sold it to Thorn EMI. The money has been used in part to help develop Virgin Atlantic Airways. In 1986 Richard Branson floated Virgin as a public company only to buy it back in 1988. Virgin's style of management never fitted comfortably with the expectations of the City financial institutions.

All of these examples illustrate different types of change to **corporate strategies**. In every case they represent an attempt to manage the organization's links with its external environment more effectively. The decisions themselves are also a reflection of the styles and preferences of the key decision-makers, the strategic leaders.

The next group of examples are really attempts to strengthen **competitiveness** through more effective exploitation of particular business functions. The corporate perspective remains largely unaltered.

Rover Cars, like Ford and its other rivals, has systematically sought to improve the quality and reliability of its cars to ensure that they are not perceived as inferior. New models have been introduced, and older ones withdrawn. Extended warranty schemes have been introduced, and more recently customers have been offered the option of returning new cars if they are not immediately satisfied. At the same time, but independently, a number of main dealers have extended their service facilities to include tyre and exhaust businesses. These are competitively priced activities which require high levels of customer service, and which have traditionally been monopolized by specialists such as Kwik Fit.

Certain **retail stores**, such as the DIY superstores and those in the new shopping malls, have extended their opening hours. Some are open most evenings; others trade on Sundays. Supermarkets have agreed to accept credit and Switch cards (and provide a cash facility) rather than insist on cash or cheque. These are all examples of attempts to improve the perceived level of customer service.

The total service package that manufacturing and service businesses provide to their customers is dependent upon the way they handle marketing and operations. These functions frequently provide new competitive strengths. New products are one example. **Instant tea** granules have been introduced by TyPhoo and its competitors alongside leaf tea and tea bags; packets of instant cappuccino have been added to the range of Nestlé's coffee products. A new product which represents a new level of service is **Pizza Hut** guaranteeing selected pizzas within ten minutes at lunchtimes.

In the majority of these examples rivals will be able to copy the initiatives. Few changes are incapable of replication. The most successful competitors are those who take a lead through imagination and innovation, and then seek to stay ahead of their rivals by more and more creativity and change. Increasing competition has meant that speed and timing have become potent competitive weapons. Unlike decisions about major changes in corporate strategy, which need to be taken at senior levels of the organization, changes in competitive and functional strategies are frequently delegated. Managers throughout the organization can contribute ideas and champion changes.

It should now be apparent that the idea of strategic change can incorporate a wide range of examples. The real challenge is understanding how the process of change is managed in the most successful organizations and evaluating the lessons ■

THE BUSINESS ENVIRONMENT

Benson Engineering was in difficulty because it was no longer satisfying its major **stakeholders** – those people with an interest and an involvement in the firm. The lack of recent innovation meant that a number of customers were switching to competitors' products, many of which now offered superior quality. Competitors who had invested in new production and information technology would be able to offer added value without any price premium. In addition the distributors the company used for some of its sales would almost certainly have lost faith as its competitiveness declined. Its bankers would have seen the overdraft climb and also lost confidence. Price reductions and lower sales must have affected the cash flow adversely. Special Components would, though, be able to provide cheaper corporate finance from its parent company, leading to lower costs.

Shareholders also constitute a critically important stakeholder. The institutions which hold blocks of shares in organizations such as Universal Engineering will have expectations for turnover, growth, profitability and debt levels. If these expectations are not met they may be inclined to sell their shares and this could lead to a loss of confidence and a decline in the stock market value of the business. Strategies, especially in the short term, are influenced by this.

As well as external parties, there are also internal stakeholders. Employee morale, for example, would have been affected by the decline and the uncertainty, and the new owners would have to work hard to restore their confidence and motivation.

Benson Engineering is typical of a company which fails to respond to change pressures, and eventually faces a crisis. In contrast, companies which are strategically effective seek to be more responsive to new opportunities and threats, and to initiate changes in their products and services.

In recent years the external environment of most companies has become increasingly dynamic, turbulent and difficult to forecast. Economic cycles are notoriously complex in nature. Industries and countries are all affected by recessions and periods of real growth, but these do not always coincide. Governments around the world will have differing political and economic objectives, and their chosen strategies will impact upon those companies which manufacture and market in their country.

In a recession companies have to cut costs wherever practical as order books thin down, in order to improve productivity. Competitive advantage cannot be gained from such improvements, but they are essential if a company is to remain competitive. Sometimes plants will be closed down and peripheral businesses sold off. At the same time it is important to continue the product development programme, and to search for opportunities for improving the overall service offered to customers.

Products in general are now being replaced by improved versions far more quickly than in the past – especially where electronics or other new technologies are involved – although some of the changes are only minimal. Both industrial and consumer products and markets are affected. Speedy response and faster change are now essential for companies who wish to remain competitive, but this must never be at the expense of lost quality or control.

Environmental issues are common to many industries, but every company needs to be aware of the changes in its own particular environment. For some companies changes in customer tastes can have both quick and dramatic effects; for others a focus on ethics and social responsibility can enhance their image and win them orders.

There are several frameworks for studying the environment of an organization. In addition to considering the company's **stakeholders** in terms of their relative power, influence, needs and expectations, a **PEST analysis** can also prove useful. This is an objective and straightforward consideration of changing political, economic, social and technological influences. This review should help to clarify changing opportunities and threats.

Chart 1.4 summarizes these points and also highlights that the *nature* of the stakeholders and the environmental forces is a useful indicator of the most appropri-

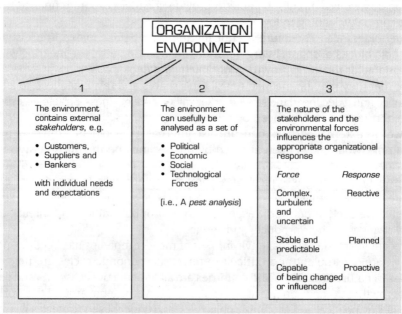

Chart 1.4 The organization and the environment

ate strategic approach for the organization to take. Where the environment is *complex, turbulent and uncertain* it will be necessary for the organization to be vigilant and speedily *reactive*. A carefully *planned approach* is ideal in *stable and predictable* circumstances; and a positive and *proactive approach* should be adopted where the environment can be changed or influenced.

THE COMPETITIVE ENVIRONMENT

One major aspect of the business environment is competition. The nature of competition in an industry affects the profit opportunities for the rival companies involved. Box 1.2 describes how we might evaluate industry competitiveness.

---

1 2 ANALYSING AN INDUSTRY

Michael Porter (1980) argues that five forces determine the profitability of an industry.

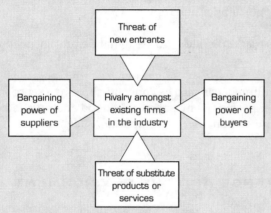

At the heart of the industry are rivals and their competitive strategies linked to, say, pricing or advertising; but, he contends, it is important to look beyond one's immediate competitors as there are other determinants of profitability. Specifically there might be competition from substitute products or services. These alternatives may be perceived as substitutes by buyers even though they are part of a different industry. An example would be plastic bottles, cans and glass bottles for packaging soft drinks. There may also be a potential threat of new entrants, although some competitors will see this as an opportunity to strengthen their position in the market by ensuring, as far as they can, customer loyalty. Finally it is important to appreciate that companies purchase from suppliers and sell to buyers. If these forces are powerful they are in a position to bargain profits away through reduced margins, by forcing either cost increases or price decreases. This relates to vertical integration.

Any company must seek to understand the nature of its competitive environment if it is to be successful in achieving its objectives and in establishing appropriate strategies. If a company fully understands the nature of the five forces, *and particularly appreciates which one is the most important*, it will be in a stronger position to defend itself against any threats, and to influence the forces with its strategy. The situation, of course, is fluid, and the nature and relative power of the forces will change. Consequently the need to monitor and stay aware is continuous ■

Key Point

1.2 Organizations exist and compete within industry, national and international environments.

Political, economic, social and technological forces impact in a variety of ways, presenting both opportunities and threats.

The competitive situation is likely to be dynamic and in need of constant monitoring.

The external environment can also be conceptualized as a set of stakeholders, whose needs and expectations must be understood and satisfied. Customers, suppliers, banks and shareholders are important stakeholders.

MANAGING CHANGE AND THE ENVIRONMENT

Ideas for change and improvement can originate with managers and employees anywhere in the organization, not just the chief executive. They are the people who are closest to customers and suppliers, and who are first to realize when competitors are making changes. Their contributions must be harnessed in some way, and they must be encouraged and empowered to make any changes which can strengthen competitiveness. If they are to do this, they have to be rewarded for using initiative and taking risks, but the whole process must be monitored and controlled. Some changes, particularly major changes, will certainly start with senior managers, and they will seek to persuade others to support their ideas. They will be looking to *manage change*. Other changes will emerge from the ongoing *decision processes*, and these depend upon how good people are at learning, sharing ideas and working as a team. People can learn from colleagues in their own company, from competitors and from different organizations if they are alert and aware of events.

Changes to the corporate strategy will frequently involve some detailed analysis and planning, although on occasions some managers will act more intuitively. Once changes have been instigated it may well prove expensive if misjudgments have been made and decisions need to be reversed. However changes with functional strategies can often be made on a trial and error basis. Ideas for improvements can be tried out experimentally, and developed seriously if the trials seem favourable. Misjudgments should not prove expensive, and further tinkering can be used to improve and then consolidate the idea. Developments fermented in this way can often provide ideas for other managers, and they can sometimes blossom into valuable competitive weapons.

The success of any organization in responding to change pressures, and managing the process of change, is very dependent upon the values and the commitment of its employees – the culture of the organization. Culture is vitally important, and it is not easily changed. Langley and Marshall knew they would have to examine the existing culture and values of their new acquisition, and, even before they visited the company for the first time they envisaged that they would not be happy with all that they found.

Effective strategic management also depends upon the abilities and style of the strategic leader. Graham Benson had created a successful business, but his qualities had never been replaced and the business had declined.

The terms **strategic leader** and **strategic leadership** are used throughout this book to describe those managers who are responsible for changes in the *corporate* strategy. Responsibility will rest ultimately with the chairman and the chief executive (or, in some firms, the managing director), but other senior managers may be actively involved. In divisionalized organizations such as Universal Engineering, the general managers in charge of subsidiaries will normally play an important role.

In some centralized organizations the strategic leader will additionally determine the *competitive* strategies; in decentralized firms this responsibility will be spread more widely.

Key Point

1.3 Corporate culture and strategic leadership are at the heart of the whole strategic process. They impact directly and indirectly upon all strategic decisions, and dictate the organization's ability to manage change pressures.

The culture and style of leadership determine the role of managers and employees throughout the organization in the strategic change process. Ideas for change can originate anywhere.

A SUMMARY CHART

Chart 1.5 summarizes many of the points made in this chapter.

Strategic management involves **awareness** of how successful and strong the organization and its strategies are, and of how circumstances are changing. At any time, previously sound products, services and strategies are likely to be in decline. As

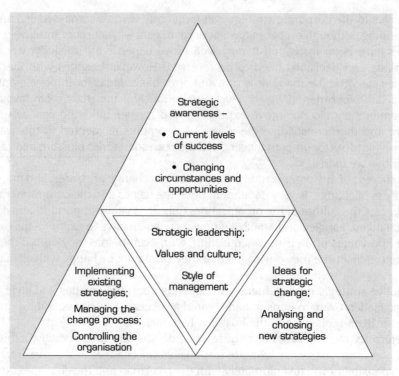

Chart 1.5 Strategic management

this happens new 'windows of opportunity' are opening for the vigilant and proactive competitors.

New strategies must be created. Sometimes this will be part of a formal planning process; at other times the changes will emerge as managers try out ideas.

The processes involved in designing and carrying through the changes must be managed, monitored and controlled.

Proper implementation is critically important.

The relative success of an organization in dealing with these strategic issues will be dependent upon the corporate culture and values, and the strength and style of the strategic leader. Consequently these are shown at the very heart of the triangle, impacting on – and ideally blending together – the other issues.

Although central to the whole strategy process, leadership is discussed in depth in Chapter 5, and culture in Chapter 8. This is deliberate, to allow the content of the book to be structured around the various ways in which strategies are created in organizations. While reading through the text it is important to remember that these issues are at the heart of strategy, and that conceptually they impact upon all strategic decision-making.

Simply, it is this 'heart' which determines the ability of the organization to **learn** from its own successes and failures, from external stakeholders, and from changes in the environmental forces – and, as a result of this learning, to act positively at the appropriate time.

AFTERTHOUGHTS

David Marshall was initially excited but back in his office he began to think more deeply, and certain doubts arose in his mind. He wondered whether he had been chosen to help Bob Langley because he was the most appropriate member of the management team, or because Bob wanted to test his managerial abilities.

A year ago he had settled quickly into his new marketing job, beginning by collating and analysing the extensive information already available on the company's major markets. The problem he inherited was that this information was fragmented, and that all-too-often Special Components was relying on facts contained only in people's heads. Several colleagues told him how useful they were finding these analyses.

David then started to explore opportunities for improving the effectiveness of overseas licensees, agents and distributors. Unfortunately he caused a ripple. One of the agents had a relatively poor record, and this had deteriorated in the last twelve months. Stocks were not moving, and the company's share of what was potentially a very profitable market was insignificant. Anxious to assert his new authority, Marshall challenged them about the situation and suggested that Special Components would have to review the sole agency agreement if improvements were not forthcoming. He never realized that the agent's sister was married to one of the group's non-executive directors! Three weeks ago he had been warned off very diplomatically by Bob, and now began to wonder if his managerial skills and judgment were being put to the test. Bob was recognized as a very astute and politically able manager, and he told David that while his analytical ability was excellent, his people skills needed polishing.

Whether or not it was a test, David Marshall knew he had to grasp the opportunity. At the same time he knew he must not neglect the other aspects of his job. The ongoing problems would not suddenly disappear.

David also wondered if this change of corporate strategy really was a golden opportunity or a pending nightmare. Universal might be buying Benson's for less than its book value, but the true worth of a company which has lost supplier and customer confidence and whose workforce is demoralized is not easily quantified.

POINTS FOR REFLECTION

- What strategic challenges relevant to your organization can you identify?

- Can you summarize the corporate strategy of your organization – together with the competitive and relevant functional strategies for the part in which you work?

- How would you evaluate the environment in which your organization operates or competes?

REFERENCE

Porter, M. E. (1980) *Competitive Strategy: Techniques for Analysing Industries and Competitors*, Free Press.

A SUMMARY OF THE STRATEGIC LESSONS

Strategies are means to ends. The ends concern the purpose and objectives of the organization. There is a broad strategy for the whole organization (the corporate strategy, which reflects the range and diversity of activities), and a competitive strategy for each activity. Functional strategies (for marketing, operations, finance etc.) contribute directly to competitive strategies.

Strategies have life cycles. Companies which fail to adapt their strategies and to innovate will eventually experience decline.

Strategic management is the process by which organizations formulate, implement, monitor and control their strategies. Changes to strategies can be dramatic and substantive, or more gradual and evolutionary.

Effective strategic management implies that companies manage their resources in such a way that they both respond to, and manage, their environment. The culture and style of management are critical factors, and the impact of an entrepreneurial strategic leader should not be underestimated. Speed is becoming an increasingly important competitive weapon.

Corporate planning is an important aspect of strategic management, but it does not fully explain how strategies are created and implemented.

The business environment can be evaluated in a number of ways:

- the expectations and influence of the stakeholders, those people/ organizations with a stake or an involvement in the business;

- political, economic, social and technological forces.

In addition, Michael Porter's Five Force model is a useful framework for evaluating the nature of competition in an industry.

All employees can contribute to strategic change. The structure of the organization (in particular, the extent to which there is decentralization and empowerment), and reward systems, will influence the contributions that people make.

2 THE CONCEPT OF STRATEGIC MANAGEMENT

This chapter explores the concept of strategy in greater detail and discusses the competencies required for strategic success in the 1990s.

CORPORATE AND COMPETITIVE STRATEGIES

On the day after Bob Langley announced that Special Components was acquiring Benson Engineering David Marshall worked on his new project. He began to prepare a series of charts for Benson's to highlight the central themes of strategic management, and to explain the current situation and strategies at Special Components. He used his MBA notes and textbooks to help produce three charts. His draft diagrams concentrated on the **concept** of strategy, rather than providing a detailed explanation of Universal Engineering's strategic planning system. He felt it was essential to begin with a description of how Special Components sought to be an effective competitor and continue to provide value for their customers.

He used the E-V-R Congruence framework, believing it to be an ideal framework for illustrating how Special Components sought to match its resources with the needs and expectations of its stakeholders. (E-V-R Congruence – environment, values, resources – together with the other concepts and frameworks mentioned in this section of the case are described in greater detail later in the chapter.) David realized that it would also be helpful if he explained the mission statements for both Universal and Special Components. He knew that a good mission statement provides a useful summary of the purpose and direction of the business and thereby helps determine appropriate objectives and strategies.

PROBLEMS WITH A NEW PRODUCT

David took an urgent telephone call from Dieter Wild, the man in charge of operations for one of Universal's main customers. Universal supplies this leading German car manufacturer with several products from different plants, but orders from the company are not a major sale for Special Components.

Wild complained that the latest batch of a new component contained too many rejects. The actual numbers meant that Special Components had failed with its recent promise to improve quality standards.

Dieter demanded an urgent meeting – either in Germany or England – with David and Ed Grey. Ed Grey is David's counterpart at Special Components' sister plant in Indiana in America.

The problems with this new product were proving expensive for Special Components, and it was losing goodwill. Ironically the component was only being produced because head office insisted that the Universal group offered Dieter's company as wide a range of products as possible – something the car company demanded from their leading suppliers. The component was barely profitable.

Special Components manufactured a wide range of precision products which were sold into a number of different industries. Over half of the sales were of standard components which were marketed through distributors. Although the range was diverse there were several common features, not least of which was the need for very high technical standards.

THE QUALITY PROBLEM

This latest problem had really arisen from two important developments in the last eighteen months. First, head office had decided to rationalize certain activities which were duplicated at the plants in England and Indiana. Marshall had been a member of the planning team which had made this recommendation. Before the change the two plants were producing essentially the same products independently and simply splitting the world market – which was easily accomplished as most of the sales were in America and Europe.

All research and development was now concentrated in the UK, and the international sales and marketing effort was led by the Americans. It was generally acknowledged that this split reflected relative strengths and expertise. Although Ed Grey held the same job title as David, he was more powerful and influential within the organization. In practice Ed concentrated his efforts on new products and opportunities and hardly interfered with existing arrangements. In cases where delivery lead times were not critical the limited opportunities for rationalizing production had been seized.

The second major development concerned one of Universal's main competitors, another American company with plants in Europe. They had recently stolen a market lead by launching a new variant of the component which offered superior properties for little extra cost. Special Components had been developing a similar new model, but it was seen as a relatively low priority because of the limited sales potential. They were at least six months behind their competitor. Dieter's company gave them three months to match the competition or they would lose the business, possibly threatening future sales of other group products.

Head office insisted on a quick and positive response to protect market share, and consequently the company was forced to launch an alternative before the development work on it was fully complete. Special Components had never taken such a risk in the past. It was a strategy dictated by a powerful external stakeholder, and it had rebounded. The technical quality of the product was not the problem, nor was safety. Special Components simply could not yet achieve a consistently high yield at the right tolerance, and the quality assurance was failing to pick up all the sub-standard components. The system had been designed to cope with Special Components' normally high and consistent yields. The customer was satisfied with the product but very dissatisfied with the overall service. It was costing them money to check for mistakes that should have been spotted before delivery. Their production schedules were also being disrupted.

The problem was compounded by two further factors.

First, Dieter's company operated plants in Germany, France and America. England was supplying the two European plants; Indiana was supplying America. The plant in Indiana was achieving a higher yield, although their costs were outside budget. Dieter knew the production problem was confined to England. Second, Special Components was dependent on a specialist sub-contractor, who helped with the specialist machining on most non-standard components. The work on this component was particularly demanding and the supplier should not have been pressed for the fast deliveries they normally provided. However they were being pressed, and in turn they were unhappy. Normally the working relationship between the companies was very harmonious, based upon mutual interdependency.

The problem clearly needed to be resolved without further delay, but a satisfactory resolution would require the co-operation of several people and departments within the plant. It would also involve their sub-contractor.

David realized that he now had a second important challenge, and he spent time planning what he would say to Ed Grey when he rang him later – Indiana is six hours behind England.

He had just returned from lunch when Bob Langley walked into his office and announced that he was flying to Indiana at short notice. He was leaving on the following day and he wanted to ensure that David would keep working on the Benson presentation while he was away. David confirmed that he would and showed the managing director the three charts he had been working on.

STRATEGIC THINKING

Langley's initial reaction was positive and complimentary, and typically his praise was followed by a new challenge. He suggested that David's charts provided a valuable conceptual framework but that alone they failed to address the real strategic issues for the 1990s.

Universal Engineering, he said, was competing in an increasingly dynamic global market and needed to work out how best to exploit its core technologies across all its businesses and develop the products which would be successful some years hence. Technological advancement would be a key source of future international competitive advantage. While the group would need to be large enough to enjoy the benefits of global scale economies, it would also need an active presence in all its markets if it was to remain close to its customers. The problems and issues were both strategic and structural, and he needed to determine what Special Components should be doing.

He asked David to make sure that he looked at all the latest ideas on strategic management to check if any of them were relevant.

David then summarized his discussion with Dieter Wild, believing it might be relevant for Bob's trip to Indiana. Langley listened, but indicated that he would not interfere at this stage – he expected his managers to deal with the problem. David was left to wonder why Bob was flying to America at short notice, and reflected that his company was sometimes poor at sharing information. He mused that another change of strategy might well be in the offing.

HELP!

David realized he needed an impartial and informed second opinion and decided to seek help from Tony Anderson, an old friend from his MBA studies who was now a strategy consultant with one of the large international firms. Tony was happy to discuss David's problems. Coincidentally Tony was also flying to America the next day and, although time was tight, he agreed to meet David and Bob Langley for breakfast at Heathrow.

After eating, Tony explained to the two men how his organization saw the current strategic demands on organizations. He began with ideas that Bob and David were familiar with. Strategies of unrelated diversification are less popular than they used to be; the anticipated synergies from diverse acquisitions are often illusory; and consequently growth should be built around a **core** of activities, perhaps related by technology or markets. He cited a number of instances where his organization had advised companies to divest non-core activities.

Tony then talked enthusiastically and convincingly about five main issues:

- adding value;
- core competencies and capabilities;
- architecture and synergy;
- competitive advantage; and
- strategic regeneration.

Tony's flight was called first, and after he left Bob and David were able to reflect upon what he had said. Langley was impressed by the consultant and congratulated his marketing manager. Perhaps they could talk to the consultant again once their ideas were firmer.

THE CONCEPT OF STRATEGIC MANAGEMENT

ENVIRONMENT-VALUES-RESOURCES

David Marshall chose the **E-V-R Congruence** framework to demonstrate the underlying concept of strategic management. Strategies are being managed effectively when the organization's resources are deployed in such a way that the business meets the demands and expectations of its stakeholders, and responds and adapts to changes in the environment. Simply expressed, it has strengths which can capitalize on opportunities and deal with potential threats in a climate of change pressures.

Our basic understanding of this comes from an analysis of the organization's strengths, weaknesses, opportunities and threats – a SWOT analysis. Sometimes a SWOT analysis is used to help clarify the current strategic situation; it is arguably more valuable when it is used as a basis for projecting forward. *Future* opportunities where the organization's strengths can be utilized for advantage should be sought; at the same time future threats which might critically expose the weaknesses of the business must be identified and dealt with.

E-V-R Congruence – see Chart 2.1 – is a refined version of this idea.

- Environment   What do customers and other stakeholders demand? Which competitor strengths have to be bettered?

- Resources   Which functions are (and will be) critically important, why, and how must they be deployed to satisfy (changing) market needs?

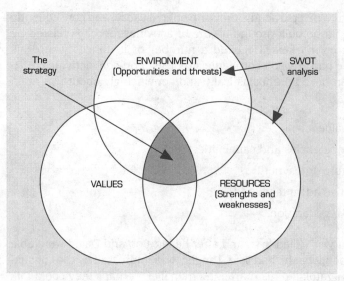

Chart 2.1 E-V-R Congruence

- Values   What will it feel like to work in the company?
  Which values and behaviours will be required for (1) adding value and (2) adapting and changing?

Strategic management is effective when resources *match* stakeholder needs and expectations. As we saw in Chapter 1, the external environment consists of suppliers, distributors and customers as well as bankers and other financial institutions and shareholders. It also includes competitors and sometimes the government. These stakeholders all expect something from a business in return for their support. If organizations are to be successful – and in many cases, profitable – they have to meet the needs and expectations of their stakeholders. Their relative demands determine what it is that a business must do well.

A company such as Special Components will have to produce to high and consistent quality levels and meet delivery promises to **customers**. Delivery times have been reducing gradually in very competitive industries. **Suppliers and sub-contractors** expect regular orders and accurate forecasting when very quick deliveries are demanded from them. Without such support just-in-time production systems are impractical. Just-in-time systems rely on regular and reliable deliveries from suppliers in order to maintain constant production without the need for high parts inventories.

Companies will try to minimize their stockholding because this helps both cash flow and costs. Special Components will have to generate a positive cash flow in order to meet the financial expectations of the **parent company** who, in effect, act as its bankers. Costs have to be controlled so that companies remain price competitive, although low prices are not always a marketing weapon.

These stakeholder requirements represent **key success factors,** those things an organization must do well if it is to be an effective competitor and thrive. In addition many companies have to be innovative and improve both their product range and their customer service if they are to remain a leading competitor in a changing industry.

The key success factors will vary between industries and sectors. For example, successful consumer goods manufacturers will needs skills in brand management.

Charities need skills in fund-raising and public relations. There is intense competition between charities for donations, and consequently they must be run as businesses. They can only spend what they can raise. It is also essential that they use their money appropriately, *are seen to be doing so and are recognized for their efforts*. The differing demands of fund raising and aid provision lead to complex cultures and organizations.

BUPA, the private medicine organization, has a similar dilemma. The business comprises two parts, insurance, with a strong commercial culture and orientation, and hospitals, which are naturally more of a caring community.

Resources must be managed with stakeholder needs in mind. Consequently it is important that everyone in the organization recognizes and is committed to meeting key success factors, and is additionally responsive to change pressures in a dynamic and competitive environment. Without this commitment companies will be unable to sustain a match with the environment as it changes.

The case suggests that market intelligence is an important resource for Special Components, and that its management team must be committed to both quality (of products and the overall service) and cost management. Change orientation and inter-departmental support are important values.

E-V-R Congruence highlights that the organizational match with its environment is a *managed process*. It does not just happen.

Key Point

2.1 Strategically effective organizations achieve a congruency between three factors:

- *environment* – the source of key or critical success factors;

- *resources* – core competencies and strategic capabilities which are required for adding value and satisfying key success factors;

- *values* – a proper match between strengths and opportunities does not simply happen. The process must be managed and the organization committed to learning and change to ensure that an effective match is sustained.

THINKING AHEAD

Strategic management is concerned with both an awareness of the current situation and an understanding of how well the company is performing in relation to its objectives and its competitors. From this the company's managers must look for ways forward which should bring new growth and prosperity, or help achieve any other objectives which are regarded as important. Awareness, formulation and implementation were introduced as three key aspects of strategic management in Chapter 1.

E-V-R can be used to focus attention on two basic questions:

1. What will our major stakeholders expect from us in the future, and how are we going to satisfy their changing needs?

2. What are our most valuable skills and capabilities, and what new opportunities are there for exploiting these abilities?

This type of analysis, however it might be carried out, should allow the organization to make decisions concerning future targets and the actions which will be required to achieve them. These points are illustrated in Chart 2.2.

This brief consideration of how strategic changes might be formulated, and how strategies are to be implemented and managed will be expanded upon later in the book.

MISSION STATEMENTS

It is useful if this thinking and analysis can take place within a clear framework of a corporate direction and purpose, the **mission** of the organization.

The corporate mission represents the over-riding purpose or *raison d'être* for the business; and ideally it should:

• define the targeted business activities;

• encapsulate long-term objectives;

• highlight how the company is differentiated from its competitors;

• be relevant for all the stakeholders, including employees, and gain their commitment and support.

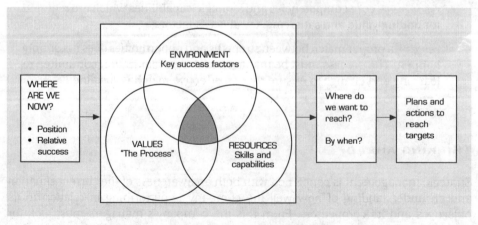

Chart 2.2   Strategic thinking

It is quite feasible for a company like Universal Engineering to have a corporate mission, and for each business in the group to also publish a mission statement.

A possible mission statement for Special Components then might be: *To be recognized as the quality supplier of (specified components) by providing customer satisfaction superior to that of all our competitors.*

This could be improved upon, but it does make explicit which businesses and products will be appropriate for the company, and what will be the key needs and values. The need for change, innovation and new product development is implicit, and the statement does not inhibit or constrain how competitive advantage might be attained. The timescale is clearly long-term and indefinite. Assuming the company does succeed in becoming the leading competitor it will then have to work hard to maintain its lead. The extent of the company's success, and its relative profitability, will also depend upon its ability to manage its costs efficiently. The opening words of the mission statement emphasize that it is essential for the company's strengths and distinctiveness to be recognized and appreciated by the stakeholders.

> *Key Point*
>
> 2.2 A corporate mission statement is useful for providing direction and guidance.
>
> Ideally the mission will state the basic purpose of the business, together with a summary of appropriate activities, how progress towards achievement of the purpose might be managed and monitored and how the company might create competitive advantage.
>
> It should be relevant for all the stakeholders, and also be understood and supported by all the company's employees.

STRATEGY STATEMENTS

The mission provides a valuable starting point for establishing more specific objectives and strategies, and in turn the performance of the organization should be assessed against both the mission and objectives. This is illustrated below:

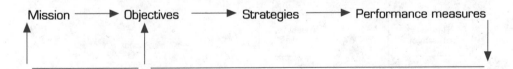

Typical objectives for Special Components will include specific targets for sales volume and revenue, costs, rejection levels, delivery lead times and the number and nature of customer complaints. It is also useful to have targets, albeit less specific, for new product developments. The end of year return on capital employed, and other financial ratios, can also constitute targets and objectives.

When timescales are applied, these specific objectives constitute *milestones*, and their achievement should be measured and recorded. Assuming that the objectives help the organization towards the achievement of its purpose, progress in this direction can also be measured.

Chart 2.3 draws upon the above points and provides an outline framework for a strategy statement. Ideally the managers in an organization will be in a position to complete a chart such as this, and agree upon the issues and their implications.

The chart begins at the top with the **corporate mission statement**. In the context of this companies should evaluate E,V and R in order to tease out any important and current **strategic issues** which need attention.

In the case, global sourcing by the car manufacturer, and the expectation that its suppliers are able to offer a wide range of important components, are strategic issues. Similarly, the increasing need for companies in the supply chain to specialize and co-operate has been critical for the successful development of just-in-time manufacturing systems.

Box 2.1 provides a hypothetical application of this for British Airways.

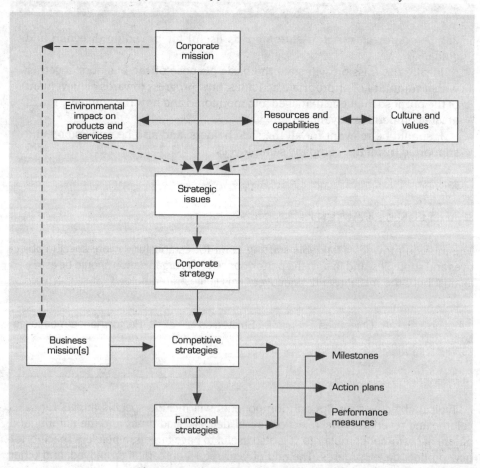

Chart 2.3 An outline strategy statement

BRITISH AIRWAYS: A POSSIBLE MISSION STATEMENT, E-V-R ANALYSIS AND STRATEGIC ISSUES SUMMARY

2 1

BA's publicity features the expression 'The World's favourite airline', and this provides a useful starting point.

What would make BA the world's favourite airline?

Safety standards would have to be high, the flights need to be reliable and on time, and generally everything should feel efficient. Friendly staff and high standards of in-flight service are also important.

(In this hypothetical analysis it is taken for granted that BA must also be profitable and productive.)

A POSSIBLE MISSION STATEMENT FOR BA

(Really this could apply to any major international airline.)
To make British Airways the most successful airline in the world by:

1. focusing on customers' needs, expectations and safety;

2. continually striving to improve the quality of our services;

3. looking for cost savings which can be passed on in lower prices – but which do not threaten our safety and quality; and

4. empowering and rewarding employees to ensure we deliver this service.

E-V-R ANALYSIS

Environment	Safety legislation
	Global demand (cyclical) and competition
	Deregulation – opening up competition
	Currency fluctuations and fuel prices
Resources	Aircraft – age; maintenance
	People
	Information systems
	Image and reputation (including livery?)
	Routes and airport slots
	Links with other airlines
Values	Customer care and service
	Recognized as being friendly and efficient
	Reliable

(This summary is not meant to be comprehensive.)

STRATEGIC ISSUES

The above E-V-R analysis helps to draw attention to four key issues.

1. New European legislation is reducing regulation and opening up competition. This will put pressure on margins.

2. Competition is also intensifying because seat supply exceeds demand on many routes. Customer care and service and efficiency are vital for survival.

3. Information technology can be used to generate greater efficiencies, say, through better control over seat sales and prices.

4. The total service provided is critical, and this includes easy access to onward flights, even if they are provided by different airlines. This suggests alliances and linkages, which might also provide access to more destinations. BA is actively looking to extend its international network of alliances. It has an alliance with US Air, for example, to provide easier passenger access to a large number of American cities ■

In the light of current and projected future issues corporate, competitive and functional strategies can be reviewed in order to establish short-term objectives (or milestones), action plans and performance targets.

Chart 2.3 thus provides both a broad outline framework for thinking and planning and a set of headings for summarizing and explaining current strategies. It would be valuable if all the managers in any organization could express the current strategic situation in this way.

This type of analysis will help determine whether current strategies are the right ones, and highlight where businesses might look to make changes. Written down and given to managers it flags where they should be vigilant and on the look-out for new opportunities and threats.

STRATEGIC SUCCESS

ADDING VALUE

A business must add value if it is to be successful. As supply potential has grown to exceed global demand in the majority of industries adding value has become increasingly important. In simple terms the extent of the value added is the difference between the value of the outputs from an organization and the cost of the inputs or resources used.

It is, therefore, important to use all resources efficiently and properly; it is also critical to ensure that the potential value of the outputs is maximized by ensuring they fully meet the needs of the customers for whom they are intended. An organization achieves this when it sees its customers' objectives as its own objectives and *enables its customers to easily add more value or, in the case of final consumers, feel they are gaining true value for money.*

The important elements are:

- understanding and being close to customers;
- a commitment to quality;
- a high level of all-round service;
- speedy reaction to competitive opportunities and threats;
- innovation.

CORE COMPETENCIES AND CAPABILITIES

Core competencies and capabilities concern the way that resources are managed for strategic effectiveness.

Successful companies develop **strategic abilities** which can be used to satisfy and exploit the key success factors in their targeted markets and industries. These can be features of the actual strategy or the structural processes.

Core competencies are *distinctive* skills, normally relating to particular products, services or technologies – Honda, for example, have such skills in engine technology – which help a company to differentiate its products or services and thereby create competitive advantage. The more distinctive and hard to copy are these skills, the greater the advantage. These competencies are often very basic and at the heart of the business; they are then exploited in a range of different end products. Honda engines can be seen in cars, motor cycles, boats and lawn mowers.

Simply having the skills is not enough, though. They have to be carefully managed and exploited, and they need improving all the time. Competitors are always going to try and match them.

Strategic capabilities are conceptually similar, but they are really process skills as distinct from core technologies and products. They can again be used to create competitive advantage because they add value for customers.

The ability to develop new products quickly is an example. Skills and best practice developed in one area of a business can be transferred to others if there is a deliberate attempt to learn and share. Information management, harnessing the potential of new technologies, is an increasingly critical skill.

Distribution channel management is an important skill for Special Components. The business is heavily dependent on its distributors and agents around the world, and they will differ markedly in ability, commitment and expectation. A few are likely to be excellent, working closely with their supplier and achieving a lucrative share of the markets they serve; others will be better at earning money for themselves rather than Special Components! Similarly there will be close links with some of the direct customers, whose needs will be recognized and satisfied; and again there will be other customers who just seem to buy the product – and might easily buy from a competitor. There is no real *relationship*.

Special Components should really regard its distributors and major customers – together with its suppliers – as partners in an alliance. Clearly this view needs to be shared by the partners!

ARCHITECTURE AND SYNERGY

Chart 2.4 expands this argument. Universal Engineering is an organization which consists of several discrete businesses. It would be unusual if there were no interdependencies between the various divisions, and opportunities to work together closely. There will be potential benefits from sharing knowledge and skills, and from seeing each other as members of the same team. Companies in the group should be actively looking to exploit these linkages. A great deal will depend upon the way head office manages the business and seeks to both control and integrate the various parts.

This issue, which will be considered in detail in later chapters, is known as internal architecture.

External architecture is equally important and relates to the added value or supply chain. This is represented by the strong horizontal line through the middle of Chart 2.4, and it links suppliers, manufacturers, distributors and finally customers.

This is a second network of mutually interdependent partners, and again organizations can benefit from establishing and nurturing close links. Alliances enable companies to focus on their core skills and competencies. Nike, for example, a leading company in sporting and leisure footwear, focuses on product design, marketing and personality endorsements; it avoids manufacturing, which it sub-contracts to specialists worldwide. Partners have to support each other, though, and understand each other's various needs and expectations. The main benefits will come from sharing information, which in turn should enable companies to respond more

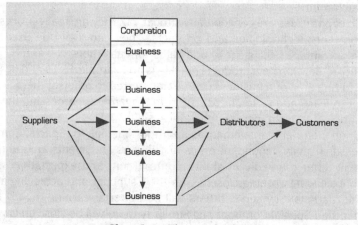

Chart 2.4   The supply chain

quickly to new opportunities and threats. Alliance partners can also be an excellent means of overcoming relative weaknesses.

COMPETITIVE ADVANTAGE

Competitive *advantage* implies a distinct, and ideally sustainable, edge over competitors. It is more than the idea of a competitive strategy, which may or may not prove distinctive.

Porter (1985) has shown how companies can seek broad advantage within an industry or focus on one or a number of distinct segments.

Porter argues that advantage can accrue from:

1. **cost leadership**, whereby a company prices around the average for the market (with a 'middle-of-the-road' product or service) and enjoys superior profits because its costs are lower than those of its rivals;

2. **differentiation**, where value is added in areas of real significance for customers, who are then willing to pay a premium price for the distinctiveness. A range of differentiated products (or services), each designed to appeal to a different segment, is possible, as is focus on just one segment.

Speed (say quicker new product development) and fast reaction to opportunities and threats can provide advantage, essentially by reducing costs and differentiating.

Real competitive advantage implies companies are able to satisfy customer needs more effectively than their competitors. Because few individual sources of advantage are sustainable in the long run, the most successful companies innovate and continually seek new forms of advantage in order to open up a competitive gap and then maintain their lead. Successfully achieving this is a cultural issue, as we have seen.

Key Point

2.3 Competitive advantage can be achieved through low cost and differentiation. Speed of action and reaction is also a very potent competitive weapon.

The real challenges lie in creating a real advantage which competitors cannot easily replicate, and sustaining a competitive lead once a gap has been opened up.

ACHIEVING COMPETITIVE ADVANTAGE

Competitive advantage, then, does not come from simply being different. It is achieved if and when *real* value is added for customers. This often requires companies to **stretch their resources** to achieve higher returns. Improved productivity may be involved; ideally employees will come up with **innovations**, new and better ways of doing things for customers.

This innovation can result in lower costs, differentiation or a faster response to opportunities and threats, the bases of competitive advantage; and it is most likely to happen when the organization succeeds in harnessing and exploiting its core competencies and capabilities.

It also requires that employees are **empowered**. Authority, responsibility and accountability will be decentralized, *allowing employees to make decisions for themselves*. They should be able and willing to look for improvements. When this is managed well, a company may succeed in changing the rules of competition. Basically organizations should seek to encourage **ordinary people to achieve extraordinary results**.

This will only happen if achievement is properly recognized, and initiative and success rewarded. Some people, though, are naturally reticent about taking risks.

3M (Post-It Notes), Sony, Hewlett-Packard and Motorola are four organizations which are recognized as being highly creative and innovative. In each case employees are actively encouraged to look for, and try out, new ideas. In such businesses the majority of products in the corporate portfolio will have only existed for a few years. Effective empowerment can bring continual growth to successful companies and also provide ideas for turning around companies in decline.

Competitive advantage is also facilitated by good internal and external communications – achieving one of the potential benefits of linkages. Without this businesses cannot share and **learn** best practice. Moreover information is a fundamental aspect of organizational control. Companies can learn from suppliers, from distributors, from customers, from other members of a large organization – and from competitors.

Companies should never overlook opportunities for communicating their achievements, strengths and successes. Image and reputation are vitally important; they help to retain business.

Chart 2.5 summarizes these points diagrammatically.

STRATEGIC REGENERATION

Organizations have to deal with dynamic and uncertain environments, as we have seen already. They should actively and continuously look for opportunities to exploit their competencies and strategic abilities, adapt and seek improvements in every area of the business – gradual change, building on an awareness and understanding of current strategies and successes. One difficulty is the fact that organizations are not always able to clarify exactly why they are successful.

At the same time it is also valuable if they can *think ahead discontinuously*, trying to understand future demand, needs and expectations. By doing this they will be aiming to be the first competitor with solutions. Enormous benefits are available to the companies which succeed.

In a sense this process is an attempt to invent the future, and the resources of the organization, its people and technologies, will need to be applied creatively. Caution is necessary when ideas are implemented because markets and customers are likely to resist changes which seem too radical.

In summary, organizations are searching for:

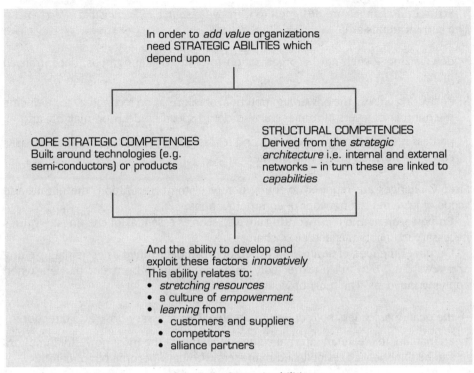

In order to *add value* organizations need STRATEGIC ABILITIES which depend upon

CORE STRATEGIC COMPETENCIES
Built around technologies (e.g. semi-conductors) or products

STRUCTURAL COMPETENCIES
Derived from the *strategic architecture* i.e. internal and external networks – in turn these are linked to *capabilities*

And the ability to develop and exploit these factors *innovatively*
This ability relates to:
• *stretching resources*
• a culture of *empowerment*
• *learning* from
  • customers and suppliers
  • competitors
  • alliance partners

Chart 2.5   Strategic abilities

• long-term product or service leadership, which is dictated by the **environment**

• long-term cost leadership, which is **resource**-dependent;

• product and service excellence, doing things faster than competitors without sacrificing quality – essential **values**.

Strategic regeneration refers to simultaneous changes to strategies and structures (organizational processes) in this search.

Strategies have to be re-invented. New products and services should be created by questioning how and why existing ones are popular and successful, and looking for new ways of adding extra value. Electronic publishing and CD-Rom technology, for example, have enormous potential for dramatically changing the ways people learn. Rewards are available for those companies which learn how to exploit these *environmental opportunities*.

In thinking ahead, companies should consider both products (or services) and core competencies. Concentrating on products encourages a search for new competitive opportunities; thinking creatively about competencies (which transcend individual products and businesses) can generate radically new opportunities for adding value and establishing a different, future 'competitive high ground'.

Structural changes are designed to improve *resource efficiency and effectiveness*. The current trends are:

1. down-sizing – splitting the organization into small, autonomous, decentralized units;

2. delayering – using the power and potential of information technology for reducing the number of layers of managers, in order to speed up decision-making; and

3. process re-engineering – reviewing and re-designing processes in order that tasks can be performed better and quicker.

Simply, changes are required to the structure of the organization, the nature and scope of jobs and the network of communications.

Empowerment and teamworking are also seen as essential for creating the **values** necessary to enable this degree of change.

On paper the idea of strategic regeneration can be justified as essential, exciting and rewarding, but, not unexpectedly, there are likely to be major barriers when applying the ideas. The most obvious hurdles are:

• the quality of leadership required to provide the necessary drive and direction;

• an inability to create an internal culture of change – the most powerful inhibitors will be experienced, established managers who have become out-of-date;

• uncertainty about changing needs and competitor activities.

Sony's mini disc (small compact discs) are competing with Philips' digital compact cassettes (DCCs) to be a leading recorded music format in the 1990s. Which of the two formats consumers will eventually favour is still unresolved, but the uncertainty did not inhibit these two innovative organizations.

Pascale (1992) uses the word *transformational* to describe organizations which succeed with simultaneous strategic and structural change. They become **learning organizations** which 'encourage continuous learning and knowledge generation at all levels, have processes which can move knowledge around the organization easily to where it is needed, and can translate that knowledge quickly into changes in the way the organization acts, both internally and externally' (Senge, 1991).

A VIEW OF STRATEGY

This chapter has introduced a number of key themes which we shall return to through-out the book. The main case study will illustrate how they might be applied in organizations. In the Preface we suggested that these themes comprise the **content** of strategy, and explained that the structure of the book is based on the **processes** involved in strategic decision-making – strategy creation, implementation and change. In Chapter 1 we also highlighted that the strategy process reflects how organizations choose to deal with a series of dilemmas and issues. These dilemmas will be illustrated at various stages in the text, and they are summarized in Table 10.1 in the final chapter.

Consequently we can summarize the strategic challenge for organizations in terms of:

- process;
- content;
- issues and dilemmas.

Strategic decision-making reflects a process by which organizations use a variety of tools (the content) to deal with the issues and dilemmas they face in a changing and competitive environment. This is illustrated in Chart 2.6.

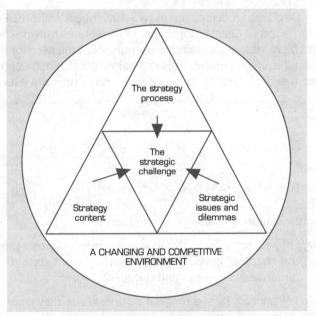

Chart 2.6 The strategic challenge

Key Point

2.4 Organizations which aim to be successful during the turbulent and competitive 1990s must address five critical issues:

- adding value;
- core competencies and capabilities;
- architecture, linkages and synergy;
- competitive advantage;
- the possible need to be strategically regenerative.

REFLECTIONS

David tried to make sense of the situation and decide which of Tony's points were the most critical and useful as far as Special Components and Benson's were concerned. The principles were straightforward, but there were no easy answers or options!

Tony's argument that many British companies do not think strategically about the future – they are metaphorically navigating in the dark, with neither a map nor a compass, hoping to find competitive survival – was clearly valid. Benson's was one of these companies; and although Universal Engineering was better, there was still considerable room for improvement. It was certainly not going to be easy to change the habits and practices at Benson's.

David also reflected on his two challenges. While the Benson acquisition affected Special Components' *corporate strategy*, the new product problem was about *competitive strategy* and the need for integrated *functional strategies*. Bob Langley's final words to him had emphasized that he was being held responsible for co-ordinating the relevant managers.

POINTS FOR REFLECTION

- Does your organization achieve E-V-R Congruence?

- Are you aware of your organization's mission statement? Does it satisfy the criteria discussed in the chapter? If your organization does not state its mission, how would you summarize the mission and purpose?

- What are the key success factors for your business? Are they changing? What are your core competencies and strategic capabilities? How do you add value? Can you think of ways in which you could enhance the value you add for your customers?

- Do you believe you enjoy any real competitive advantage?

REFERENCES AND FURTHER READING

Ackoff, R. L. (1986) *Management in Small Doses*, Wiley.
Kanter, R. M. (1989) *When Giants Learn to Dance*, Simon & Schuster.
Kay, J. (1993) *Foundations of Corporate Success*, Oxford University Press.
Ohmae, K. (1988) Getting back to strategy, *Harvard Business Review*, November–December.
Pascale, R. T. (1992) Paper presented at the Strategic Renaissance Conference, Strategic Planning Society, London, October.

Porter, M. E. (1985), *Competitive Advantage: Creating and Sustaining Superior Performance*, Free Press.

Prahalad, C. K. and Hamel, G. (1989) Strategic intent, *Harvard Business Review*, May–June.

Prahalad, C. K. and Hamel, G. (1990) The core competence of the corporation, *Harvard Business Review*, May–June.

Prahalad, C. K. and Hamel, G. (1991) Corporate imagination and expeditionary marketing, *Harvard Business Review*, July–August.

Prahalad, C. K. and Hamel, G. (1993) Strategy as stretch and leverage, *Harvard Business Review*, March–April.

Senge, P. (1991) *The Fifth Discipline: The Art and Practice of the Learning Organization*, Doubleday.

Stalk, G. *et al.* (1992) Competing on capabilities – the new rules of corporate strategy, *Harvard Business Review*, March–April.

A SUMMARY OF THE STRATEGIC LESSONS

An analysis of strengths, weaknesses, opportunities and threats (a SWOT analysis) is a useful framework for strategic awareness. Organizations need to match their resources with their environment.

Because the environment can be unpredictable and changing this matching process needs to be managed. Values and culture determine the organization's ability to create and maintain an effective match. A more useful framework, which encapsulates this theme, is E-V-R Congruence.

The environment, and the organization's stakeholders, determine the key success factors – those factors that an organization really needs to address for long-term competitive advantage and strategic success.

A clear, shared and understood mission statement, which explains the basic purpose of the business, is helpful both for strategic planning and for explaining current strategies.

Strategic success is very dependent upon architecture. This relates to internal linkages between businesses and functions, and external alliances between members of the added value (or supply) chain. Interdependencies must be fostered if potential synergies (the added value from linkages) are to be attained. In large organizations these linkages, and especially internal links, are influenced by the style of control adopted by the head office.

The organizations which are most successful in meeting key success factors are those which harness their core competencies and strategic capabilities to add value for customers.

The basic themes of competitive advantage are lower costs, differentiation and speed – these again must represent added value for customers.

Innovation, empowerment and the ability to learn and share are critical for achieving and maintaining competitiveness.

The real challenge for many organizations is strategic regeneration – simultaneously changing strategies, structures and styles of managing the organization.

3

STRATEGIC SUCCESS

This chapter discusses how strategic success might be achieved and evaluated. Organizations must satisfy their stakeholders and out-perform their competitors.

This requires organizations to address and satisfy the five key issues discussed in Chapter 2 and summarized at the end of the chapter in Key Point 2.4.

COMPETITIVE AND FUNCTIONAL STRATEGIES

The internal discussion about the new component took place on Friday morning. Around the table were David Marshall, Susan Scott (sales manager), Roger Ellis (production manager), Stephen Wood (purchasing) and Paul Adams (quality control). Wood and Adams reported directly to the production manager.

David arranged to visit their sub-contractor with Roger Ellis early the following week; and a week later he was due to fly to Germany, where Ed Grey would join him. The problem was being taken very seriously.

DIFFERENT PERSPECTIVES

It quickly became apparent that the managers disagreed about the relative importance to their division of the new component and the significance of Dieter Wild's complaint. David and Susan found themselves agreeing on the need to take a corporate perspective; Roger Ellis and his people had a narrower view. It was low volume and low profitability, they argued. Moreover it diverted attention away from those products which really earned revenue and profits for Special Components.

Roger Ellis joined Special Components as a graduate engineer 25 years ago, and he has been in charge of operations for the last 15 of these. He runs a very efficient and harmonious plant; the latest production technologies and up-to-date working practices are in evidence. Roger has no ambitions to progress further, and he is increasingly reluctant to take risks. While he recognizes the level of service expected by distributors and customers he has not always co-operated – he argues that sales and marketing personnel should also be listening to his problems and considering the advice of his operators.

Susan Scott's relationships with Special Components' main customers are excellent; and established business is rarely lost. She is ambitious for promotion within Universal Engineering and spends a considerable proportion of her time away from the plant. Susan is always hounding Roger to speed up deliveries and provide a better level of customer service, but she is less comfortable talking with engineers and production operatives than she is with customers. Roger feels that some of her requests are disruptive and push up his costs. David Marshall can see both sides. Selling is easier with competitive, fast deliveries – and service is more important than price to the majority of Special Components' customers – but cost control and reliability cannot be sacrificed. David also feels strongly that Special Components has tended to undersell its abilities and achievements.

Paul Adams was very defensive throughout the meeting. He knew that his staff had been failing to spot all the defective components, but argued that the real cause lay elsewhere. Quality control should not take the blame. Stephen Wood constantly complained that the company's close relationship with its sub-contractor was the most important issue at stake.

THE DISCUSSION

The managers acknowledged that mistakes had been made and argued about causes and culpability. They agreed that there had been a lack of customer care, but disagreed on why it had happened. In part it was clearly a marketing problem. They had failed to satisfy their customer. Their competitor had been first to launch the new product, which might imply shortcomings with research and development. Their yields were too low, and the responsibility for this lay with production. It was also possible that their sub-contractor had let them down. They also discussed whether the problem was a one-off or a symptom of more deeply rooted issues. It was commented at one stage that an outsider listening to the arguments would never believe that Special Components was a successful company.

Nevertheless there clearly was room for improvement, especially as competition in the industry was intensifying. Japanese component suppliers provide high quality, and quick, reliable deliveries; their standards are now the industry norm. Companies which fail to match these standards will not survive in the long term.

Roger Ellis explained why the development engineers believed the yields had been low, and how the operations were being changed. With more time there would never have been a problem at all. Paul Adams described the new testing procedures which would be used. Trials were already in progress and more definite information would be available on Monday. The production staff were confident about the outcomes.

A RESOLUTION

The meeting finished harmoniously. The managers disagreed about a number of issues, but recognized that they all faced different constraints and pressures. The varying demands from the company's stakeholders constrained them; everyone could not be fully satisfied all the time. Compromise was necessary, and mistakes would be made. The important thing was to deal with them quickly. Roger Ellis was promising that the production aspects of this particular problem had now been resolved.

The managers agreed upon the actions they would each take to repair the damage. Their attitude and thinking, in the end, had been short-term and pragmatic – a fact they all realized. They knew instinctively that a longer term perspective was required, together with a commitment to work together more closely to ensure that the mistakes they had discussed were not repeated. Improvements to both the internal and external architecture were required if they were to add value for Dieter Wild and satisfy their customer's needs and expectations.

STRATEGIC SUCCESS

Strategic success requires the following:

- clear direction, which is communicated through the organization, understood and supported; this relates to the corporate mission;
- the 'right' corporate strategy – a portfolio of businesses/products/services which

  1. capitalize upon the organization's core competencies and strategic, capabilities;

  2. generate synergy from linkages and interdependencies; and

  3. individually benefit from being part of the organization.

- competitive and functional strategies which enable the organization to satisfy its stakeholders and out-perform its competitors;

- the successful implementation of these strategies in order to obtain the potential benefits;

- the ability to change these strategies when necessary and appropriate.

Essentially these imply **common sense and competence.** Many companies have the competencies, but arguably fail to apply them effectively. The fundamental challenge is *to make common sense common practice.*

The case shows that Special Components is failing to satisfy three important stakeholders with its strategies for the new product – its customer, the car company; its parent, Universal Engineering; and the sub-contractor upon whom it depends. It is being out-performed by one of its competitors.

Understanding strategic success is complicated by the different perspectives and objectives held by the various interested parties. The result can be disagreements about the appropriate way to evaluate performance and success. Two areas of conflict are highlighted in the case: internal differences, perspectives and ambitions within Special Components; disagreement with Universal Engineering about the importance of the new component.

Universal Engineering needs an organization where the individual businesses support each other and co-operate; Special Components needs a co-ordinated team of managers. Achieving these ideals is difficult. Special Components will be seen as successful by Universal Engineering if it achieves revenue and profit targets; internal linkages are less likely to be monitored. Special Components' managers are individually successful, but they are not a co-ordinated team. While a situation such as this is not ideal it is not exceptional.

MONITORING AND EVALUATING PERFORMANCE

In this chapter we will look at how organizations might measure and evaluate their performance, and compare it with that of their competitors. Initially it is important to emphasize the issue of **timing.** Good performance needs to be recognized quickly so that it can be built on. Poor performance must also be spotted so that it can be dealt with sooner rather than later. Few organizations are like the professional football teams who know very quickly after a match whether they have moved up or down their league.

Chart 3.1 explains the role of information feedback and the importance of measuring the most critical variables. Ideally the organization will continuously measure customers' perceptions of the level of service they are receiving, highlighting both the need and opportunities for improvement. Speedy action then can follow. Satisfied customers will help the organization to achieve its other objectives such as high and sustained profits. This is the top half of the diagram.

The bottom half illustrates the danger of relying on other performance measures, which, although essential yardsticks, are inappropriate for stimulating action at the right time. Poor service, relative to that provided by competitors, will lead to systematic reductions in sales, market share and profits. If the organization waits for these

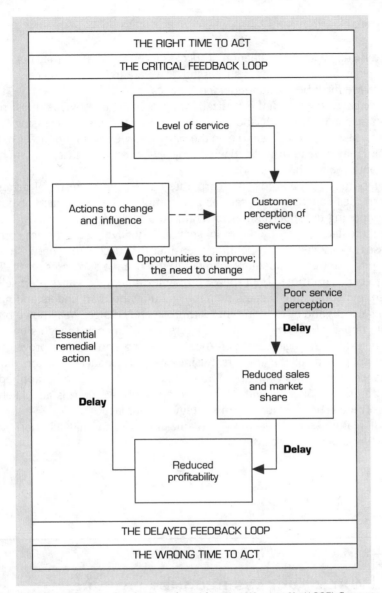

Chart 3.1 Managing service levels. Based on ideas in: Warren, K. (1993) Strategy research: improving the rear view mirror, paper presented at the British Academy of Management conference, Milton Keynes.

indicators, bearing in mind that there will be a delay before the information is fed back and analysed, it may be too late to recover the lost market share.

Accurately measuring customers' perceptions of service is, however, likely to prove more difficult than monitoring, say, sales and profit figures. The data must be collected externally and it will be subjective. Nevertheless, in many instances, it is perfectly feasible to stay aware informally and be ready to react.

LEARNING

Another difficulty with the evaluation of success is the fact that we may not be able to wholly explain why something is successful. If we are to build on success, and remedy failure, we must be able to understand the causes.

The *outcomes* of significant organizational problems are obvious – lost revenue, market share and profits; high labour turnover and absenteeism; increasing customer complaints. Managers may disagree on the *causes*, as we saw in the case. Companies in difficulty may have to respond to what they *believe* are the causes – there may not be sufficient time for thorough analysis.

Managers may also assume that corporate success is the result of actions they have taken. Self-congratulation can lead to complacency and a lack of hunger to improve, opening up opportunities for competitors. However the success may not have been created directly by the managers; it may have resulted from competitor weaknesses or mistakes. If competition intensifies the success may prove short-lived. It is also possible that competitors who study the relative successes and failures of their rivals can learn more about these companies than they realize themselves.

Growth and continuing success therefore requires both an understanding of the underlying causes and a commitment to improve and change. Well-known businessmen write books which describe their careers and offer their thoughts on effective management and strategic success. While interesting and thought-provoking such books cannot provide all the answers. Businesses and key success factors differ, and circumstances are always changing. Strategies and ideas have to be **applied** to the particular situation. Success without change and improvement is also likely to be transient. There is no ideal long-term strategy or approach.

Box 3.1 features three well-known organizations which enjoyed enormous success which was to prove relatively short-lived.

WHEN SUCCESS BECOMES FAILURE

1. THE LAKER SKYTRAIN

Freddie Laker launched his Skytrain service in the 1970s. He offered cheap trans-Atlantic flights and opened up the market to many people who previously had been unable or unwilling to pay the ticket prices of the leading airlines. The service was very basic and the airports used were not the 'first choice' of many passengers. However Skytrain was initially very successful and received enormous publicity. Laker was tempted to borrow money to expand the numbers of flights and destinations.

Laker's competitive strategy was based wholly on low prices, and consequently it was easily copied. When the major American airlines and British Airways realized that Skytrain was a competitive threat they cut their trans-Atlantic fares in an attempt to win back the lost business. Their pre-flight and in-flight services were superior to those of Skytrain, and they succeeded in driving Laker out of business.

Richard Branson learnt from Skytrain when he started Virgin Atlantic Airways. Virgin's prices would also undercut the leading carriers, but Branson ensured that his overall service package was at least as good as, and for many passengers, better than, that of his rivals.

2. LESNEY MATCHBOX TOYS

During the 1960s the success of Matchbox Toys, small-scale models of cars, made Lesney one of the most successful and fastest growing British companies. The company's production systems were modern and efficient; two new models were launched, and two withdrawn, every month; the products were widely available because distribution was not restricted to toy shops but included newsagents and confectioners; the pricing strategy made them affordable. Matchbox Toys quickly became collectables.

Demand for the product seemed to exceed the company's ability to supply. Lesney appeared to be doing everything right as it expanded rapidly.

At the end of the 1960s an American competitor, Mattel, launched a rival product. Hotwheels featured innovatory plastic friction-free wheels and their cars ran further along a table or floor once they had been pushed. They were over twice the price but much more fun to play with.

Lesney lost sales and market share, but responded very quickly. Friction-free wheels were added to Matchbox Toys and the low price was maintained.

Lesney 'came back' but at the expense of lost revenue, profits and reputation. Their *marketing skills* had been questioned. Lesney continued to survive and grow but they never recovered the image they enjoyed in the 1960s. Eventually they were acquired by a Hong Kong-based manufacturer.

3. BURTON

Burton's is a long-established clothing retail chain which became well-known and very successful for made-to-measure men's suits, which it also manufactured. At the end of the 1970s Burton's profits were depressed, and, despite some diversification, the company's image was outdated. The company was in need of a strategic turnaround, and this came with a new, more flamboyant chief executive, Ralph Halpern.

Burton was able to capitalize on the fashion changes and the retail spending boom of the mid 1980s and positioned itself to appeal to both men and women with casual but fashionable clothing and accessories. The image was revitalized with names such as Principles, Top Shop, Dorothy Perkins and Harvey Nichols all complementing the Burton brand.

Burton became second only to Marks & Spencer for high-street clothes. E, V and R were congruent; the new strategies proved effective. Further proactive strategic developments then destroyed this congruency. Growth and success led to over-expansion and the acquisition of new sites with very high rent and lease costs. Burton moved into property and the development of shopping centres; and in 1985 they bought Debenhams. These moves away from the core business implied new key success factors and changes of values, and they have never proved wholly successful. Borrowing increased and Burton has had to face high debt payments when trading conditions have deteriorated in the early 1990s.

Resources and environment became mismatched. This has also led to an inability to refocus and redesign the portfolio as fashion trends have changed once again. Critics have described Burton as having 'half a dozen tired retail formulas which were right for ther 1980s, wrong for the 1990s'.

Sir Ralph Halpern retired in 1990 and Burton has been forced to rationalize, closing and selling sites in order to fund investment in the stores which remain ■

MEASURING SUCCESS: EFFICIENCY AND EFFECTIVENESS

There are four important measures of performance although we normally attach most significance to just two of these.

- **Efficacy** – the chosen strategy is capable of fulfilling the purpose for which it is intended.

- **Economy**, which means *doing things cost effectively*. Resources should be managed at the lowest possible cost consistent with achieving quantity and quality targets.

- **Efficiency**, which implies *doing things right*. Resources should be deployed and utilized to maximize the returns from them.

    For measuring economies and efficiencies, quantifiable objectives and targets will be set and agreed with managers. Progress can be measured and relative success evaluated. Economy and efficiency measures are essentially objective.

- **Effectiveness**, or *doing the right things*. Resources should be allocated to those activities which satisfy the needs, expectations and priorities of the various stakeholders in the business.

Effectiveness invariably involves *subjectivity* as the measures concern perceptions of outcomes; and the variables being measured are mostly external rather than internal to the organization. For these reasons it is generally more difficult to measure effectiveness, and consequently some organizations will need to rely on *indicators* rather than formal measures. Some companies will concentrate on resource efficiencies simply because they are easier to deal with. In this latter case the real interests of stakeholders may be overlooked.

	Ineffective	Effective
Inefficient	Corporate collapse	Survival
Efficient	Gradual decline	Growth and prosperity

Chart 3.2   Efficiency and effectiveness

Chart 3.2 highlights that organizations which are efficient but not effective are likely to experience gradual decline as E, V and R (environment-values-resources) become less congruent. Effective organizations, whose strategies do address the expectations of stakeholders, but which are being run inefficiently, will survive but not prosper and grow to the extent they might. Growth and prosperity requires organizations to be both efficient and effective.

In February 1991, in its Report to Shareholders, BT (British Telecom) stated that it was 'determined to continue improving service levels for all customers, and where it falls short of its own high standards, is improving its handling of customers' complaints'. Specific measures included the percentage of calls connecting at the first attempt; the percentage of public payphones operational at any one time; the percentage of orders completed by the customers' confirmed date; and the percentage of business faults cleared within 5 working hours. In isolation these measures relate to efficiency; if the selected target service levels are acceptable to customers (not too low, and at the same time not in excess of what people would be satisfied with) they are also measures of effectiveness.

> ### Key Point
>
> 3.1 Strategic success implies that stakeholder needs and expectations are being satisfied, and that an organization is out-performing its competitors.
>
> Measuring *resource efficiencies* is both essential and relatively straightforward, but in isolation it is not an indicator of strategic success. Organizations need to also be *effective* if they are to grow and prosper, which implies meeting the needs of their important stakeholders.

E-V-R CONGRUENCE

Efficiency measures are primarily concerned with the utilization of **resources** and effectiveness measures relate to the **environment**, the organization's ability to satisfy its stakeholders.

It is important not to forget **values**

Organizations which attempt to measure values will first need to clarify which values and behaviours are critical for carrying out corporate and competitive strategies, and pursuing the mission, both now and in the future. The extent to which they are present will then be measured, and any changes tracked. There may also be attempts to change the values, which is difficult but by no means impossible.

SPECIFIC MEASURES

Box 3.2 provides a list of possible economy, efficiency and effectiveness measures for an international airline.

 PERFORMANCE MEASUREMENT FOR AN AIRLINE

An airline is a people-dependent service business. Unquestionably its revenue, profits, profitability, liquidity and market share are all important. But alone they are inadequate for assessing the overall performance.

The following list contains examples of appropriate measures which might also be used.

ECONOMY MEASURES

- costs – e.g. the cost of fuel;
- the cost of leasing aircraft;
- staff levels and costs – slimming these is acceptable as long as the appropriate quality of service is maintained. This could be measured as an overhead cost per passenger.

EFFICIENCY MEASURES

- time-keeping;
- utilization of aircraft/seat capacity – in total for the aircraft, and also by individual class or section – first, business and economy;
- average revenue per seat – this implies maximizing the return from each flight, given that on any aircraft there are likely to be several pricing schemes in operation.

  (The last two points are essential if the airline is to run at all profitably. Passenger needs vary, and consequently success will depend in part on the seating configuration of the aeroplane chosen for particular routes. On long-haul flights, for example, business passengers want space to sleep, while on short-haul they want space to work.)
- income (from all sources) related to the numbers of employees;
- reliability of the aircraft – i.e. continuous flying without breakdown (as a result of efficient maintenance – see below);
- the number of complaints; the number in relation to the number of passengers.

EFFECTIVENESS

- ability to meet all legislative requirements;
- image – which is based on several of the factors listed in this section;
- staff attitudes and contributions – both on the ground and on board the aircraft – care, courtesy, enthusiasm, friendliness, respect and efficiency;
- the aeroplane itself – does it look and feel new and properly looked after?;
- other aspects of the on-board service, such as the cleanliness of the seating and toilet areas, food and entertainment;
- innovation – new standards of passenger comfort;
- safety record;
- the number of routes offered, the timing of flights and the general availability of seats (this requires good links with travel agents);
- recognition of, and rewards for, regular and loyal customers;
- having seats available for all people with tickets who check-in; while airlines, like hotels, often overbook deliberately they must ensure they are not 'bumping' people onto the next available flight at a level which is causing ill-will and a poor reputation;
- the compensation package when people are delayed;
- time taken at check-in;
- reliability of baggage service – particularly making sure bags go on the right flight; this also involves the issue of bags being switched from one flight to another for transit passengers;

- the time for baggage to be unloaded (this is partially in the hands of the airport management);
- the absence of any damage to luggage;
- the systems for allocating particular seats in advance of the flight and at check-in;
- the way complaints are handled;
- the ability to balance the cost of maintenance with the costs incurred if things go wrong. If there is inadequate maintenance there are likely to be incidents or accidents which are costly in lost revenue and goodwill. At the same time airlines could 'over-maintain' to a level where they are no longer able to compete because of too-high costs ■

The following measures would be typical and appropriate for Special Components – the list is not exhaustive.

EFFICIENCY

- Head Office sales revenue targets;
- return on capital employed;
- stock and debtor turnover ratios;
- production capacity utilization;
- rejection rates.

Success in meeting targets will depend upon good management control and sound budgeting.

EFFECTIVENESS

- satisfying all Head Office expectations
- consistently meeting customers' quality and delivery requirements;
- good internal co-operation and close linkages through the supply chain; this suggests that every person involved understands the needs and expectations of their own customer and those of the next in line in the chain – specifically asking, 'Who is my customer's customer?';
- innovation – improving products and service on a continuous basis.

Most organizations can build extra value into a product and improve the level of service. The secret of success lies in finding those opportunities for adding value which are most important for customers and which do not increase costs such that profitability is compromised. While it is necessary to consider all the stakeholders, most organizations need to concentrate on satisfying the requirements of their customers more successfully than their competitors.

Trade-offs between efficiency and effectiveness are both commonplace and difficult. Some would argue, for example, that **charitable organizations** should seek to constrain their advertising and administrative expenses in order that a substantial proportion of their income, however generated, is available for the charitable work. This would indicate efficiency. Others would argue that there needs to be generous spending on advertising in order to generate even more income, and a sufficiently large administrative structure to make sure that the charity is run both effectively and efficiently, with money spent where it is most needed.

Local authorities together with organizations within the **National Health Service** normally have a demand for services which exceeds the ability to supply. Resources are limited and finite. High costs incurred in providing any one service can indicate either inefficiency or a high level of provision. High provision would be an indication of high priority – at the expense of satisfying other needs. Priorities have to be determined and resources allocated accordingly, recognizing that many stakeholders will disagree with the priorities chosen. The extent to which the various interested parties can be satisfied is an indication of effectiveness.

The measure which is commonly used is **value for money**, the perceived value of the outputs divided by the cost of the resources utilized.

THE BALANCED SCORECARD

We saw in Chapter 2 that performance measures relate to objectives and milestones. Kaplan and Norton (1993) suggest that organizations should focus their efforts on a limited number of specific, critical performance measures which reflect stakeholders' key success factors. In this way managers can readily concentrate on those issues which are essential for corporate and competitive success.

Kaplan and Norton use the term 'balanced scorecard' to describe a framework of four groups of measures, and argue that organizations should select critical measures for each one of these areas. The four groups, and examples of possible measures, are:

- Financial   Return on capital employed
                      Cash flow

- Customers   Perceived value for money
                      Competitive prices

- Internal processes Enquiry response time
                      Enquiry $\longrightarrow$ order conversion rate

- Growth and improvement   Number of new products/services
                      Extent of employee empowerment

It can be seen that these measures encapsulate both efficiency and effectiveness.

DIFFERENT PERCEPTIONS OF QUALITY

Measuring effectiveness requires a recognition that *quality* does not mean the same things for every customer. Organizations must determine what will generate repeat business and seek to provide it. Supermarkets, for example, can offer service in the form of a wide range of products, brand choice for each product in the range, low prices, fast check-out and ample car parking. Stores can focus aggressively on one or more of these or seek a balanced profile. The major chains will have a basic competitive posture and then tailor each store to meet local conditions.

CUSTOMER CARE AND TOTAL QUALITY MANAGEMENT

There are four essential principles to effective customer care:

- recognizing the importance of the customer to the long-term health of the business;
- involving all employees in meeting customer requirements;
- seeing every activity as part of a process designed to satisfy customers;
- seeking continuous improvement.

Quite simply, total quality management is knowing what is required to satisfy customers and out-perform competitors, and doing it – first time and every time, consistently. It is much more than quality control, which is concerned with ensuring that products and services have been produced to the correct specification and standards.

The need for service occurs whenever a customer 'meets' an organization. These 'moments of truth' might occur when dealing with a sales person, when receiving a delivery or an invoice, or when making a complaint. Consequently no one person or function is responsible for all these moments of truth; they are incorporated within processes and across departments. The process of meeting a customer's order, for instance, will embrace order processing, pricing, production planning, production itself, packing, distribution and invoicing. **A business is only as strong as its weakest link**. Customers will not care about which link is weak but about the outcome of the weakness. Improving customer service requires the members of an organization to operate as an integrated team – a point demonstrated in the case.

> *[Many] organizations are not built to serve customers, they are built to preserve internal order. To customers, the internal structure may not only mean very little, it may serve as a barrier. Organization charts are vertical and serving the customer is horizontal* (George Fisher, Chief Executive Officer, Motorola).

Key Point

3.2 Competitors' strategies should be evaluated, and competitors should be benchmarked against customer key success factors.

It is vitally important for an organization to stay aware of how actions and reactions by the various rivals in an industry constantly change the competitive environment.

COMPETITIVE SUCCESS

In many industries the competitive environment is dynamic and uncertain. Changes by any single competitor at any time impact upon rival organizations who may be forced to react. Their reactions introduce further changes to the competitive environment, which may be in a state of perpetual flux. Chart 3.3 summarizes this idea, and the significance is debated at greater length in Chapter 7. Clearly some competitors will be more proactive than their rivals, attempting to *manage their competitive environment*; and some will be in a position to react more quickly and positively to threatening changes.

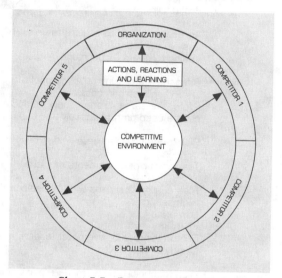

Chart 3.3   Dynamic competition

If we are to out-perform our competitors we must first identify who they are and how and why they are successful. Table 3.1 provides a possible framework for such an analysis. Organizations which appreciate the competitive structure of their industries and markets will be in a better position to clarify competitive threats and opportunities.

Competitive success, as we saw in Chapter 2, requires organizations to control their costs and to differentiate their products and services in order to add value. Table 3.2 lists a number of ways in which individual functions can contribute to this competitive advantage.

A strategy of **cost leadership** necessitates the management of essential cost drivers (*efficiency*) and the avoidance of unnecessary costs, by eliminating product or service benefits which are not required for efficacy, and not seen as important by customers (*effectiveness*). **Differentiation** is achieved by concentrating on features which do matter to certain customer segments, if not to all customers, especially those features which competitors cannot copy easily, and for which customers will pay a premium price (*effectiveness*). At the same time it is important to manage the operations *efficiently*.

Table 3.1 A framework for evaluating competitive strategies

Scope	Global; industry-wide; niche Single or multi-product/service Focused or diversified Vertical linkages with suppliers/distributors
Objectives	Ambitious for market or segment leadership Market presence just to support other (more important) activities
Success	Market share Image and reputation Profitability
Commitment	Agressive: willing to acquire to grow Passive survivor Willing to divest if opportunity arises
Approach	Offensive – attacking other competitors Defending a strong position (Note: the same strategy (new products, price cuts) can be used both offensively and defensively) Risk-taking or risk-averse Teasing out new segments or niches
Strategy	High quality – perhaps with technological support High service Low price
Position	Cost advantage or even cost leadership enjoyed Clearly differentiated
Competitive resources	High technology base; modern plant Location relative to markets Quality of people (ability to add value) Reputation

The examples provided for each of the eight criteria are not offered as an exhaustive list.

COMPETITOR BENCHMARKING

Chart 3.4 shows how we might benchmark competitors for comparison with an organization and with customer preferences. The key order criteria – key success factors – are listed down the left-hand side and ranked in order of their importance to customers. Their relative significance is plotted against the horizontal axis. The ability of different competitors to meet these key success factors is illustrated by the dotted lines. Competitor A is clearly relying on its quality and technical back-up, for which it has a good reputation, but is it truly satisfying customer needs? Competitor B seems to offer an all-round better service, and in a number of areas is providing a service

Table 3.2 Functional strategies and competitive advantage

	Competitive strategy	
Functional strategy	*Low cost*	*Differentiation*
Marketing	Large companies can obtain media discounts	Image – reinforced by well-known strategic leader
Operations	Efficient plant management and utilization (productivity)	Low defect rate and high quality
	Re-engineered processes which reduce costs	Re-engineered processes which add extra value
Human resources	Training to achieve low rejections and high quality	Incentives to encourage innovation
	Policies which keep turnover low	
Research and development	Reformulated processes which reduce costs	New, patented breakthroughs
Finance	Low cost loans (improves profit after interest and before tax)	Ability to finance corporate strategic change, investments and acquisitions
Information technology	Faster decision making in flatter organization structure	Creative use of information to understand customer needs, meet them and out-perform competitors
Distribution/ logistics	Lower stock-holding costs	Alliances with suppliers and/or distributors which are long-term mutually supportive

This list of examples is indicative only, and not an exhaustive set of possibilities

beyond that demanded. Given the areas, this actually may be good as it will indicate a reliable supplier.

It should never be forgotten, of course, that future competition may not always come from existing rivals. New competitors can emerge, breaking into the industry, often by rewriting the rules of competition. Virgin Atlantic Airways, mentioned in Box 3.1, challenged British Airways with a new and different service package – first-

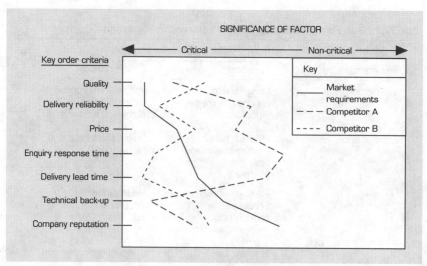

Chart 3.4   Competitor gap analysis

class seats at business-class prices and innovative in-flight entertainment systems. Similarly Microsoft, a manufacturer of computer software such as Windows, emerged to challenge the more diversified and established IBM (Box 5.3); discount retailers such as Aldi, and more recently American food discount warehouses, have begun to challenge the dominance of Sainsbury and Tesco.

BUSINESS FAILURE

Having examined strategic success we conclude this chapter with a very brief summary of the main reasons why businesses fail. Companies fail for a variety of reasons, and normally more than one factor is in evidence. The main ones are:

- Poor management — either at strategic leader level or through the heart of the organization – which again indicates weak leadership

- Poor financial control — weak budgeting and cost management

  an inability to cover overheads

- Competition — the company's competitors have become relatively stronger

- Declining profitability — resulting from either stronger competition or lax cost control

- Declining demand — with no suitable replacement products or services

The last three factors above all relate to *poor marketing*.

- Acquisitions or other changes in corporate strategies which overstretch the company's resources and detract attention away from existing activities, products and services.

3.3 The main causes behind **business failures** are normally:

- poor strategic leadership;
- poor financial controls;
- intensifying competition.

POINTS FOR REFLECTION

- Does your organization achieve internal cohesion and synergy? What improvements could be made?

- What are the important efficiency and effectiveness measures for your organization? How successful are you against the measures? Are your conclusions based on objective analyses or subjective opinion?

- How would you rank your organization against its leading competitors? From where do you see future competition for your organization's products or services?

- Can you identify and explain any noteworthy business failures?

REFERENCES AND FURTHER READING

Drucker, P. F. (1989) What businesses can learn from non-profits, *Harvard Business Review*, July–August.

Kaplan, R. S. and Norton, D. P. (1993) Putting the balanced scorecard to work, *Harvard Business Review*, September–October.

Jackson, P. and Palmer, R. (1989) *First Steps in Measuring Performance in the Public Sector*, Public Finance Foundation, London.

Oakland, J. (1989) *Total Quality Management*, Heinemann.

PA Consultants (1987) *How to Take Part in the Quality Revolution* – A Management Guide, Dr Steve Smith, PA Management Consultants.

Slatter, S. (1984) *Corporate Recovery: Successful Turnaround Strategies and their Implementation*, Penguin. (A useful reference text on business failure.)

A SUMMARY OF THE STRATEGIC LESSONS

Strategic success implies that stakeholder needs and expectations are being satisfied, and that an organization is out-performing its competitors.

Feedback of progress is essential if organizations are to build on success and remedy weaknesses. Vigilance is important, and it is necessary to determine the most appropriate factors to measure.

Strategies have life cycles and success can quickly become failure. This is compounded by the difficulties involved in understanding the reasons behind success and failure.

Strategic success requires that value is added for customers through the supply chain. This implies internal and external linkages and co-operation.

Success is more likely if the organization's managers work as a cohesive team, with a shared and understood purpose. Functional strategies should be co-ordinated. Without this there is a real chance that managers will pursue personal objectives, when their different perspectives concerning which factors are most significant may bring them into conflict.

Measuring resource *efficiencies* is both essential and relatively straightforward. In isolation it is not an indicator of strategic success. Organizations need to also be *effective*, doing the right things and meeting the needs and expectations of the various stakeholders, if they are to grow and prosper.

Measuring effectiveness is more subjective, and quite possibly indicators, as opposed to definitive measures, may have to be used.

Competitors' strategies should be evaluated, and competitors should be benchmarked against customer key success factors.

The E-V-R Congruence model can help an understanding of strategic success. It suggests that resource efficiency, stakeholder satisfaction and values are important constituents which need evaluating.

Business failures are normally caused by poor strategic leadership, poor financial controls and intensifying competition.

STRATEGY CREATION

This chapter introduces three distinct but complementary approaches to strategy creation. These approaches are examined individually in Chapters 5, 6 and 7.

We also look at a range of alternative strategic options and the criteria which might be used for selecting strategies.

THE THREE MODES OF STRATEGY CREATION

David Marshall was determined to relax and forget about work over the week-end. On the Saturday afternoon he joined a small group of friends at a nearby Premier League football match. He thoroughly enjoyed the game, and on Sunday morning he eagerly turned to the match report in his newspaper.

Yesterday's intriguing top of the table clash kept a capacity crowd on the edge of their seats. From the kick off it was clear that City were content to settle for an away draw. It was one-way traffic as the international array of talent in City's line-up looked ill at ease with defensive tactics at odds with the creative, open style of play which has witnessed their rise to the top of the table.

United, clearly intent on three points to enhance their championship challenge, were ahead in the seventeenth minute through a goal, seemingly designed and executed to grace this Premiership shop window. Ten minutes later, they were two up, from a hotly disputed penalty, City's clumsy defender, Peters, arriving so late for a challenge that there was some doubt he had made contact at all. The means of their lead may have been dubious but no one but the most ardent City fan could have begrudged them the two goal margin.

What was said in the changing rooms at half time we may never know, but it was two different teams that emerged for the second half. As United tried to kill the game by packing the defence, and closing down on every yard of space, City rediscovered their flair and vitality. In the engine room of midfield, their England under 23 international played with a maturity and vision that belied his years. Within fifteen minutes of the restart, he had almost single-handedly put them back on level terms. After making the first goal for City's leading scorer, he followed up with an inspirational strike from fully 35 yards.

An increasingly charged atmosphere saw both managers on the touchline, screaming new instructions to their players. United, stunned into action by City's second, rediscovered an understanding crucially missing for the twenty minutes on which the game had turned.

When the final whistle blew, honours remained even, and the rival tribes of supporters filed away knowing that the championship as a whole is likely to be as closely contested and entertaining as this tactical game of cat and mouse.

As he read the summary David recalled the recent discussion when Tony Anderson had commented that strategic change in organizations is similar to a game of football. He realized the consultant was right.

Strategies are means to ends. The two football teams had devised game **plans** to fulfil their objectives for the match. United wanted to win; City did not want to lose and would be content with a draw. But 'the best laid schemes o' mice an men gang aft a gley'. In the first half United's competitive strategy proved more appropriate than City's, and City were forced to **adapt** and change to stay in the game. The strategies were revised at half time and throughout the second half of the match as the managers shouted fresh instructions and the individual players, empowered to exercise some personal initiative, experimented and learnt in the dynamic and turbulent situation.

The result was really decided by the **vision** and leadership skills of City's midfield star.

STRATEGY CREATION

David Marshall had seen applications of the three major modes of strategy formulation at the football match:

1. tactics had been **planned**, but the plans were seen as flexible if the assumptions on which they were based changed;

2. there was **visionary leadership** from one outstanding player who had the ability to inspire others; and

3. the players **adapted** and changed their approach in a dynamic, competitive situation. They were empowered to exercise initiative.

The situation is exactly the same for organizations which compete in a dynamic, turbulent and uncertain environment. They need:

• purpose, direction and strategic intent – which in turn requires both **planning and vision**

- flexibility to **adapt and change** in response to competitive pressures; and

- a commitment to achieve their objectives and implement their chosen strategies. This requires effective **leadership**

Good and bad examples of each of these themes can be seen in the major case study.

In this chapter we will introduce the three modes in greater detail after we examine the range of possible alternative options from which new strategies might be selected.

We saw in Chapter 1 that strategic management comprises three integrated elements:

- **Awareness**   Understanding the strategic situation

- **Formulation**   Choosing suitable strategies

- **Implementation**   Making the chosen strategies happen.

In this chapter we are concentrating on formulation.

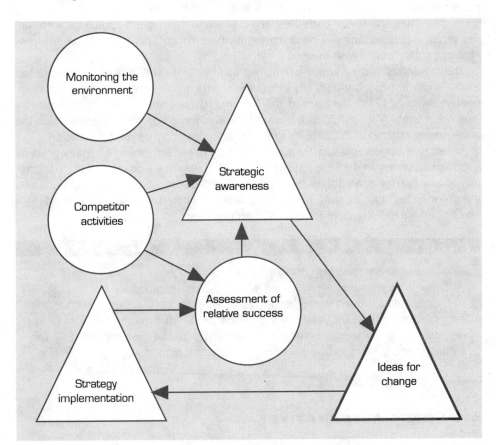

Chart 4.1   Strategic change

Chart 4.1 (which is an extension of Chart 1.5) shows that the ideas for strategic change are dependent upon managers' awareness of the company's strategic situation. This requires an objective appraisal of the organization's current situation and relative success, changing trends in the environment and competitor activity – the subject of Chapters 2 and 3. Once new strategies are selected and implemented they will affect the company's strategic success, and consequently the process of strategic change is continuous and dynamic.

STRATEGIES, OBJECTIVES AND CONSTRAINTS

Strategies are means to ends, which would seem to imply that strategies will be carefully selected with clear objectives in mind. Theoretically this is both sensible and justifiable, but reality is more complex.

On occasions it will be **constraints** rather than freely set objectives which determine strategic choices. Proactive companies will set ambitious objectives and create and implement strategies to achieve the objectives. If they are successful at the expense of their rivals, these competitors will be pushed to react and change their strategies. They will revise both their objectives and strategies because they are under threat. Their actions will be designed to meet constraints rather than any new objectives they might wish to set.

The regulators of the various **privatized utilities** – including water, gas and electricity – can impose statutory price formulae, which influence corporate and competitive strategies. The decision of the **Natural History Museum** to charge visitors was not a strategy it wished to introduce – it was forced on the Museum when the government refused to increase its grant-in aid by the current rate of inflation.

When new opportunities arise suddenly and are seized, strategies really precede specific objectives. In the case study Universal Engineering was offered the opportunity to buy Benson's, an acquisition which fitted the corporate mission and enabled the group to build an existing business. It was highlighted that buying a competitor was not an agreed objective for Special Components.

> *Key Point*
>
> 4.1 Strategies are means to ends.
>
> These ends may be objectives set within the organization.
>
> On occasions though strategies are designed to meet constraints, such as the expectations of powerful stakeholders. These demands limit the freedom of an organization to pursue alternative objectives, which might be preferred by the strategic leader. Competitive pressures impact in a similar way.

STRATEGIC ALTERNATIVES

In choosing a suitable strategy the three main questions are:

- **What?**   Which option is most suitable?

- **How?**   The best way of implementing the choice.

- **When?**   Timing and opportunity.
               Good ideas cannot always be carried through.

While we outline all the main strategic alternatives in this chapter, it is important to appreciate that only a selection of these options will be available to, and appropriate for, an organization at any given time.

THE PLANNING GAP

The idea behind the planning gap is an examination of the organization's need for strategic change. Some possible strategic changes will imply relatively high risks for the organization but offer potentially high rewards if they can be implemented successfully. The choice should balance need with risk. Gap analysis encourages an evaluation of the strategic alternatives required and available to close any gap which might exist between the forecast results which the organization can expect to obtain from present strategies continued forward, and the results the strategic leader would ideally like to attain.

It requires three inputs:

- an honest assessment of the current strategic position, together with an evaluation of the future potential of existing products, services and strategies;

- a statement of the ideal future strategic position and results;

- an evaluation of the alternatives for closing the gap between these, considering the extent of any changes and the risks implied.

By **risk** we mean the magnitude of the possible loss or costs if the chosen strategy does not work out, and the likely impact of this loss on the business as a whole. Sometimes organizations will resist choosing a strategically attractive opportunity if the downside risk is too great. On other occasions organizations will pursue high-risk opportunities either because their range of options is severely limited or because the strategic leader is a risk-taker.

Chart 4.2 illustrates how we might use the concept of the planning gap. We start on the left-hand figure with a statement of where we are now and where we are going. This is shown as the bottom of the three lines. A decline is illustrated, but it does not follow that this would always be the case. To this is added an ideal end point – the top line of the three. As we explore the strategic options for achieving this end we may well revise our objectives if the changes and risks are greater than those we feel happy with – shown as a realistic forecast which is less ambitious (and risky) than the ideal.

The growth vector drawn on the right hand side has been developed from a simpler version devised by Ansoff (1987). It allows us to consider the implications of the

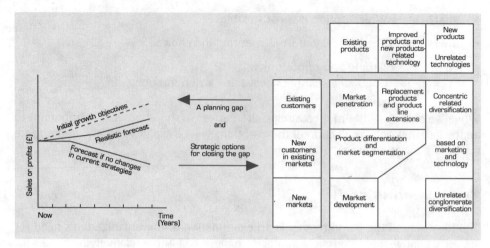

Chart 4.2 The planning gap

alternatives which might be used to close the gap. The least-risk alternative is market penetration, an attempt to manage present products and services more effectively, aiming to sell more of them and to reduce costs in order to generate increased sales and profits.

Growth from this alternative is likely to be limited and consequently it can be extended to strategies of market and product development, which imply respectively:

- new customers, or even new market segments, for existing products, which might be modified in some way to provide increased differentiation; and

- new products, ideally using related technology and skills, for sale to existing markets.

The highest risk alternative is diversification because this involves both new products and new markets simultaneously. When considering this high-risk option, it is important to distinguish between concentric diversification, where the new products are related to existing ones by say technology or marketing, and conglomerate diversification. This encompasses completely new and unrelated products for sale to new customers, and it is frequently implemented by an acquisition.

Key Point

4.2 The planning gap highlights the magnitude and nature of the strategic changes which would be required for the organization to achieve its ideal growth objectives.
Some possible changes will imply high risk.
The outcome should be realistic objectives and means for achieving them.

Box 4.1 explores these four strategies in the context of retailing. The Sainsbury examples illustrate that over a period of time an organization may pursue all four options.

4 1 APPLYING THE SIMPLE GROWTH VECTOR TO RETAILING

1. MARKET PENETRATION

A department store attempts to increase market penetration when it leases specialist concessions for, say, cosmetics, clothes and shoes without changing the overall range of products in any significant way. These concessions introduce greater *product knowledge* which should lead to a better service to customers.

When the major supermarket chains increase the number and volume of their own label products they should be more profitable – the margins will be higher than those for the major brands, which, of course, they will also wish to retain. In 1993 Sainsbury 'permanently reduced' the relative prices of own-label products as a competitive reaction to the growing presence of discount retailers such as Kwik Save, Aldi and Netto and the new threat from American food warehouses. This was a clear attempt to prevent *market erosion*.

A third example is the use of information technology and electronic point-of-sale systems. These improve stock management and reduce costs at the same time. Most large retailers have gone down this route, and some have gone a long way down. Tesco, for example, is linked to all its main suppliers with electronic data interchange, and this really streamlines their relationship by providing fast and accurate information on forecasts, requirements and deliveries.

2. PRODUCT DEVELOPMENT

Examples include the introduction of furniture into Marks & Spencer stores and newspapers, books and cut flowers in Sainsbury's.

In the past supermarkets increased the range and variety of wines, spirits and beers to accommodate the growing incidence of people drinking at home rather than visiting pubs.

3. MARKET DEVELOPMENT

George Davies revitalized the chain of Hepworth's menswear shops, which lost their way and became dowdy and old fashioned, as Next and developed a group offering fashionable clothing for both younger men and women. However, the business grew too quickly and failed to consolidate all the changes and acquisitions. Next bought out Grattan (mail order), but eventually sold it on. Davies became a casualty.

Asda have changed a number of their smaller stores into a discount format, again to compete with the specialist discount retailers, while the large stores still compete with Tesco and Sainsbury.

Marks & Spencer have expanded overseas, opening stores in Europe and Hong Kong, for example. Sainsbury's have bought two supermarket groups in America.

4. DIVERSIFICATION

Marks & Spencer's expansion into America was achieved with the acquisition of Brooks Brothers. This represents related diversification – Brooks is primarily menswear, and it has a prestigious, up-market position. It is quite different from normal M & S stores but it is related because Marks' retailing expertise can be transferred.

The Marks & Spencer chargecard, and their unit trust, constitutes unrelated diversification.

DIY stores provide another example of diversification. Do It All (a joint venture owned by W H Smith and Boots) requires different retail skills from the high-street Smith's and Boots' stores. Competition with B & Q and Texas is very price and discount oriented – supply basically exceeds demand – and the major groups have found it very difficult to establish any real differentiation. Sainsbury's Homebase is a little different as it focuses on gardening and home furnishings rather than covering the whole DIY market ■

The planning gap is basically straightforward and simple to apply. It can be extremely valuable as part of a formal planning process, as it helps an organization to deal with the important issue of objectives, as well as providing a framework for evaluating alternatives. It is also useful for just *thinking* about options.

STRATEGIC ALTERNATIVES

The growth vector provides an outline of the basic expansion strategies; Chart 4.3 is a more detailed summary of the possible strategic alternatives.

From origins in a single business concept, market penetration and product and market development are shown as level-one growth strategies as they mainly affect competitive strategies rather than imply major corporate change.

The level-two growth strategies imply more ambitious and higher risk expansion which is likely to change the corporate perspective or strategy. These options, explained below, may involve either a strategic alliance or an acquisition, and these *strategic means* are discussed in the next section.

We established in Chapter 1 that it is important for organizations to seek competitive advantage for each business in the portfolio. Consequently, once an organization has diversified, it will be necessary to look for new competitive opportunities – or level-one growth strategies – for the various individual businesses. This is illustrated by the dotted line on the chart.

THE LEVEL-TWO GROWTH STRATEGIES

Vertical integration occurs when businesses diversify into different parts of the supply chain, such as components supply (making instead of buying) or distribution. It implies different skills and competencies, and it is often achieved with a strategic alliance rather than a full acquisition or merger. **IBM**, the world's leading computer company which is radically changing both its corporate strategies and structures in the early/mid 1990s, has diversified vertically into semi-conductors, disk drives, computer assembly, software and distribution. In contrast the very successful Microsoft (MS-DOS and Windows) has stayed firmly focused on operating systems.

Related diversification relates to the critical issue of building upon *core competencies* and *key strategic abilities*, which was introduced in Chapter 2. **Canon**, for example, has developed technical competencies in precision mechanics, fibre optics and microelectronics which it has exploited in various products for consumer and office markets. The range includes cameras, calculators, printers and photocopiers.

Horizontal integration is the term used to describe the merger between firms at the same stage of the supply chain. Such firms may be direct competitors or concentrate on different niches. Examples in **financial services** include National Westminster Bank (National Provincial and Westminster banks), the Alliance and Leicester and the Nationwide Anglia building societies. A proposed merger between the Leeds Permanent Building Society and the National & Provincial (itself an earlier merger) was abandoned in 1993 because of cultural differences.

Electrolux is a company which has horizontally integrated and built upon core engineering competencies to become a major global producer of domestic appliances. The acquisitions have included Zanussi of Italy, Tricity in the UK and the Hungarian Lehel, a leading East European producer. Unrelated businesses are now being systematically divested. A global structure has been created deliberately to exploit the potential synergies.

Unrelated diversification can be high-risk but very profitable if the appropriate structure and style of control is adopted. Generally this implies that the businesses are run independently, with the corporate head office providing only limited centralized serv- ices. This point is taken up later, in Chapter 9.

At its height **Lonrho** consisted of some 800 companies in 80 countries. The activites spanned mining, agriculture, steel, oil, textiles, retailing, brewing, motor vehicle distribution, publishing, freight forwarding, hotels, casinos and property management. In the 1990s there has been some limited divestment to give the group more focus.

An excellent example of a diversified conglomerate which has horizontally inte- grated and divested unrelated activities simultaneously is **Grand Metropolitan**. In the mid-1980s Grand Met encompassed hotels (its original business), restaurants, brewing (Watney-Mann), foods (Express Dairies) and leisure (Mecca, William Hill). Most of these have since been sold as the business has been strategically restruc- tured around foods (with the purchase of the American company Pillsbury (Green Giant, Burger King and Häagen Dazs), and a number of spirits brands. Smirnoff vodka, J & B whisky, Gilbey's gin, Croft, Malibu and Bailey's Irish Cream are all Grand Met products. Competitive advantage is being built around marketing and brand man- agement skills which Grand Met believes are transferable across frontiers and be- tween businesses. The company has decentralized more responsibilities to its businesses in an attempt to *strategically regenerate* – see Chapter 2.

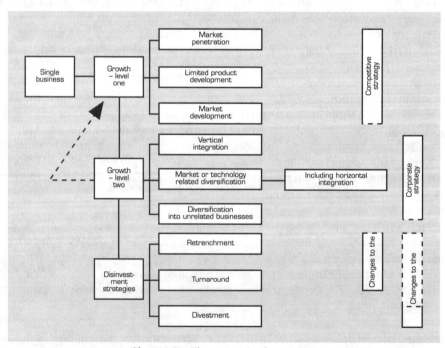

Chart 4.3   The strategic alternatives

Key Point

4.3 Growth objectives can be separated into two groups:

- those which focus mainly on *competitive strategies*;
- *corporate strategy changes* – which normally implies greater risk but potentially higher rewards.

At times growth may not be realistic and organizations will look to rationalize and refocus their strategies.

DISINVESTMENT STRATEGIES

The bottom section of Chart 4.3 illustrates the three main strategies for corporate reduction.

Divestment of non-core or unprofitable businesses is really a disinvestment strategy designed to give the organization either more strategic focus or cash to redeploy. It is sometimes chosen freely; on other occasions it is forced on a company in financial difficulty.

The other disinvestment strategies can be applied at both the competitive and corporate levels. **Retrenchment** involves cost or asset reduction in order to reduce the scale of the organization to a sound basis. **Turnaround** strategies are concerned with finding a new strategic position for a company in difficulty. Burton (Box 3.1) provides a useful example.

Disinvestment and downsizing is frequently straightforward and chosen by companies in a recession and organizations experiencing competitive or financial difficulties. The reduction opportunities, however, may be finite; assets cannot be cut back indefinitely. The real challenge lies in re-creating growth opportunities from the reduced size, and this may imply a change of leadership and values. The skills and approach required for improving productivity is different from that required for creating new and imaginative competitive strategies.

While the various strategic alternatives have been discussed individually, it should be recognized that a number of them overlap and that many organizations pursue several strategies at the same time.

Having discussed the 'what' aspects of strategic alternatives it is now important to evaluate 'how' the option might be implemented.

STRATEGIC MEANS

Chart 4.4, Market Entry Strategies, summarizes the various ways in which an organization might implement its chosen strategies. It should be appreciated that any strategic alternative can be international in scope, rather than focused on a single country or market, and that as we move from the top to the bottom of the chart the inherent scope, risk and potential benefits all increase.

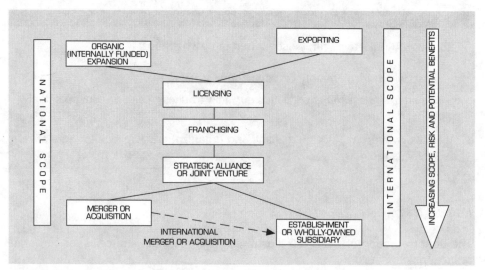

Chart 4.4 Market entry strategies

Organic or internal growth should be low-risk and it should enable ongoing learning and effective control. However it is likely to prove slow, allowing competitors time to prepare their reactions. Moreover new skills may be needed, and these may prove difficult to obtain or learn.

Exporting begins with the search for overseas markets which can absorb any surplus capacity. At this level of commitment it is low-risk but unlikely to yield substantial rewards. Organizations wishing to build and maintain overseas sales will normally utilize the services of agents or distributors. Such arrangements may prove very fruit-ful, but often they can be disappointing. The company's business may not be a major earner for the independent agent/distributor who consequently sees it as low prior-ity. This difficulty can be overcome with a strategic alliance – see below.

Licensing is ideal for an organization which is seeking fast penetration of a market without major investment. Other companies are allowed to manufacture a product or service which is protected by patent in return for royalties. Pilkington achieved a global presence for float glass with licensing; Glaxo used the strategy to launch its anti-ulcer drug, Zantac, in several countries simultaneously. Companies like Walt Disney allow selected clothing and gift manufacturers to use the Disney characters in return for a licence payment. The company is then earning money from activities it is not personally interested in developing itself.

Franchising is another rapid expansion strategy which does not require substantial investment. Examples, which are predominantly service businesses, include McDonald's in America (but not everywhere around the world), Kentucky Fried

Chicken, Thornton's Chocolate Cabins and Fastframe picture framing. The franchisor provides expert training and the exclusive local marketing rights for an established service or brand. The franchisee pays an initial lump sum and royalty payments.

Acquisitions (agreed corporate purchases), **take-overs** (hostile acquisitions) and **mergers** (the integration of two companies) are fast market entry strategies. Companies are simply buying market presence and share, using new debt or equity capital. The strategy has proved very popular with growth-oriented British companies, who, until recently, have mainly concentrated on North America. European acquisitions have been more evident as the single European market has become established. However, valuing a company is never easy, and too high a price may be paid, especially if there is a rival bidder. In addition there may be implementation problems after the acquisition or merger if the two businesses have different cultures which prove difficult to integrate. These problems are explored further in Chapter 10.

Porter (1987) has suggested three important tests for a diversified acquisition.

- The new industry should offer profit potential in excess of the cost of capital (debt or equity) involved.

- The entry cost (acquisition price) should not compromise the future profit stream.

- Both companies should benefit from the merger. There should be true synergy from transferring skills or sharing resources.

Strategic alliances and joint ventures are sometimes an attempt to obtain the benefits of integrating two businesses without the potential drawbacks of a full merger. The term strategic alliance covers a variety of linkage opportunties for strengthening the *external architecture* we discussed in Chapter 2. Joint ventures are regarded as the strongest type of alliance because they require the partners to take equity stakes in each other's company. There may be tensions if the perceived benefits are not of the same magnitude for each partner; and there may still be difficulties in linking two distinct cultures. However it is generally easier to abandon a difficult alliance than to re-sell a problematical acquisition.

Rover and Honda have worked together, mainly in joint product development, for a number of years. Rover has obtained access to Japanese technology, working practices and quality systems; Honda gained a base in Europe. British Airways is using alliances and minority shareholdings to extend its market access and strengthen its position as a leading global carrier. BA owns 25 % of US Air, the fifth largest American carrier, 25 % of Qantas (Australia's international airline), 49 % of TAT (France) and is also allied with Deutsche Air and Air Russia. Sony and Apple are working together on small, personal communications devices with audio and visual facilities. Each company has distinct and relevant core competencies, and together they hope to generate the potential synergy from linking them.

There are four main criteria for successful alliances and joint ventures:

1. both (or all) companies must be committed, allocating time and resources, and trusting their partners;

2. mutual needs and benefits – sacrifices will be required, and these must be rewarded;

3. flexibility – the circumstances and priorities of each partner are likely to change;

4. any cultural differences must be reconcilable.

The highest risk strategic alternative is unrelated diversification through hostile take-over. It is selected because it offers instant growth and is often feasible when more related expansion is not. Acquisitions in related businesses may be unavailable or subject to scrutiny by the Monopolies and Mergers Commission in the UK and similar bodies elsewhere. Such take-overs can also be prompted by an acquisitive strategic leader who simply wants to own the other business, convinced a merger can be made to work. However the success rate remains relatively low at around 50 %; and subsequent divestments often imply substantial losses on the venture. This joint strategic alternative has been less popular during the economic recession of the early 1990s, as companies have chosen to focus more on businesses which relate to their core competencies and strategic abilities.

Key Point

4.4 Vertical integration, often involving a strategic alliance, implies changes to the **external architecture**.

Related diversification seeks to build on **core competencies**, normally in marketing and technology.

Synergy is being sought.

Synergy from unrelated diversification is more elusive.

Mergers and acquisitions require the fusion of two distinct cultures, and consequently the highest risk, most challenging strategic change is unrelated diversification via acquisition.

The chosen strategy should be appropriate, feasible and desirable.

We mentioned earlier that **successful** diversified conglomerates can be very profitable. Hanson (discussed in detail in Chapter 7) and BTR (which includes Dunlop and Hawker Siddeley in its portfolio) are notable examples. They succeed because they:

• carefully target their acquisitions;

• avoid paying too much (normally);

• adopt an appropriately decentralized structure and control systems; and

• corporately add value.

Head office capabilities and contributions include low cost financing for the subsidiaries and skills in trading assets and improving operating efficiencies. In other words, these organizations have developed a strategic expertise in running a diversi-fied conglomerate, skills not matched by many organizations which choose this stra-tegic alternative.

> *As soon as things go wrong, companies start talking about focus. Focus is the crutch of mediocre management ... If you are trained in the techniques of management ... you should be able to apply them across a range of companies. Diversified companies possess both defensive qualities in recession and a springboard for new ventures in more expansive times* (Sir Owen Green, previously Chairman, BTR, quoted in *Management Today,* June 1994, p. 40).

STRATEGY EVALUATION

There are three broad criteria for evaluating strategies: appropriateness, feasibility and desirability.

APPROPRIATENESS

- Does the proposal fit – and strengthen – the existing portfolio of activities?
- Is it compatible with the mission of the organization?
- Does it address any targeted opportunities, or help redress any critical weaknesses?
- What impact would the change have on E-V-R Congruence?
- Is this an opportunity for stretching our resources and exploiting our core competencies? or:
- Does it imply diversification?

FEASIBILITY

- Can we implement the strategic change successfully, and without any detrimental impact upon our existing products, services and markets?

(Sometimes an acquisition might be seen as desirable but infeasible. The targeted company cannot be acquired.)

- Do we have the required skills and competencies, or must we develop new ones? And: Is this feasible in the timescale available to us?
- Can we afford any costs involved?
- Is there an opportunity for us to create (and sustain) competitive advantage?

DESIRABILITY

• Does the option truly help to close the planning gap?

• Are we comfortable with the risks?

• Is this a justifiable (or, in certain cases, the most profitable) use of any spare resources?

• Is there any potential synergy we can exploit?

• Which stakeholder needs will be addressed and satisfied?

These tests can be applied to any change opportunities either formally and objectively, or informally; the ideas are also useful for considering the suitability and value of existing businesses, products and services.

When reviewing options, it is rare that any one alternative will appear to be the most appropriate and the most desirable, and be perfectly feasible. The most desirable strategy for the strategic leader, for example, may not be objectively appropriate for the organization's resources; equally it may be difficult to implement. Normally subjectivity will be involved, and trade-offs between the criteria will have to be made.

On occasions managers will see the 'easiest', most feasible, least risk option as the most desirable. The strategy will be rationalized as appropriate, although with more objective appraisal it may not be the most appropriate for all the stakeholders and the long-term interests of the business.

Having examined a range of strategic possibilities and possible criteria for evaluating their suitability, it is now appropriate to look in greater detail at how strategic change decisions are actually made. We start by looking at three basic modes; organizations are complex and will typically exhibit aspects of all three.

STRATEGY FORMULATION

All managers plan. They plan how they might achieve objectives. Planning is essential to provide direction and to help ensure that the appropriate resources are available where and when they are needed for the pursuit of objectives. Sometimes the planning process is detailed and formal; on other occasions planning may be informal, unstructured and essentially 'in the mind'. In the context of strategy formulation a clear distinction needs to be made between the cerebral activity of informal planning and formalized planning systems.

Formal strategic planning systems are most useful in stable conditions. Environmental opportunities and threats are forecast, and then strategies are planned and implemented. Strategies which are appropriate, feasible and desirable are most likely to help the organization achieve its mission and objectives.

Where the environment is more turbulent and less predictable, strategic success requires flexibility, and the ability to learn about new opportunities and introduce appropriate changes continuously. Planning systems can still make a valuable contribution but the plans themselves must not be inflexible.

In addition it is important not to discount the contribution of visionary strategic leaders who become aware of opportunities – and on occasions, create new opportunities – and take risks based on their awareness and insight of markets and customers.

PLANNED STRATEGIES

Formal planning implies determined actions for achieving stated and desired objectives. For many organizations these objectives will focus on sales growth and profitability. A detailed analysis of the strategic situation will be used to create a number of strategic alternatives, and then certain options will be chosen and implemented.

Planning systems are useful, and arguably essential, for large groups such as Universal Engineering which has a number of businesses which, although largely independent, do need integrating on occasions. There are, though, a number of possible approaches. Head office can delegate the detailed planning to each division, offering advice and making sure the plans can be co-ordinated into a sensible total package. Alternatively the planning system can be controlled centrally in order to establish priorities for resource allocation.

While the discipline of planning and setting priorities is valuable, the plans must not be inflexible and incapable of being changed in a dynamic competitive environment. During implementation it is quite likely that some plans will be discarded and others modified.

VISIONARY LEADERSHIP

Planning systems imply that strategies are selected carefully and systematically from an analytical process. In other instances major strategic changes will be decided upon without lengthy formal analysis. Typically such changes will reflect strong, entrepreneurial leadership and be visionary and *discontinuous* – 'I have seen the future and this is it!'

To an outsider it can often appear that the organization is pursuing growth with high-risk strategies, which are more reliant on luck than serious thought. This can under-estimate the thinking that is involved, because quite often these visionary leaders have an instinctive feel for the products, services and markets involved, and enjoy a clear awareness and insight of the opportunities and risks.

This mode of strategy creation is most viable when the strategic leader has the full confidence of the organization, and he or she can persuade others to follow his or her ideas and implement the strategies successfully. Implementation requires more detailed planning and incremental changes with learning – initially it is the broad strategic idea that is formulated entrepreneurially.

The case suggests that Graham Benson was a visionary leader, but the second generation lacked his flair. Their failing, common in many small businesses, was that they failed to replace the lost entrepreneurialism with an effective alternative.

ADAPTIVE STRATEGIC CHANGE

In dynamic and turbulent competitive environments detailed planning is problematical. The plans are only as good as any forecasts, which must be uncertain. It can make sense, therefore, not to rely on detailed plans, but instead just plan broad strategies within a clearly defined mission and purpose.

Having provided this direction the strategic leader will allow strategies to emerge in a decentralized organization structure. Managers will be encouraged and empowered to make changes in their areas of responsibility, and, ideally, rewarded for their initiatives. The implication is that functional changes will impact upon competitive strategies in a positive way as the organization adapts to its changing environment.

Learning is at the heart of this mode. Managers must learn about new opportunities and threats; they should also learn from the successes and mistakes of other managers. Managers must be willing to take measured risks; for this to happen understandable mistakes and errors of judgment should not be sanctioned harshly.

Change is gradual and comes from experimentation; new strategies involve an element of trial and error. The success of this mode is very dependent upon communications. Managers must know of opportunities and threats facing them; the organization must be able to synthesize all the changes into a meaningful pattern, and spread learning and best practice.

It is quite feasible to find all three modes in evidence simultaneously in an organization, although, of course, there is likely to be one dominant mode. *Moreover different managers in the same organization will not necessarily agree on the relative significance of each mode; their perceptions of what is actually happening will vary.*

Chart 4.5 summarizes these ideas and Box 4.2 applies them to Virgin and McDonald's.

The chart indicates that *intended strategies* can be the outcome of both a formal **planning process** and **visionary leadership**. On implementation some of these intended strategies will be discarded – they turn out to be based on misjudgments, or changing circumstances make them less viable. Meanwhile, in this changing environment, the organization does two other things as a result of learning. First, it **incrementally changes** the intended strategies as they are implemented. Second, it introduces new **adaptive strategies** when fresh opportunities are spotted. Consequently the *actual strategies* pursued will relate to, but differ from, the intended strategies.

Chart 4.6 further relates the ideas to the three levels of strategy: corporate, competitive and functional. In large organizations much of the responsibility for corporate strategic change will be centralized at the head office, although the businesses and divisions can be involved or consulted. Competitive and functional change decisions are more likely to be decentralized, but again, not exclusively. Corporate policies, discussed in the next section, can require or constrain changes at these levels.

In Chapters 5, 6 and 7 we will examine the three modes in greater detail; Chapter 8 will present a number of additional themes to enhance our understanding of how strategies are created in practice.

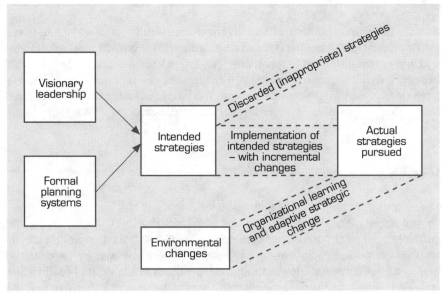

Chart 4.5   Strategy creation

4 2   VIRGIN AND MCDONALD'S: APPLYING THE THREE MODES OF STRATEGY CREATION

VIRGIN

Richard Branson is a well-known entrepreneurial businessman. He became prominent through the growth and success of his Virgin record label and music stores during the 1970s and '80s.

He decided to begin a trans-Atlantic airline in 1984. The move had been prompted by an American who approached him with an idea, and Branson took just a few weeks to make his decision. In this short period Branson analysed why small airlines had previously failed with similar ventures. In particular he focused on Freddie Laker's Skytrain which had competed with a basic service and low prices (Box 3.1). When the major airlines reduced their prices Skytrain was driven from the market — it had no other competitive advantage. Virgin Atlantic Airways would offer added value and superior service at competitive prices, and concentrate on a limited number of the most lucrative routes. Branson had both a *vision* and many critics, who argued he lacked the requisite skills.

More detailed *planning* came later after he began recruiting people with expertise in the industry. In this case the planning concentrated on the implementation of a visionary strategy. The airline has grown steadily over a ten-year period, and won a number of awards for the quality of its service. Additional aircraft have been leased and new routes added. The growth has been in limited, incremental steps as Virgin Atlantic has learnt from experience and adapted in a very dynamic environment. The major carriers such as British Airways have clearly seen Virgin as a threat, and the whole industry has been affected by the Gulf War and the worldwide economic recession.

McDONALD'S

McDonald's, begun by a visionary, the late Ray Kroc, has become a very successful international company, popular with large numbers of customers, and certainly not just children. There are now over 13 000 branches worldwide, up to 1000 are added each year, and the *formula* works as well in Moscow and Beijing as it does in America. Although the products available are broadly similar in America and Europe, menus are seen as flexible in other parts of the world. 9500 stores are franchises, 2500 are company-owned and the rest are joint ventures.

The growth and success in an industry where 'fast food is a by-word for low wages and an unskilled temporary workforce' is not accidental. It has been very carefully planned and managed, although McDonald's relies a lot on the people at the sharp end.

Ever since it began in 1955 McDonald's has been driven by a simple vision, known internally as Q, S, C and V – quality food; fast, friendly service; restaurants known for their cleanliness; and menus which provide value for money.

McDonald's is profitable because it is efficient and productive; and it stays ahead of its competitors by being innovative and looking for new opportunities.

A lot of the developments are planned and imaginative. McDonald's does not move into new countries without thorough investigation of the potential; the same is true for new locations. There are now McDonald's branches in American hospitals, military bases and zoos; worldwide they can be found in airport terminals, motorway service stations, supermarkets (Tesco), and on board cruise ships and Swiss trains.

McDonald's relies heavily on its suppliers for fresh food; again arrangements are carefully planned, monitored and controlled. The in-store systems for cooking and running branches are very tight – to ensure that products and service standards are the same worldwide.

New product development has utilized all the group's resources. The Big Mac, which was introduced nationally in America in 1968, was the idea of a Pittsburgh franchisee who had seen a similar product elsewhere. The aim was to broaden the customer base and make McDonald's more adult-oriented. The company allowed the franchisee to try the product in his restaurant in 1967, although there was some initial resistance amongst executives who wished to retain a narrow product line, and it proved highly successful.

Egg McMuffins in the early 1970s were a response to a perceived opportunity – a breakfast menu and earlier opening times. Previously the restaurants opened at 11.00 am. Although the opportunity was appreciated the development of the product took place over four years, and the final launch version was created by a Santa Barbara franchisee who had to invent a new cooking utensil.

When Chicken McNuggets were launched in 1982 it was the first time that small boneless pieces of chicken had been mass-produced. The difficult development of the product was carried out in conjunction with a supplier and there was immediate competitive advantage. The product was not readily copied. From being essentially a hamburger chain McDonald's quickly became Number 2 to Kentucky Fried for fast food chicken meals.

McDonald's continually tries out new menus, such as pizzas, in order to extend its share of the overall fast food market. To enhance its image of good value, and to compete in a very dynamic industry, McDonald's offers 'extra value meals', special combinations at low prices. There is innovation and the ability to create and adapt strategies to capitalize on opportunities. In addition there is a continuous pressure to reduce costs. Success with these strategies has been achieved partly through serious attempts to share learning and best practice throughout the global network ■

Key Point

4.5 Strategic change decisions can result from:

- formal planning which examines a range of options for achieving strategic objectives;

- visionary leadership which focuses the organization's resources on seizing opportunities;

- ongoing **learning**, **innovation** and adaption in a dynamic environment.

Elements of all three will be found in an organization at any one time.

STRUCTURES AND POLICIES

A clear mission and purpose for the organization are very important, and a visionary approach to changes in the corporate strategy can bring real success. It is also impor-

	CORPORATE STRATEGY	COMPETITIVE STRATEGIES	FUNCTIONAL STRATEGIES
PLANNING	Formal planning systems	Planning the detail for implementing corporate strategies	
VISIONARY	Seizing opportunities – limited planning only	Innovation throughout the organization	
ADAPTIVE/ INCREMENTAL	Reacting to environmental opportunities and threats e.g. Businesses for sale; divestment opportunity	Reacting to competitor threats and new environmental opportunities — — — — — — — — — — Learning and adjustment as planned and visionary strategies are implemented	

MODES OF STRATEGY CREATION

Chart 4.6   Levels of strategy and modes of strategy creation

tant for the strategic leader to have a *vision* concerning the future organization **structure** as well as the strategy. In other words, the type of organization he or she wants; the ways people will work together; where decision-making is to be centralized and where decentralization is more appropriate; issues of empowerment, communications and reward systems. Then, it is important to *plan* how to make this happen. This, in turn, will incorporate alliances and linkages with suppliers, distributors and customers – *external architecture* – and **policies**

Policies are guidelines relating to decisions and approaches which support organizational efforts to achieve stated objectives. They are basically *guides to thoughts (about how things should be done) and actions*. Policies can be mandatory (rules which allow little freedom for original thought or action by managers) or advisory. They can be formally written down, or understood informally, as part of the culture. If managers are substantially empowered to change functional and competitive strategies the policy is really to require managers to 'use their best judgment at all times'.

Finally, decisions and outcomes need to be monitored and controlled, and the strategic leader must put the appropriate mechanisms in place. Structures, systems and policies must also be *adaptive* if strategies are to be adapted and changed incrementally.

POINTS FOR REFLECTION

- Can you think of other examples of visionary, planning and adaptive strategies in action?

- How would you evaluate your organization's strategy creation processes? How much do you think other people's views might differ from yours?

- How do you personally impact upon strategy creation?

- What strategic alternatives and strategic means have been selected in the past by your organization? What future opportunities do you believe exist for the organization and for your business area?

- Are you able to apply the strategy evaluation criteria to any particular strategies, especially ones you might have been instrumental or involved in creating?

REFERENCES AND FURTHER READING

Ansoff, H. I. (1987), *Corporate Strategy*, revised edition, Penguin.

Bailey, A. and Johnson, G. (1992) How strategies develop in organizations. In *The Challenge of Strategic Management* (eds G. Johnson and D. Faulkner), Kogan Page.

Lewis, J. (1990), *Partnerships for Profit*, Free Press (for strategic alliances).

Lowe, J. F. (1986), *McDonald's: Beneath the Arches*, Bantam.

Mintzberg, H. (1973), Strategy making in three modes, *California Management Review*, **16**(2) Winter.

Mintzberg, H. and Waters, J. (1985), Of strategy deliberate and emergent, *Strategic Management Journal*, **6**(3).

Porter, M. E. (1987), From competitive advantage to corporate strategy, *Harvard Business Review*, May–June.

Tilles, S. (1963), How to evaluate corporate strategy, *Harvard Business Review*, July–August.

A SUMMARY OF THE STRATEGIC LESSONS

Strategies are means to ends; the ends can be either objectives or constraints.

The planning gap is a useful concept for exploring the organization's need to change. Strategies for closing a conceptual gap between the expected outcomes from not changing existing strategies and the ideal objectives of the strategic leader can be reviewed. This assessment should balance potential outcomes and risks.

Strategic alternatives can be categorized into relatively low risk growth strategies, higher risk/higher potential growth options and strategies for disinvestment and corporate restructuring.

As well as deciding 'which' strategy, it is also necessary to consider 'how' the preferred strategy might be implemented.

The highest risk strategy is normally diversification via acquisition.

There are three main criteria for evaluating strategies: appropriateness, desirability and feasibility.

Strategy creation is complex and multi-faceted; three themes summarize the alternative basic modes. These are planning, visionary and adaptive strategy creation. All may be present in an organization, although there will be one dominant mode, but managers are likely to disagree on their relative prominence.

The themes of planning, vision and adaptive change can be applied to corporate structures as well as strategies.

Policies are important for guiding the actions and decisions taken by managers. Policies can be loose and empowering, or much tighter.

5

VISIONARY LEADERSHIP

In this chapter we look at the contribution made by an effective strategic leader and at the visionary aspects of strategy creation. Visionary leaders provide a suitable purpose and clear direction for the organization and ensure that the necessary structures are in place for transforming creative ideas into strategic successes.

TWO CONTRASTING STRATEGIC LEADERS

Early the following week David Marshall and Roger Ellis went to their sub-contractor's factory. Roger knew the company well, but it was David's first visit. Clark Precision Engineering was housed in a smart but unpretentious factory unit on a new industrial estate; the equipment inside represented up-to-date technology and the atmosphere was 'busy'.

Tom Clark, the managing director, and his partner had bought the business from their previous employer, which was rationalizing its interests. Tom's partner was the finance director, and it was his nephew, a graduate engineer, who was being groomed for eventual succession.

The previous owner, KB Equipment, which manufactured earthmoving equipment and agricultural vehicles, decided to concentrate on assembly and buy-in specialist components. Tom Clark was general manager of the company's gear box division, and he bought this business and expanded it. He still manufactured a range of gear boxes for KB and one other customer, and used his surplus capacity and specialist skills for sub-contract work. In total he had only six customers, all of whom he dealt with personally. He recognized the significant importance of every customer to his business; he also attempted to ensure they were similarly dependent upon his contribution.

STRATEGIC ABILITIES AND EXTERNAL ALLIANCES

Tom explained:

- Competition in the gear box industry is based upon technological abilities, but customization and service are also crucially important.
- For his sub-contract work technological ability is really a 'given' – you simply must have the competency to win any business. Differentiation is based upon service.
- Consequently his company concentrates upon three main strategic abilities: product development (essentially continuous improvements in performance), quality improvements and operational flexibility (to fit in with customer requirements). Cost control is also treated seriously.
- Internally he personally seeks to ensure there is co-operation between design and development, production and sales. Information technology is used to keep everyone up-to-date.

The company understands gear boxes, but there is no wish to diversify into the design and manufacture of other components. By limiting the number of customers they believe they can offer a high quality, reliable service, and they retain business by understanding and consistently meeting customers' needs. The product development for gear boxes is allied to ongoing research at KB and their other customers – first, to ensure Clark Precision Equipment will be in a position to meet their customers' future needs; second, to help their customers add value by providing the 'best available' gear box. Tom Clark has fostered and re-tains close links with the mechanical engineering department of a local university, and he aims to be innovatory in a very limited field. In sum-mary, Clark Precision Engineering aims to (1) add value for its custom-ers and (2) help its customers add further value.

David felt that Clark was not complacent about the need to adapt and change continuously, and he intended that the company would grow. The growth would be gradual and organic. He did not want the company to be so stretched that it would be unable to cope with the economic recessions which plagued many engineering businesses. His management style was open and informal. His employees were mostly highly skilled and experienced, and he sought to use their knowledge, abilities and creativity as much as possible.

SHARING THE PROBLEM

The managers discussed Special Components' new product. Tom be-lieved that in this instance his customer, Special Components, had failed to appreciate his difficulties. They had reacted to an ultimatum from their customer in Germany, simply passing their own problems further down the supply chain. The work on the new component was complex and demanding, and development work was needed to determine the most efficient way of achieving the quality standards speedily. At the moment he was having to commit too many resources to the work and this was proving both expensive and threatening to his other orders.

He appreciated that Special Components was under pressure from Germany and from Universal Engineering but felt nothing valuable would be achieved until all the parties concerned properly shared their concerns, fully recognized their mutual interdependency and agreed a suitable way forward. Hasty promises and a reluctance to deal with the critical issues would cause a breakdown in the close working relationships along the supply chain, and this would only benefit their competitors.

Afterwards Roger and David talked about the clear picture Tom Clark had of his company's strengths and abilities, and upon the interdependencies along the whole supply chain. David knew he must discuss **external architecture** with Dieter Wild.

THE BUSINESS THAT FAILED

David was very impressed with Clark Precision Engineering; it seemed markedly different from what he had learnt about Benson Engineering. Tom Clark was clearly focused, and in control of both the strategy and the organization.

Graham Benson was an energetic, forceful and creative engineer who could spot the market opportunities for new technologies. He too had been focused, and concentrated on a single range of products which he developed systematically. He was not, though, without faults. He used the success of his company to help finance his personal interest in motorsport, and this had drawn his attention away from building a sound team of managers and planning for his succession. When he died suddenly it was apparent that the business was too dependent upon one person. Another strong and influential leader was needed to take over and give the company fresh ideas and direction. Two uninterested sons could not provide that leadership. In recent years the limited investment in the business had mainly been spent on the administrative building. Visitors to the plant were impressed by the external appearance and amazed that inside the equipment and layout was old-fashioned.

VISIONARY LEADERSHIP

The case has identified that strategic leadership involves elements of vision and action. An organization needs a purpose and direction, together with strategic ideas that are capable of implementation. In most organizations the leader is dependent upon other people for some of the ideas and certainly for successful implementation. Consequently the structure and style of management are critical issues. Tom Clark has a clear and focused strategy and understands that successful implementation requires co-operation with his customers. He also recognizes the important contribution his employees can make. His vision appears to be long-term. Graham Benson was a *visionary engineer* but he lacked Clark's *strategic vision*. His sons failed to grasp which factors were critical for strategic success.

These same themes can be applied to all types and sizes of business.

There is no single profile for a successful strategic leader. Some industrialists enjoy a very high public profile; low-profile leaders can be found at the head of many successful organizations. Some are cautious while others are more adventurous and risk-oriented. Some are well-known personally to many managers and employees throughout the organization, and in touch with day-to-day happenings; others prefer to be detached from ongoing operations, concentrating instead on long-term strategic developments. Personable, easy-to-approach leaders contrast with those who are more authoritarian. Certain leaders are loners who appear to be largely self-dependent; some are good listeners who work closely and openly with their senior management team. The extent and type of experience and the personal power bases vary markedly.

It is therefore more important to examine the **contribution** required from an effective strategic leader.

It was mentioned at the end of Chapter 1 that the term *strategic leader* is being used to describe the chairman, chief executive or managing director who is clearly responsible – and accountable – for corporate level strategic decisions and changes. The *leader* can be a single person or a team of executives, and he or she is responsible to the Board of Directors, and through the Board, to the stakeholders of the business.

STRATEGIC LEADERSHIP

An effective strategic leader ensures the organization has a strategic vision and a structure which allows successful implementation. See Chart 5.1. The important direct or personal contributions concern vision and action, but the leader must also ensure the other key aspects are in place.

There are seven identifiable themes.

STRATEGIC VISION

At the heart of this is a clear, understood and supported mission for the organization. Employees must appreciate the fundamental purpose and be committed to its achievement; the mission will provide guidance and direction when managers make decisions and implement strategies determined by others. The mission may be the vision of the current strategic leader; equally it may have been established by a predecessor. Similarly, the actual strategies – corporate and competitive – for achieving long-term

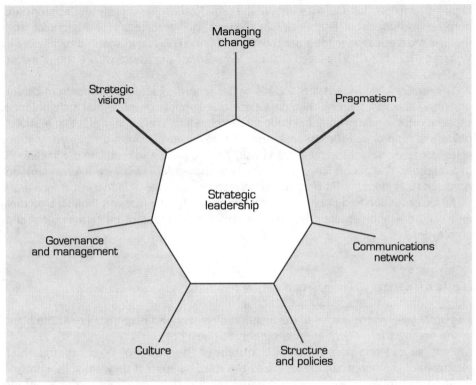

Chart 5.1 Strategic leadership

objectives may be created personally by a strong or visionary strategic leader, or they may be ideas from anywhere inside the organization. It is simply the responsibility of the strategic leader to ensure that strategies are in place, communicated and understood, together with processes for managing strategic change. The more feasible and achievable the objectives and strategies seem, the more likely they are to be supported.

PRAGMATISM

This is the ability to make things happen and bring positive results. Some strategic leaders will be doers, active in carrying strategies through; others will be delegators who rely instead on their skills for motivating and inspiring. Control systems for monitoring results and strategic effectiveness are also important.

Some corporate leaders, then, will be strategic visionaries who are also active in operations; others will contribute ideas and leadership but be happy to devolve operational responsibility. It is possible for pragmatic but non-visionary leaders to be highly effective as long as they ensure the organization has a clear and appropriate purpose and direction. Bennis (1988) suggests, however, that vision is crucial and that the most effective leaders are those with ideas. This accords with the view of Sir Winston Churchill who believed that the 'emperor of the future will be the emperor of ideas'.

The strategic leader's vision and his or her record of achievement are critical for obtaining and maintaining the confidence and support of influential stakeholders, especially the very important institutional shareholders. The willingness of large share-holders to hold or sell their shares, and their expressed support for company strat-egies, are essential for maintaining a healthy share price and reducing the likelihood of a takeover. Their confidence in the ability of the leader is a major determinant; on occasions it is shareholder pressure which forces a change of leadership.

As well as vision and pragmatism it is necessary for the leader to build a structure and culture which captures the abilities and contributions of other managers and employees.

GOVERNANCE AND MANAGEMENT

Corporate governance relates to the location of power and responsibility at the head of the organization. There are two significant questions.

First, should one person act as chairman of the Board of Directors and chief executive of the organization, or should the roles be split? If they are split, strategy creation can to some extent be separated from current operations, and allow for healthy questioning and debate. However it is vital that the two people concerned can work together amicably. One person combining the roles can provide clear and firm direction and control, but can sometimes become very powerful. In such cases the organization might become too dependent on one person.

Second, what contributions can be made by part-time, non-executive directors? Experienced people who are detached from daily responsibilities and pressures within the organization can often be objective and a source of fresh ideas. Frequently the non-executive directors will either be members of several boards or active as an executive in another non-competing company.

Related to this issue, it is vital that the strategic leader ensures that there is a strong, competent and balanced executive team at the head of the organization.

STRUCTURE

It is the strategic leader who decides upon the appropriate structure for carrying out existing strategies and ensuring there is proper momentum for change.

The issues are:

- Should the organization be relatively flat and informal or have several layers of management and more formality?

- Should it be split into individual businesses or divisions?

- How much power and responsibility should be delegated and decentralized?

- What is the appropriate role for the corporate headquarters?

- To what extent should managers and other employees be empowered to take more responsibility?

- What structures and mechanisms are required to ensure that managers in different business areas and different functions integrate and plan how they can help each other? In other words, planning synergies through effective organizational teamworking.

- What policies are necessary and appropriate for guiding and directing decision-making?

These issues are explored in greater detail in later chapters.

THE COMMUNICATIONS NETWORK

Effective communication systems, both formal and informal, are required to share the strategic vision and inform people of priorities and strategies and to ensure strategies and tasks are carried out expeditiously. Where the organization is decentralized an effective communications network is vital for feeding information *upwards and laterally* inside the organization; without this control will be lost. Good lateral communications also help managers to learn from other parts of the business; this in turn can lead to 'best practices' being shared.

CULTURE

To a great extent the culture of the organization is dictated by the strategic leader. The attitudes and behaviours of people are affected as well as their willingness to accept responsibility and take measured risks.

The strategic leader may have very clear or specific values which influence his or her style, and the culture of the organization. For example if the leader has a financial background and orientation, this may prove important. Financial targets and analysis may be crucial elements in the management of strategy. Similarly if the leader has a marketing background this could result in a different style of leadership, with perhaps more concentration on consumers and competition. An engineer may be very committed to product design and quality. These comments are generalizations, and will not always prove to be true.

If a new strategic leader is appointed from another company it is inevitable he or she will bring values which have been learned elsewhere, and these may involve change. Logically the person will be chosen because of his or her successful record in one or more previous companies; and the newcomer may be determined to establish his or her presence by introducing changes.

MANAGING CHANGE

The organization must be able to respond to the change pressures of a competitive environment. Curiosity, creativity and innovation become critically important values, and it is important for the strategic leader to ensure they become part of the corporate culture. However, while learning and incremental change are crucially important they may not be sufficient. As we saw in Chapter 2, *discontinuous change* and **strategic regeneration** will be necessary for organizations at certain stages in their life cycles. When this is the case, and strategies, structures and styles of management need re-inventing simultaneously, an effective, visionary leader will be essential.

Box 5.1 describes aspects of the structural vision of John F. Welch, strategic leader at General Electric in America.

5 1 GENERAL ELECTRIC

General Electric (GE), which manufactures aircraft engines, defence electronics and household consumer goods and owns NBC Television in America, has recorded annual revenues in excess of $50 billion. Until October 1994 GE also owned the Kidder Peabody Investment Bank.

The company is decentralized and employees are encouraged to speak out and pursue ideas. External contacts and sources are constantly monitored for new leads and opportunities. 'We'll go anywhere for an idea.'

The chief executive officer, John F. Welch, believes 'the winners of the 1990s will be those who can develop a culture that allows them to move faster, communicate more clearly, and involve everyone in a focused effort to serve ever more demanding customers'.

The decentralization aims to 'inject down the line the attitudes of a small fast-moving entrepreneurial business and thereby improve productivity continuously'. Integration strategies promote the sharing of ideas and best practices.

There is a developed strategy of moving managers between businesses and countries to transfer ideas and create internal synergy, together with a reliance on employee training. Welch regularly attends training courses to collect opinion and feedback. 'My job is to listen to, search for, think of and spread ideas, to expose people to good ideas and role models.' GE's 'work out' programme involves senior managers presenting GE's vision and ideas to other managers and employees, and then later reconvening to obtain responses and feedback on perceived issues and difficulties. External advisers (such as university academics) monitor that communications are genuinely two-way.

Managers are actively encouraged to work closely with suppliers and customers, and they have '360 degree evaluations', with inputs from superiors, peers and subordinates. 'People hear things about themselves they have never heard before.'

Welch summarizes his philosophy as follows:

If we are to get the reflexes and speed we need, we've got to simplify and delegate more – simply trust more. We have to undo a 100 year old concept and convince our managers that their role is not to control people and stay on top of things, but rather to guide, energize and excite. But with all this must come the intellectual tools, which will mean continuous education of every individual at every level of the company.

(Strategic regeneration at General Electric is examined in Chapter 10, Box 10.3.) ■

The importance of an *effective* strategic leader cannot be stressed too highly, but of course an individual leader cannot and should not attempt to 'do everything'. An important skill is the ability to understand personal strengths and limitations and appreciate the most appropriate ways of contributing. The rest of this chapter examines the visionary element of strategy creation and strategic leadership and includes short cases on a number of leaders who are recognized as visionaries.

Key Point

5.1 An effective strategic leader will ensure the organization has a clear purpose and direction and the means to achieve the purpose. In other words he or she will provide the 'where' and the 'how'. In addition the organization's resources will be focused towards seizing opportunities.

Lord Hanson, founder and executive chairman of the renowned and very successful Hanson plc, believes that he has personally been a successful strategic leader because he has:

- ensured he has stayed informed;

- wanted to actually do things in business;

- deployed his not inconsiderable energy into making things happen;

- been able to inspire others to do things;

- stayed responsive to change pressures.

VISIONARY LEADERSHIP AND STRATEGY CREATION

Visionary leadership implies a strategic leader with a vision for the future of the organization and at least a broad idea of the strategies for pursuing the vision. Such leadership often appears to be based on intuition and possibly experience rather than detailed analysis, but truly visionary leaders possess strategic awareness and insight and do not require extensive analyses to understand key success factors and how the organization can use its abilities and competencies to satisfy needs and expectations. There is a 'feel' for which strategies will be appropriate and feasible and for the potential of the opportunity.

When a visionary leader pursues new opportunities and introduces changes the detailed plans for implementing the new strategies are unlikely to be in place; instead there will be a reliance on incremental learning, flexibility and adaption. For the approach to succeed, the leader must be able to inspire others and persuade them of the logic and merits of the new strategies. This is true for all important strategic changes, of course, but when new proposals have emerged from a more formal strategic planning system there will be substantive detail and analysis to justify the case instead of a strong reliance on vision and intuition.

Where major changes to the corporate strategy are being considered it may be necessary for the strategic leader to convince other members of the Board of Directors and, if new funding is needed, the institutional shareholders and bankers.

The strategy cannot be successful until it has been implemented and has brought the desired results and rewards. Such outcomes require the support and commitment of other managers, and consequently effective visionaries are often articulate, communicative and persuasive leaders.

In simple terms, then, visionary strategic leadership implies three steps: step one is the vision; step two is selling it to other stakeholders and managers; and step three is making sure it happens. Aspects of vision, communication and pragmatism.

Richardson (1994) suggests the following factors are typical of visionary leadership:

- 'covert' planning – planning is often cerebral rather than formal and systematic, such that planning **systems** are not a major aspect of strategy creation;
- a passion about what they are doing and their business;
- they are instrumental in creating and fostering a particular culture;
- they are highly persuasive when encouraging others to implement their ideas and strategies;
- they rely on charisma and personal power.

(Culture and power are explored in Chapter 8.)

Box 5.2 considers one visionary strategic leader whose creative ideas have often been thwarted at the implementation stage.

EXAMPLES OF VISIONARY LEADERSHIP

Founders of successful, fast-growing businesses are frequently visionary. As we have seen in the case study, when these companies are family businesses the issue of leadership succession is critical if the growth momentum is to be maintained.

5 2 VOLVO

Volvo was led from 1971 to 1993 by Pehr Gyllenhammar, a lawyer who was married to the daughter of the previous chief executive. Gyllenhammar has been credited as a visionary leader who failed to implement many critical strategic proposals.

In the early 1970s he realized Volvo was reliant on a limited product range (essentially large cars, trucks and buses) and constrained by Sweden not being a member of the European Community. He acquired Daf from the Dutch government; a prolonged learning curve was required before Volvo's subsequent range of small cars proved successful. He began to build the first foreign-owned car assembly plant in America; production never started. He opened the revolutionary Kalmar assembly plant in Sweden in 1974, based on autonomous work groups rather than the traditional assembly line; the idea was successful, but not outstandingly so, and Kalmar was closed in 1993. In 1977 a proposed merger with Saab-Scania was abandoned when Saab had second thoughts. In 1978 Gyllenhammar agreed to sell 40% of Volvo to the Norwegian government in exchange for oil rights; Volvo's shareholders revolted.

In the 1980s Volvo acquired an American truck business and diversified into the food and drug industries in Sweden, but not without some friction with the Swedish government.

In 1989 Volvo and Renault cemented a strategic alliance with the exchange of minority shareholdings; and in 1993 a full merger was proposed. Fearing the future role of the French government (Renault was nationalized but due for privatization), Volvo's shareholders again refused to back Gyllenhammar. After this defeat he resigned. Despite all the setbacks, Volvo has proved to be robust and, under Gyllenhammar, has grown into one of Sweden's leading businesses.

The diversification strategies have been focused on less cyclical industries to offset the uneven cash flow characteristics of car manufacturing, but a new corporate strategy was announced in April 1994. Non-vehicle interests would be divested systematically. Vehicle joint ventures with a **series** of companies worldwide would be sought ■

In successful businesses which grow and become public companies the challenge is to find the right leader to replace anyone who retires or resigns. Whenever a visionary leader leaves or joins an organization there is likely to be a change in strategy and possibly structure, with the consequent risks.

Grand Metropolitan has had three chief executives since it was created in 1957. The first was the founder, Sir Maxwell Joseph, who ran the business for 23 years. He started with hotels, later diversifying into restaurants, brewing, spirits, foods and leisure. When he retired in 1980 Grand Met was 90 % dependent on the UK; and his successor, Sir Stanley Grinstead, was determined to reduce this. Grand Met began to invest in America. Sir Allen Sheppard took over in 1986 and his strategy was to focus where Grand Met could attain world leadership. This would be selected branded foods – Pillsbury (Green Giant foods, Burger King and Häagen Dazs ice cream) was acquired – and spirits. Remaining non-core businesses have been divested. In recent years Grand Met has been increasingly decentralized to speed up decision-making.

Box 5.3 features three well-known visionary strategic leaders who have founded – and still control – their successful businesses. The leaders represent different backgrounds, styles and strategies, but they all have a clear vision and focus. Their organizations have been built around identifiable competencies and strategic abilities.

 THREE VISIONARY STRATEGIC LEADERS

BILL GATES – MICROSOFT

In the early 1990s there are over 100 million personal computers in use around the world. 90 % of them run on Microsoft operating systems. Bill Gates, the founder and current strategic leader, is one of the richest men in America. He will be 40 years old in 1995.

Gates had a vision – a computer on 'every' desktop in every office, providing timely information. These computers would all need software. He saw this need ahead of any real market penetration by personal computer hardware, and he took risks in his desire to break into the market. He also had a share of good luck.

When the first commercial micro-computer (the Altair) needed a customized version of the Basic programming language Gates accepted the challenge. His package was later licensed to Apple, Commodore and IBM, the companies which developed the personal computer market. When IBM decided to seriously attack the personal computer market Gates was commissioned to develop the operating system. He made a number of innovative improvements to an existing off-the-shelf package and renamed it MS-DOS (Microsoft Disk Operating System). Manufacturers of IBM-clones, who could undercut IBM's hardware assembly costs, also chose MS-DOS.

IBM, seeking to protect their niche, jointly developed a new system with Microsoft, the OS/2 system. While perfectly satisfactory other manufacturers were not interested in licensing it; Microsoft then went it alone and eventually launched Windows in 1985. Windows allows easy switching between software packages and the ability to mix text and graphics. Windows resembles the Apple Mackintosh operating system and there have been legal battles in America concerning copyright infringement.

By nature Gates is a competitive person with a strong will to win. His background is 'middle class America'. His father is a successful corporate lawyer and his mother is very active in community work.

ALAN SUGAR – AMSTRAD

In contrast to Gates, Alan Sugar was brought up in East London in a relatively poor estate. His background is working class. He founded Amstrad in 1968 (he was 21); he is still in firm control of the company, which is now quoted on the Stock Exchange. In recent years the company's performance has been cyclical – in 1994 Amstrad reported its third consecutive pre-tax loss – and Sugar did try and reprivatize Amstrad, but he offered less than the original selling price for the shares and the shareholders turned him down. Sugar is one of Britain's richest men; he is also the largest shareholder and chairman of Tottenham Hotspur, the football club and leisure business.

Amstrad's early business activity was the buying and selling of audio equipment, later followed by the manufacture of low cost amplifiers and speakers. Sugar's breakthrough really came when he persuaded Comet to stock his products.

Sugar's strategy from the early days has been to identify new electronics products with mass market potential and design versions which are cheaper than the competition. Low-cost parts, sourced worldwide, and aggressive marketing underpin the strategy. There are three principles: cost-cutting, simple designs for mass markets and speed. Sugar has an unequivocal view on technology: 'I don't care if they have rubber bands, as long as they work.'

By the early 1980s Amstrad had entered the computer industry, and Sugar envisioned a computer where the screen, printer and control mechanisms were run from a single box, thereby saving components and costs. He marketed a high-capability computer as a word-processor, a typewriter-substitute, to allay consumer fears about using high technology.

Amstrad has also manufactured aerial dishes for BSkyB satellite television, fax machines, video cassette recorders (Amstrad pioneered a double-deck model where tapes can be edited and two programmes recorded simultaneously) and, in 1991, laptop computers.

There have been mistakes. Arrangements with Far Eastern suppliers have broken down on occasions, for example, resulting in late deliveries and poor quality. But Amstrad and Sugar have survived the setbacks. In the early 1990s Amstrad's competitive strategy of low-price personal computers (there is no technical superiority) looked vulnerable as global over-supply has driven down market prices.

Sugar now looks to acquire and 'glue on to the core businesses others that have a synergy with electronics and electrical goods'. Cellular phones are one example and in 1994 Amstrad bought the personal computer manufacturer

Viglen. There is no intention of moving up-market. 'Our vocation is always in the lower end of the market.'

ANITA RODDICK – THE BODY SHOP

Anita Roddick was born in 1944, the daughter of Italian immigrant parents who ran a successful café. She trained as a teacher, but then chose to travel and work around the world. She returned to the UK, taught English for a while, and then set off again. She spent time in the Polynesian Islands, New Caledonia and Australasia, where she learnt about natural skin and hair care products.

Back home again she married Gordon Roddick and they ran a small hotel and restaurant before opening a shop in Brighton. They sold natural products. Large companies refused to produce for her, and consequently she initially used herbalists as suppliers. Body Shop is now vertically integrated into manufacturing. The real growth of Body Shop has been facilitated by franchising – Gordon's idea – and the UK market is approaching saturation. Both Boots and Sainsbury's now have ranges of natural cosmetics and toiletries. Most of the company's growth in the 1990s is being achieved with international expansion. The company has succeeded in penetrating Japan, for example.

The company's success has been based on:

* simple systems;
* a high public profile built on the respect the company enjoys for its ethical and environmental beliefs;
* an informal style of management;
* a willingness to always ask for outside help;
* a strong focus on people inside the business.

One Body Shop director has commented: Anita Roddick 'is so far ahead of the rest of the market that she will never have competitors – only imitators.' It appears that Anita Roddick understands the market and is the creator of the competitive strategies; Gordon contributes ideas for corporate strategic changes and runs the control systems. An ideal partnership.

Partnerships pervade the Body Shop. Franchises are partnerships, after all. Distribution is handled by an independent company, the Lane Group, with whom Body Shop co-operates very closely. There is a 'partnership document' which requires that 99.7% of deliveries will take place within a two-hour window. Achievements above this level attract bonuses – which the distributors earn frequently ■

Some strategic leaders who turn round companies in a crisis situation and restore growth are also visionary. However it does not follow that visionary leadership is essential for new ventures and turnaround situations; good analytical 'company doctors' who can restructure, rationalize and refocus a troubled business can be equally effective.

In reality a visionary leader can emerge at the top of almost any organization if the Board of Directors choose to select such a person. Some of the largest public companies around the world are led by charismatic visionaries; others have leaders who are more analytical and reflective.

Key Point

5.2 Visionary leaders possess strategic awareness and insight and do not seem to require extensive analyses to understand key success factors and how the organization can use its abilities and competencies to satisfy needs and expectations.

Visionary leaders are able to inspire others and persuade them of the logic and merits of their strategic ideas.

MAJOR PROBLEMS

- Unless proper plans are made succession can be a critical issue.

  In 1993 Grand Metropolitan Chairman Sir Allen Sheppard relinquished his additional chief executive role. Organized succession seems to be in hand.

- Visionary leadership is frequently associated with entrepreneurial strategies for companies enjoying prosperity in growth markets. As the organization continues to grow a more formal structure, together with robust control systems, will be required. The leader must therefore be flexible, capable of adapting and willing to relinquish some personal control. Ideally other managers will be empowered and encouraged also to be entrepreneurial and visionary.

  This will not always happen – some visionary leaders tend to be inflexible. In such circumstances a change of leader would benefit the organization.

- Visionary leaders can become too confident with their current success and fail to build new strategies and new futures. Ideally they should have confidence, and a strong commitment to their business and where it is going; at the same time it can help to be humble, and recognize that there are competitors who are just as strong and who can change situations very quickly.

- Strategies have life cycles, and the leader may run out of fresh ideas. Without a change of style the future may be jeopardized; past successes can turn to failure. Coloroll (Box 5.4) illustrates a successful company whose growth strategy was inappropriate for a changing economic climate.

- Powerful, visionary leaders can act against the best interests of the organization as well as for it, especially if their power is unchecked.

The late Robert Maxwell is an example of this. Maxwell was both charismatic and very successful, but his ambition to build a global communications empire led to over-expansion and financial difficulties. Secretly and unethically he 'borrowed' money from pension funds to try and prop up other businesses inside his corporation. In the end he failed and his whole business empire crumbled.

5 4 COLOROLL

Coloroll was an established business in Manchester when John Ashcroft, a 30-year-old MBA, became managing director in 1979. In the next ten years Coloroll expanded and acquired aggressively.

The company's share of the UK wallpaper market grew from 3% to 30%; pottery and earthenware (Denby and Staffordshire Potteries) were added; Edinburgh Crystal and Fogarty duvets and bed linen were acquired; and finally Coloroll bought John Crowther (Kosset carpets).

Ashcroft successfully identified and exploited an opportunity for providing a range of attractive and affordable household products for young consumers who were either first-time home owners or removing for the first time.

There were tight financial controls; managers were required to achieve stretching targets in a very decentralized organization; the head office comprised just four executives and a small support team. Ashcroft commented:

I have a clear perception of where the business is going. Every year we debate it, but once I decide, then everyone has to go along with it. There is a lot of nonsense talked about democracy. I believe management democracy is everyone agreeing to do what the leader wants.

The company grew exceptionally quickly and it was profitable – until too high a price was paid for John Crowther. When the economy moved into recession, and demand for Coloroll's products fell – the house market collapsed – Coloroll struggled to meet the interest payments on the borrowing which had been incurred to pay for Crowther.

Ashcroft's aggressive, acquisitive style worked successfully in an expansionary market. His approach was unsuitable for a recession, when cost cutting and rationalization was needed. In addition, he had lost the confidence of Coloroll's financiers. He resigned in 1990.

Receivers eventually split the business into eleven separate parts. Five were sold to their managements; three to other companies; and the remaining three were closed ■

THE PRICE OF FAILURE

Strategic leaders often pay the ultimate price for strategic failure. They either resign or they are dismissed by the Board of Directors. Ironically they are often rewarded with a generous golden handshake to compensate for the termination of their contract. Financially they suffer far less than those employees who lose their jobs, and sometimes the shareholders. A new leader may restore any lost value of the shares.

VISIONARY LEADERSHIP IN CONTEXT

A visionary leader who possesses the characteristics we defined earlier is not essential for an organization. Equally this style of leadership is not appropriate for all circumstances. Companies which rely more on planning (see Chapter 6) and adaptive strategy creation (Chapter 7) will typically feature a different style of leadership. Visionary leaders are usually associated with entrepreneurial growth, and, as we have seen, sometimes organizations need consolidation rather than growth, which really requires a different style and different characteristics. Companies in trouble, facing a strategic crisis or which need rationalizing require a leader who is skilled at managing detail and resources to generate productivity improvements – again different characteristics from the visionary. However, once such an organization has been successfully rationalized, fresh growth requires vision, and here a more visionary leader can again prove ideal.

In a perfect world, as Richardson and Thompson (1994) argue, leaders will be flexible and adaptive and they will ensure the organization as a whole possesses a multiplicity of strategic skills and competencies such that it can adapt and deal with the various issues and challenges it faces. Where leadership is inflexible, and where skills do not match those required at a particular time, the organization might be best served by a change of strategic leader. But this will not always be easily brought about – especially, as is often the case with visionary leaders, the strategic leader owns the company.

Finally, it is important to emphasize that visionary, leadership and innovation skills should not be present only at the head of an organization. It is important that they permeate the whole business if the company is to remain an effective competitor in a dynamic environment.

Key Point

5.3 The major problems with visionary leadership are:

- succession;
- ensuring the style is appropriate for the company's strategic needs and circumstances;
- loss of vision;
- the pursuit of personal objectives to the detriment of the long-term interests of the organization.

PLANNING AHEAD

David Marshall knew Bob Langley would be returning from America before the end of the week. He also knew that Bob's secretary had arranged their visit to Benson's for the following Tuesday, the day before David was going to Germany.

David studied the preparations he had made for their Benson presentation. He had covered:

- the meaning of 'strategy' and 'strategic management';

- evaluating strategic success;

- strategy formulation.

His previous experience would enable him to describe the Universal Engineering planning system, the process through which Special Components and the other divisions annually agree their performance targets and outline strategies with the Universal Board.

David realized that their **planning challenge** required them to work out how to rescue the most valuable parts of Benson's, integrating these with Special Components in order to exploit their combined strengths, competencies and strategic abilities. The two businesses, with different histories and cultures, had to be allied. They had to learn how to work together and to think and act like Clark Precision Engineering if they were to generate synergy from the combined businesses.

POINTS FOR REFLECTION

- Can you identify any important external alliances your firm has set up? Are they managed effectively? Does your organization see itself as part of a systemic network, closely linked to, say, its suppliers, distributors and customers?

- How would you evaluate the role and contribution of the strategic leader in your organization?

- Identify other (successful or failed) visionary leaders ... how would you describe their style and approach? Why are they successful? Unsuccessful?

REFERENCES AND FURTHER READING

Bennis, W. (1988) Interview recorded in Crainer, S., Doing the right thing, *The Director*, October 1988.

Richardson, B. (1994) Towards a profile of the visionary leader, *Small Business Enterprise and Development*, **1**(1), Spring.

Richardson, B. and Thompson, J. L. (1994) *Assessing Strategic Competencies: A New View of the Role of Strategy Performance Evaluation*. Paper prepared for the British Academy of Management conference, Lancaster, September.

Warren Bennis has written a number of useful books on leadership, including Bennis, W. and Nanus, B. (1985) *Leaders: The Strategies of Taking Charge*, Harper & Row (which is not his latest book but which provides a useful introduction).

The semi-autobiographical books on business written by such British authors as Sir John Harvey-Jones (past Chairman, ICI), Lord Sieff (past Chairman, Marks & Spencer), George Davies (Next) and Debbie Moore (Pineapple), together with a biography of Alan Sugar by David Thomas, all provide insight into the perspective and strategies of individual leaders. Similar American books include ones by Lee Iacocca (Chrysler) and Victor Kiam (Remington). Swedish authors Borgström and Haag have written a biography of Volvo's Pehr Gyllenhammar.

Readers interested in leadership and strategic regeneration are referred to: Goss, T., Pascale, R. and Athos, A. (1993) The reinvention roller coaster: risking the present for a powerful future, *Harvard Business Review*, November—December.

A SUMMARY OF THE STRATEGIC LESSONS

There is no single profile for a successful strategic leader. What matters is not the leader's personality or style, but his or her overall contribution.

The key aspects of **effective leadership** are vision and pragmatism. It is necessary for the leader to ensure the organization has a clear direction and purpose and is action oriented. Strategic decisions must be capable of implementation. The organization must be able to respond to competitive and change pressures in the appropriate timescale. Potentially valuable opportunities must be seized.

In addition the strategic leader must take responsibility for:

* corporate governance;
* a strong and balanced senior management team;
* the structure of the organization;
* the communications network;
* the culture;
* managing change.

In simple terms, the leader ensures the needs and expectations of important stakeholders are being met.

Visionary leaders have a vision for the future of the organization, and a commitment to making it happen. They seem to understand intuitively which strategies will satisfy important stakeholders. They also rely heavily on other people, and consequently their skills at motivating and inspiring others are critical issues.

There are three steps to visionary leadership:

* the vision;
* selling it to stakeholders and managers;
* making it happen.

Leadership succession is always important. The appointment or retirement of a strong, visionary leader will imply strategic change.

It is important to ensure the style of leadership fits the strategic circumstances. Leaders must be flexible and capable of adapting.

The power of strong leaders should be checked to ensure they act in the long-term interests of the organization.

6

PLANNING STRATEGIES

In this chapter we evaluate (1) the contribution of planning to strategy creation and (2) the need to plan the consequences of intended strategies, however they might have been created. Strategic planning techniques are introduced; and the case is used as a vehicle for explaining a typical large organization planning system.

IMPLEMENTING A MERGER

Bob Langley and David Marshall made their presentation to the Benson management team exactly two weeks after Bob had announced the acquisition. The purchase had been finally completed on the previous Friday. Bob used David's charts and notes to help explain strategic management and strategy creation. He outlined how Universal Engineering would evaluate the success of the merger with Special Components and what was expected from the combined business. Bob then asked David to describe Universal's corporate planning system, the company's framework for strategic *analysis*.

David introduced his presentation with a brief summary of the history and structure of Universal Engineering.[1] Universal started as a manufacturer of electrical equipment, specifically motors and control systems. The German conglomerate, of which Dieter Wild's company is a subsidiary, was an early customer – their domestic appliance division bought Universal motors. A bearing company, which already supplied both Universal's electric motors division and the European automotive industry, later constituted a major acquisition. As the German conglomerate was primarily a car manufacturer – requiring bearings – they now became a very important customer for Universal.

---

[1] An organization chart was provided in Chapter 1.

The bearings and electrical equipment businesses currently comprise two of the three divisions in Universal's structure; the third is Special Products, of which Special Components is just one discrete business unit. Like bearings, a number of Special Products' activities support electricals, although the majority of their sales are outside the group.

Universal Engineering's corporate planning system is designed to allow the businesses in the group to operate independently but at the same time harness the *synergy* potential from linkages ·and inter-divisional support. Fostering this *internal architecture* is one of the ways head office can *add value* to the group.

A CORPORATE PLANNING SYSTEM (SEE TABLE 6.1)

David explained the work of the Universal corporate planning group at head office. The team contains both planners and analysts. The analysts

Table 6.1 The Universal Engineering corporate planning timetable

	Universal Engineering corporate planning team	Individual businesses
March	Review of progress and corporate objectives	
April	Strategic review for the group ⟶	
May		Strategic review for each business and
June		Presentation to divisional boards
	⟵ Divisional strategies and bids presented	
July/ August	Search for new strategies – growth and divestment	
September	Final corporate plan agreed ⟶	
		Action plans and target milestones
October ⟶ March	On-going search for further strategic opportunities; monitoring, control and change	

are responsible for monitoring the external environment, searching for new opportunities and threats. They also model the implications of possible future events and scenarios for the group. The planners consolidate the individual plans for every business in the group to create the overall corporate plan. Group progress against the plan is continuously monitored and evaluated by the planners.

The company's financial year end is 31 March. Around this time, when the relative success of the group for the year is becoming clear, the planners produce a final review of progress towards corporate objectives. They evaluate where the group is doing well and where it is less successful, and the extent to which it is satisfying its major stakeholders. To this is added a rigorous internal (corporate resources) and external (environmental developments) assessment of the group, provided by the analysts. They specifically highlight the important **strategic issues** facing the group – appropriate and feasible opportunities and critical threats.

During April the group chief executive (the strategic leader) convenes his corporate strategy committee, which comprises senior Board members and the head of the corporate planning group. The divisional managing directors are not members, although on occasions they are asked to attend. They are excluded on the grounds that when bids from the divisions for additional investment capital are being considered later in the year, they would all support each other's projects. Any opposition by one divisional head would provoke counter-hostility from the others.

The outcome of the April meeting is a preliminary statement of corporate objectives for the year ahead. Typically these will summarize:

- growth and profit aspirations;

- the company's strategy for exploiting core competencies and capabilities and its willingness to diversify (possible acquisition targets and divestments may be discussed but not announced);

- international objectives;

- the commitment to, and standards for, quality, service and customer care;

- the resources available to support expansion.

This is broadly equivalent to the top line of the planning gap – see Chart 4.2.

During May and early June each business unit finalizes its own strategic review, which is presented to the relevant divisional board of directors. Each company in Universal Engineering carries out comprehensive SWOT and portfolio analyses (portfolio analysis is explained later in the chapter) and indicates:

1. the anticipated revenue and profit targets if there are no **major** changes to competitive and functional strategies;

2. the requirements for the company to achieve or maintain competitive advantage;

3. strategic changes it would like to make, the anticipated returns and the resource implications (all significant investments must be justified in detail; the assistance of the head office planners can be enlisted in formulating proposals).

(1) and (2) will be used immediately for updating the company's action plans and budgets, recognizing that these may have to be adjusted later.

The role of the divisional board is to question and challenge before reaching a set of recommendations for the chief executive. The strategy committee meets for a second time at the end of June to discuss these recommendations, which may be accepted (and the necessary resources provided) or rejected. Portfolio analysis is again used to consider the current and emerging state of the group; and strategic opportunities for inter-divisional support and internally generated synergies are sought.

At the same time the committee compares the promised returns from all the businesses with their own initial growth objectives. If a gap remains, and further resources are available or can be found, the corporate analysts will be asked for costed options and recommendations. The strategic leader may, of course, have ideas of his own to input. In addition the analysts will be asked for recommendations concerning how the group might rationalize and achieve further cost savings, beyond those being offered by the divisions. Divisional boards may suggest the divestment of particular businesses, but this is unusual; such decisions are more likely to start with the strategic leader or the analysts.

This evaluation takes place throughout the summer, and the strategy committee meets for a third time in September to agree the corporate strategy. Final targets are issued to the divisions and business units, enabling them to review, and if necessary change, their current plans and budgets. It is these final plans which are co-ordinated by the head office planners into the corporate plan and used for committing and managing the group's strategic resources.

David commented upon the different reactions provoked by these strategic decisions. Business units which are allocated resources and given support for their proposed strategies tend to be euphoric; those which see themselves as 'losers' are frequently demotivated, an inevitable drawback of this approach.

The divisions and individual businesses are not precluded from changing functional and competitive strategies at any time in response to competitive threats and opportunities, but if they require additional resources, outside their budgeted allocation, they have to apply to the chief executive.

David concluded his presentation by commenting that the planning system is basically a process which forces managers to address key questions and issues. Head office finds the detailed plan to be a useful document for explaining their basic intentions to the major shareholders. The value of the finished plan to the individual subsidiaries – as distinct from the *process* of planning its content – is more questionable. They see the document as a *summary of thinking* and a statement of intent, rather than a rigid plan that must be executed.

The corporate strategy may also be changed by the strategic leader at any time during the year if new windows of opportunity become available. The Benson acquisition is evidence of this.

In addition the planning exercise is seen as essential for providing a framework against which the strategic leader can monitor the commitment of resources and the emergent outcomes.

MERGING THE BUSINESSES

After answering a number of questions David sat down and Bob Langley took over again. He confirmed that the head office analysts who evaluated the acquisition had produced a preliminary set of target figures for sales and profits, which he showed to the Benson managers. This provoked an immediate response; they were ambitious targets. The reaction was not wholly negative and a number of useful ideas emerged.

Langley explained that any decisions about rationalization and possible redundancies would have to be taken sooner rather than later, but he wanted to give the Benson people, in conjunction with David, an opportunity to work out whether the targets could be achieved without cutting back. He commented that this was another important planning task – planning the detailed implementation of strategic change. Initially the ex-Benson sales and production directors would have day-to-day responsibility and the two businesses would remain separate. Special Components would take over all financial controls.

Typically he left the Benson managers with a number of challenges and a request that they liaise directly and frequently with David Marshall. He wanted:

- confirmation that existing customers would be retained through *adding* further *value* for them, and providing higher levels of product quality and service;

- ideas for new customers, market development and cost reduction; he was looking for realistic targets which would *stretch the resources*;

- possibilities for linking the product ranges of Benson and Special Components to provide an even better service – *internal synergy and architecture*;

- opportunities for sharing skills and abilities to foster *innovation, learning and competitive advantage*.

He accepted that a considerable shake-up was implied and that the culture at Benson's would have to change. Hopefully the Benson people would react favourably, accepting that a new attitude and commitment was needed for survival. Competitive success would, in turn, bring rewards.

NOTE

The corporate planning system described in the case is typical of certain large company systems. The procedures described are not being put forward as a 'best practice model'. Some of the advantages, limitations and drawbacks are brought out in the chapter text.

PLANNING STRATEGIES

All managers plan; they think about what the organization should be doing and how objectives might be achieved. Planning contributes to strategic management in several ways. Strategic or corporate planning systems of the type described in the case study *underpin* – but do not fully account for – strategy creation in most large organizations. Also, as we saw in the case, the implementation of intended strategies, however they might have been created, needs careful planning. Chapter 7 will consider adaptive and incremental changes to strategies as managers and organizations act on opportunities and threats, often at short notice, in a learning context and a dynamic environment. Here an organization is exhibiting *planned flexibility* – a mixture of limited planning and intuition leads to experimentation and innovation. Hence the planning is 'cerebral' rather than rigorously analytical. This chapter, however, is specifically concerned with the more formal and systematic approach of strategic planning systems.

We have seen from the case study that:

- Planning systems represent analytical strategy creation and they lead to a statement of intent. These plans are the output of an organization's learning about an uncertain future – further learning as plans and strategies are implemented will generate changes.

- Planning systems provide a useful framework for managing the organization's strategic resources – they can provide a means of controlling resource allocation and fostering internal linkages.

- The strategic leader is in charge of the system and the chief 'strategic architect'. Ideas for strategic change, possibly involving a visionary approach, can be input by the strategic leader, other managers and members of the planning team. The implementation of an idea for, say, an acquisition must then be planned in detail; targets might be tracked for several months.

- Ideally any documented plan will be seen as a set of intentions and guidelines, and it will be flexible. Changes to corporate, competitive and functional strategies can be made as new strategic issues emerge. Managers are empowered to make changes within their budgets and the company's policy guidelines.

Key Point

6.1 The primary benefit of planning is that it forces people to think.

Planning is everything; plans are nothing (Dwight D. Eisenhower).

Effective planning can stimulate positive action.
    Too much bureaucracy and detail will paralyse activity. Over-emphasis on planning at the expense of vision and learning can have a similar effect.

- Planners can offer valuable advice and help other managers to clarify their strategic thinking and draw up plans for their divisions and businesses. They should not be personally responsible for *creating* the strategies.

The planning system described in the case is *one* way in which large, diverse organizations might manage the analytical aspects of strategy creation. Other approaches are described in Chapter 9. The key issue concerns the role of the corporate head office. How can it best add value? To what extent is strategy creation centralized? How much autonomy is delegated to divisions and business units? How is strategic change controlled? How are business unit strategies co-ordinated to harness internal synergies?

DAVID MARSHALL'S PERSONAL VIEW

David Marshall felt that the Universal Engineering corporate planning system did succeed in the essential task of co-ordinating the plans for all the divisions and businesses, enabling the strategic leader to exercise control over the conglomerate. In addition, the system did not prohibit vision and learning within the corporation, which is important as these are the two modes of strategy creation most likely to take the organization forward in a competitive and uncertain environment. Unfortunately the vision and learning was concentrated in each division; it did not permeate the whole organization as effectively as it might.

The system used to be much more formal. All ideas from the individual businesses had to be supported by comprehensive, documented analyses. Now it was accepted that many proposals could not be fully justified quantitatively; instead the assumptions and justifications were probed and challenged by divisional boards.

However, Universal still tends to use the performance targets as the primary means of control. David is concerned that this sometimes results in short-term thinking. Once a business drops below its target it is put under considerable pressure to reduce costs, and this may restrict its ability to be creative and innovative. He also believes the system would be improved if the head office corporate planners had more contact and involvement with the businesses; they tend to be remote and detached.

In summary: the system may be imperfect, but a system of some form remains essential for control and co-ordination. Alone it cannot enable the company to deal with competitive uncertainties and pressures. Vision and learning are essential. But planning must not be abandoned.

CORPORATE PLANNING

In the 1960s and early 1970s corporate planning was seen as the most logical and appropriate means of creating strategy. It provided an analytical, intentional process through which success could be planned and brought about. The process was systematic and controlled; the explicit plans would lead directly to actions. Managerial actions and decisions were directed by the plan. Positive outcomes required correct assumptions and forecasts concerning future demand, appropriate (winning) strategies, and competitor actions and responses. Strategic leaders who placed great emphasis on corporate planning systems were regarded as tacticians rather than visionaries.

It became apparent in the 1970s that such systems implied slow response to environmental changes – and industries and markets were becoming more turbulent. Competitor actions were not always predictable; and implementation problems, not foreseen when the plans were drawn up, reduced their value. Companies realized that corporate planning **alone** is inadequate for effective strategy creation, but this does not mean it cannot make an important contribution.

Key Point

6.2 Organizations must establish plans or intentions for:
- the overall corporate strategy;
- competitive strategies for each business;
- the way in which synergies will be generated within the structure;
- dealing with competitive and change pressures.

Visionary aspects may be involved, but some form of planning system can provide a valuable framework for thinking and analysis.

It is important that the outcomes are flexible guidelines rather than firm plans which 'must be implemented'.

Ackoff (1970) suggests that systematic 'commitment' planning is appropriate for a stable, predictable, certain environment. When the environment is uncertain but understandable the organization should use scenarios to plan for a number of eventualities, so that it will be in a strong position to exploit whatever does happen. In more turbulent and unpredictable situations it is more important to *plan an organization* that will be able to deal with the unexpected.

Drawing on the work of Ansoff (1990) we can summarize this section by concluding that organizations should plan:

- **strategies** to meet environmental opportunities and strategic issues;
- the **resource ability** to implement these strategies – specifically *competencies and strategic capabilities*;
- the ability to respond to, create and manage **change**.

The time available between 'find out', 'interpret' and 'act' is critical when deciding the most appropriate role for planning systems. It is frequently necessary to decentralize some responsibility for strategic changes and empower managers – the subject of Chapter 7 – but there will still need to be mechanisms for allocating and controlling corporate strategic resources.

PLANNING IN DIFFERENT TYPES OF ORGANIZATION

Strategic planning is useful and relevant for all types of organization. It is appropriate, for example, in **local government** where a variety of complex strategic issues have to be tackled. Invariably the demand for services from a local authority exceeds the supply potential of its available resources. Government applies constraints: spending must be limited if capping is to be avoided; services must increasingly be put out for tender and private sector providers invited to compete with the authority's own staff; certain minimum provisions must be made. The planning challenge concerns the allocation and prioritization of scarce resources.

The individual service areas are similar to the business units of large manufacturing and service organizations. They compete for the limited corporate resources, and they will be expected to agree service and cost targets and operate within budgets. Like Special Components they will be free to alter priorities and change their strategies as long as they keep to their budgets and operate within corporate policy guidelines. A major difference is the role of the key stakeholders. Company shareholders have chosen to invest *financially* in a business, knowing that they could lose money; and customers can invariably change to a competitive supplier if they are dissatisfied. Elected Councillors have no financial involvement and may have strong personal feelings about service priorities, driven by their political convictions; recipients of the services may not have an option to switch.

The planning challenge for **small businesses** is similar to that facing Special Components. Major *corporate changes* frequently imply large injections of capital, and this will not be readily available to a typical small business. Consequently such companies need to plan:

- how to implement the entrepreneurial vision of the strategic leader;
- how to create and sustain a competitive edge in the segment of the market in which they focus.

Box 6.1 explores the planning challenges facing British Airways.

THE PLANNING CHALLENGE FOR BRITISH AIRWAYS

Lord King was recruited from outside the industry to become Chairman of the nationalized British Airways in 1981. He turned the ailing company around, and in 1987 BA was successfully privatized. Five years later BA was ranked seventh among world airlines when measured by revenue. In terms of passenger miles flown BA was 5th behind the four leading American airlines, all of whom benefited from the huge domestic route networks. Only Swire Pacific (Hong Kong) and Singapore Airlines, both considerably smaller than BA, recorded higher profits. Many leading competitors, including those in the US, lost money.

THE VISION

Lord King wanted BA to become the first truly global airline, a vision the company pursued through most of the 1980s. In the mid-1990s, after King has been succeeded by Sir Colin Marshall, the vision is close to fruition. For several years BA has promoted itself as 'The World's Favourite Airline'.

THE CORPORATE STRATEGY

BA has recognized that it needs to establish a strong presence in Europe, North America and the Asia/Pacific region if it is to be a global carrier. This has been accomplished by a series of acquisitions and alliances:

- BA has purchased 25% of US Air, the fifth largest American airline. US Air operates a hub-and-spoke route strategy whereby passengers are flown into and out of key cities – hubs – where they transfer between short- and long-haul flights. US Air has four hubs: Pittsburgh, Philadelphia, Charlotte and Baltimore, all in the East. Joint ticketing arrangements have given BA's transatlantic passengers easier access to significantly more American cities.
- BA has also acquired 25% of the Australian national airline, Qantas, from the Australian government.
- 49.9% of the French regional carrier, TAT, has been obtained, together with an option to buy the remainder in 1997.

- BA also owns 49% of the German regional airline, Delta, which has been renamed Deutsche BA; and has entered into a joint venture with Aeroflot. The new airline, Air Russia, is based in Moscow.
- BA intends to use these alliances to operate a hub-and-spoke strategy for selected European cities.
- BA acquired Dan Air to strengthen its UK-based domestic and European services and reinforce its presence at Gatwick in addition to Heathrow.

These moves all needed careful and detailed **planning** and negotiations, particularly as governments are always involved, either as owners of airlines or regulators.

There were also disappointments. In 1989 an earlier arrangement with United Airlines, number two in America, was abandoned; and attempts to form alliances with Sabena (Belgium) and KLM (Holland) both failed. A gap still exists in the North Pacific region to facilitate stronger access to Hong Kong and China.

MORE DETAILED PLANNING

It is additionally necessary for BA to plan in detail the consequences of its vision. Capacity must be matched to routes and schedules; new planes must be ordered years in advance of delivery; and future finances must be planned in line with decisions to purchase or lease the planes. Resources (planes and crews) must be allocated to ensure all flights can operate to schedule. Maintenance of the aircraft needs planning; and there need to be contingency plans for when unforeseen problems take an airliner out of service.

COMPETITIVE ADVANTAGE

Competitively BA is profitable because it is both efficient and effective. There are constant (and not always popular!) drives to cut costs and improve productivity. At the same time the 49 000 employees are seen as an important strategic resource; those who interface with customers are trained in customer care and empowered to use their initiative for improving the overall level of service.

The potential of information technology is harnessed in several ways. In conjunction with United Airlines (and a number of minority partners) BA owns one of the world's two leading reservations systems.

SCENARIO MODELLING

The international air transport industry is turbulent and very competitive. Many airlines are unprofitable and surviving only with government subsidies.

Consequently BA must consider a number of uncertain futures:

- What will be the impact of continual over-supply, especially if markets become less regulated? Deregulation in America has been partially followed in Europe.

- How might BA deal with volume crises? During and immediately after the Gulf War, for example, the number of passengers fell dramatically.

- Might the CAA (Civil Aviation Authority – the UK air transport regulator) require BA to release more of its valuable take-off and landing slots at Heathrow to carriers like Virgin, who have targeted the most profitable routes around the world, in order to foster more competition?

- Will American carriers be given greater access to the UK? They are demanding this as compensation for BA's acquisition of a stake in US Air.

- Moreover, will BA be allowed to retain its shareholding in US Air? The leading American carriers, fearing the competitive strength of BA, are lobbying the US government to introduce new restrictions.

- Is the hub-and-spoke strategy still the right approach? It seems to be successful in Europe and Asia, but it is not proving profitable for the American carriers. The strategy results in considerable activity at peak times (when feeder planes arrive and depart, matching long-haul flights) followed by quiet lulls. Staffing levels must be appropriate for the high level of activity – many people are then almost idle for costly periods of time.

- Might BA's ongoing dispute with Virgin prove damaging? BA has been accused of poaching passengers and is being sued in the American courts. Its image could be affected.

Faced with these uncertain future possibilities BA must be vigilant and flexible. New threats may emerge at any time; fresh opportunities will also arise ■

Key Point

6.3 Planning is one aspect of strategy creation.
It is also necessary for the organization to plan

1. strategy implementation; here the *consequences* of intended strategies are being planned in detail;

2. how the organization will *manage change*.

PLANNING SYSTEMS

The basic principle underpinning any planning system is:

Thinking and Ideas ⟶ Plans and budgets

Managers seek to widen their awareness of the current situation and prepare for the challenges ahead. The challenges are both external (out-performing competitors) and internal (acquiring the necessary corporate resources; achieving internal synergies and helping other parts of the organization to out-perform their competitors). It is essential to allow enough time and opportunity to evaluate the issues properly; it is also vital to ensure the thinking continues after plans and budgets are drawn up. Plans are, after all, primarily a framework for guidance.

A FRAMEWORK FOR PLANNING

Organizations will develop systems which are appropriate for their needs. Chart 6.1 illustrates the essential elements which should be incorporated in some form. The challenge is to synthesize internal and external intelligence; the contributory activities need not all be centralized at head office.

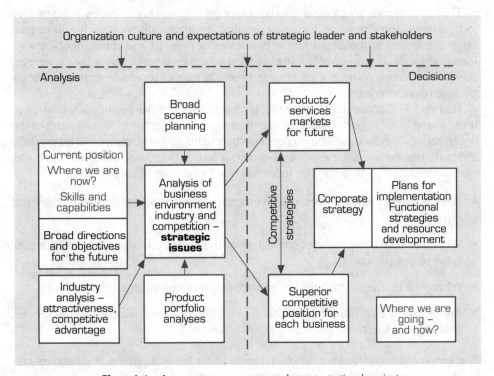

Chart 6.1 A contemporary approach to strategic planning

The organization's culture and the expectations of the strategic leader and the key stakeholders influence the whole process of analysis and decision-making. The thinking starts with an assessment of the current position of the organization, its skills and resources, and an evaluation of whether there is a clear understanding of the mission, the broad objectives and directions for the future.

Then we analyse the business environment thoroughly, concentrating on the industries in which the organization currently competes and those in which it might apply its skills and resources. Feeding into this analysis are three other analyses:

- Broad **scenario planning** – conceptualizing a range of different futures which the organization might have to deal with, to ensure that the less likely possibilities, threats and opportunities are not overlooked, and to encourage a high level of flair and creativity in strategic thinking.

    It is useful to ask a series of 'what-if' questions. What do we do if prices fall because of over supply? How would we respond if our competitors ...?

- Product (or service) **portfolio analyses**, which are discussed in greater detail in the next section; contingency and possible crisis planning considerations can be incorporated in this.

- **Industry analyses**, following the Porter criteria for judging attractiveness and opportunities for competitive advantage (discussed earlier).

This environmental analysis should focus on any **strategic issues** – current or forthcoming developments, inside or outside the organization, which will impact upon the ability of the organization to pursue its mission and meet its objectives. Ideally these would be opportunities related to organizational strengths. Wherever possible any unwelcome, but significant, potential threats should be turned into competitive opportunities.

Hamel (1994) argues that forward-looking organizations will periodically (say every three years) bring together and cross-fertilize ideas and opinions from all parts of the organization. The focus will be on core competencies and an attempt will be made to integrate the various businesses and divisions rather than keep them separate – as companies often tend to do. The following questions might be addressed:

- What new core competencies do we need to protect our existing situation and businesses?

- What new core competencies could destroy the ways in which we currently deliver value to our customers?

- What new markets could we access with our core competencies?

- Are there any new opportunities on the horizon for which our core competencies could be adapted?

The emphasis is clearly on strategic issues and on breaking down any barriers created by the structure of the organization.

From these analyses competitive strategy decisions must be reached concerning:

- the reinforcement or establishment of a superior competitive position, or competitive advantage, for each business within the existing portfolio of products and services;

- product markets and service markets for future development, and the appropriate functional strategies for establishing a superior competitive position.

Amalgamated these functional and competitive strategies constitute the corporate strategy for the future, which in turn needs to be broken down into resource development plans and any decisions relating to changes in the structure of the organization, i.e. decisions which reflect where the organization is going, and how the inherent changes are to be managed.

It is important that new strategic issues are spotted and dealt with continuously, and the organization structure must enable this to happen, either by decentalization and empowerment or by effective communications. See Chapter 7.

DIRECTIONAL POLICY MATRICES

The best known directional policy matrices, a form of portfolio analysis, were developed in the 1970s by Shell and General Electric and the management consultants McKinsey. They are broadly similar and aim to assist large, complex, multi-activity enterprises with decisions concerning investment and divestment priorities. A version of the Shell matrix is illustrated in Chart 6.2, and further details can be found in Robinson, Hitchens and Wade (1978).

In using such a matrix there is an assumption that resources are scarce, and that there never will be, or should be, enough financial and other resources for the implementation of all the project ideas and opportunities which can be conceived in a successful, creative and innovative organization. Choices will always have to be made about investment priorities. The development of an effective corporate strategy therefore involves an evaluation of the potential for existing businesses together with new possibilities in order to determine the priorities.

The matrix is constructed within two axes: the horizontal axis represents industry attractiveness, or the prospects for profitable operation in the sector concerned; the vertical axis indicates the company's **existing** competitive position in relation to other companies in the industry. New possibilities can be evaluated initially along the vertical axis by considering their likely prospects for establishing competitive advantage. It will be appreciated that Michael Porter's work links closely to this.

In placing individual products the factors listed below the matrix are typical of those which might be used. Each factor would be given a weighting relative to its perceived importance, and each product being evaluated would be given a score for every factor. The aggregate weighted scores for both axes determine the final position in the matrix.

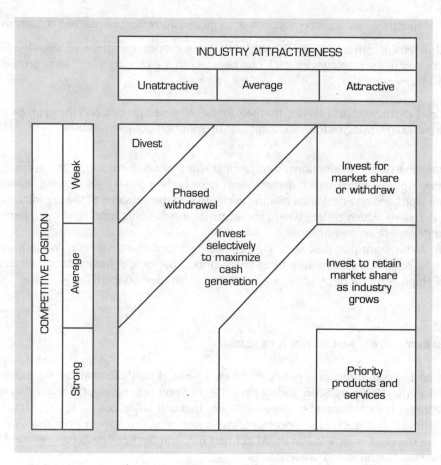

Chart 6.2 The directional policy matrix

INDUSTRY ATTRACTIVENESS

- Market growth
- Market quality, or the ability for new products to achieve higher or more stable profitability than other sectors
- Supplier pressure
- Customer pressure
- Substitute products
- Government action
- Entry barriers
- Competitive pressure

COMPETITIVE POSITION AND RELATIVE STRENGTH

- Competition
- Relative market shares
- Competitive postures and opportunities
- Production capability
- Research and development record and strengths
- Success rate to date, measured in terms of market share and financial success (earnings in excess of the cost of capital)

Chart 6.2 illustrates that the overall attractiveness of products diminishes as one moves diagonally from the bottom right-hand corner of the matrix to the top left. Priority products, in the bottom right hand corner, are those which score highly on both axes. As a result they should receive priority for development, and the resources necessary for this should be allocated to them.

Products bordering on the priority box should receive the appropriate level of investment to ensure that at the very least market share is retained as the industry grows.

Products currently with a weak competitive position in an attractive industry are placed in the top right-hand corner of the matrix. They should be evaluated in respect of the potential to establish and sustain real competitive advantage. If the prospects seem good, then carefully targeted investment should be considered seriously. If the prospects are poor it is appropriate to withdraw from the market. A weak position in an attractive industry might be remedied by the acquisition of an appropriate competitor.

Products across the middle diagonal should receive custodial treatment. It is argued that a good proportion of products are likely to fall into this strategic category, which implies attempting to maximize cash generation with only a limited commitment of additional resources.

Currently profitable products with little future potential should be withdrawn gradually, but retained as long as they are profitable and the resources committed to them cannot be allocated more effectively elsewhere.

Products for divestment are likely already to be losing money if all their costs are properly assigned.

The directional policy matrix, like other matrices, is only a technique which assists in determining which industry and product sectors are most worthy of additional investment capital. Issues of synergy and overall strategic fit require further managerial judgment before final decisions are reached.

(There are, of course, many strategic planning models and techniques, but an exhaustive coverage of these is outside the scope of this book.)

Key Point

6.4 There is no single 'best' model or framework for strategic planning. However we can identify a number of important issues which should be incorporated in any system an organization chooses to use.

A variety of techniques are available and useful; directional policy matrices are an example. These techniques cannot provide definitive answers; they simply help structure and clarify the analysis.

TWO REALITIES OF PLANNING

Business unit general managers in large organizations will realize that their bids for resources are unlikely to be successful if they are not promising substantial benefits, financial and otherwise. They may, therefore, be tempted to over-state the anticipated outcomes and under-state the downside risks involved. Afterwards they will argue that their assumptions proved to be wrong in a dynamic and unpredictable competitive environment!

Institutional shareholders and bankers expect organizations to have firm corporate plans in order to confirm they have a clear purpose and direction. Additional funding is raised on the back of these promises. One temptation might be to write the plan these stakeholders would like to see. The consequences can be faced later. If this happens the organization will really have two plans – a visible plan for external consumption and an invisible plan which managers utilize.

ASSESSING THE SITUATION

David Marshall realized that Universal Engineering, in setting target expectations for the merger with Benson Engineering, had imposed *constraints* which were now objectives for Special Components. Strategies were needed to fulfil these objectives. Hopefully the Benson managers, now free from previous restraints and a lack of encouragement, would contribute a number of useful ideas. Bob Langley would certainly offer an opinion and ideas when the situation became clearer. These would help provide a **vision** for the future of the combined businesses. A detailed analysis of the current situation, and the future prospects and opportuntities, was both essential and urgent – a planning approach.

David also knew that their initial thinking and planning would not produce all the answers; both companies (and their managers) had a lot to learn; new ideas and changes would emerge as this learning took place.

(Ongoing, emergent changes are the subject of the next chapter.)

POINTS FOR REFLECTION

- Does your organization utilize formal planning procedures? Can you describe the process in detail? What do you believe are the main strengths? Do you see any important limitations and drawbacks?
- How do you personally use planning ideas and techniques when deciding upon actions to take?
- Can you apply a directional policy matrix to your organization?
- Can you describe any important scenarios that your organization should consider seriously?

REFERENCES AND FURTHER READING

Ackoff, R. (1970) *A Concept of Corporate Planning*, Wiley.
Ansoff, H. I. (1990) *Implanting Strategic Management*, 2nd edition, Prentice-Hall.
Cohen, K. J. and Cyert, R. M. (1973) Strategy formulation, implementation and monitoring,

Journal of Business, **46**(3) – for a useful coverage of strategic planning systems.

Hamel, G. (1994) *Competing for the Future*, Economist Conference, London (June).

Mintzberg, H. (1993) *The Rise and Fall of Strategic Planning*, Prentice-Hall.

NEDO (1993) *Unplanned and Unprepared*. This research project by the consultants *Strategy for Success* examines the state of strategic thinking and planning in UK companies.

Robinson, S. J. Q., Hitchens, R. E. and Wade, D. P. (1978) The directional policy matrix – tool for strategic planning, *Long Range Planning*, **21**, June.

Rowe, A. J., Mason, R. O., Dickel, K. E. and Snyder, N. H. (1989) *Strategic Management – A Methodological Approach*, 3rd edition, Addison Wesley. This text provides an ideal introduction to planning techniques.

A SUMMARY OF THE STRATEGIC LESSONS

Planning is a second important aspect of strategy creation.

Planning is vital for thinking and learning about future strategic issues, challenges and opportunities.

The actual *process* of thinking and planning is more important than the plan itself, which really should be seen as a framework for guidance.

The rigid, systematic corporate planning approach of the 1960s and early 1970s has been made more flexible in order to deal with the turbulent business environments which characterize many industries.

Organizations must plan:

- strategies for closing the planning gap;
- resource management and the implementation of intended strategies;
- a structure that is capable of dealing with change pressures.

Large organizations will have some form of planning system. There is no 'single best approach' to this. The role and contribution of corporate head office – and its ability to add value – is an important issue. Head office can control the planning, support business units and divisions and look for synergy opportunities.

Strategic planning is also useful for small businesses – in their search for valuable competitive opportunities – and for other types of organizations such as local authorities which are faced with the challenge of allocating scarce resources between competing ends. In many respects the broad approach is identical.

A contemporary approach to strategic planning has been developed and the contribution of directional policy matrices discussed. It was highlighted that such planning techniques can make a major contribution to strategic management, but managerial judgment remains essential.

7 ADAPTIVE STRATEGIC CHANGE: STRATEGIC MANAGEMENT IN A DYNAMIC ENVIRONMENT

In this chapter we look at the **reality** of many strategic change decisions. Intended strategies are changed incrementally as they are implemented; new strategies are formulated continuously as managers adapt to a dynamic, competitive environment.

Such changes are facilitated when managers are empowered to learn in a flexible organization. Herein lies the **real strategic challenge** for many organizations.

EMPOWERMENT AND LEARNING: ADVICE FROM A CONSULTANT

David Marshall returned to his office after the Benson presentation; he had to sort through the papers he needed for his trip to Germany on the following day. Almost immediately his consultant friend rang. Tony Anderson was working with a client just a few miles away and asked David to join him for dinner that evening.

During the meal David talked about his problems and the two friends began to discuss the strategic demands facing Special Components and the skills and competencies the company needed. From his reaction David realized that Tony was able to foresee many of the hurdles his company faced.

Tony encouraged David to pinpoint Special Components' strategic tasks and challenges, and with a little prompting David produced the following:

- operationalize head office strategies, making any changes that become necessary;
- attract further corporate investment;
- find new market opportunities and appreciate the key success factors;
- monitor competitors and deal with any threatening changes;
- differentiate more effectively – by building on core competencies and adding more value for customers;
- manage and improve quality and customer service;
- reduce costs without threatening quality;
- encourage managers and employees to be innovative and look for ways of improving their job satisfaction;
- work more closely with suppliers and sub-contractors;
- manage the information flowing into and inside the organization;
- act as a conduit between the environment and corporate strategic leadership;
- look for acquisition opportunities;
- deal effectively with unexpected future events and crises.

They discussed the value of strong leadership and strategic planning and agreed that for Special Components to be strategically successful and carry out these tasks, all managers and employees would need to be involved and committed. The company must be able to:

1. capture the important **knowledge** held by all the managers; and

2. ensure that this knowledge is communicated widely so that managers can **learn** and use it positively and quickly in their search for new competitive opportunities.

In other words: people and information are critically important strategic resources.

Tony emphasized that the information links were both internal and external. Departments within the company should enjoy a co-operative supplier-customer relationship (*internal architecture*); externally Special Components, Benson Engineering and their suppliers and customers should be similarly integrated (*external architecture*).

David wondered just how feasible this really was for Special Components, agreeing that it was clearly desirable. Tony confirmed that the vast majority of organizations in his experience find this to be a difficult – but worthwhile – battle to fight. The benefits can be enormous, but major changes are implied.

Employees must be **empowered**; many are initially reluctant to accept more responsibility and accountability. David wondered how the Benson managers would respond to the new tasks given to them by Bob Langley. He knew that he had also been empowered with new responsibilities and that he would be held accountable for the outcomes.

Tony explained how the culture must become more supportive; people must work together and see themselves as members of integrated teams. Rewards must be based more on outcomes. The processes and the ways in which tasks are carried out may also have to be reviewed and re-designed using *business process re-engineering.*

(Empowerment, learning organizations and business process reengineering are discussed in this chapter; culture is the subject of Chapter 8.)

ADAPTIVE STRATEGIC CHANGE: STRATEGIC MANAGEMENT IN A DYNAMIC ENVIRONMENT

Chapter 6 highlighted the value of a clear framework for analysis and planning – we need to clarify and understand intentions. Intentions will, of course, change by necessity in a dynamic environment.

Looking at the way in which organizations and managers deal with this dynamic environment helps us to understand the **reality** of strategic management and strategic change. However, as the case points out, herein lies the **real strategic challenge** for organizations in the uncertain 1990s. Conceptually the strategic requirements for organizations are clear; the challenge lies in successful implementation and change. Strategically successful organizations will accept the challenge and seek to be environmentally vigilant, innovative and flexible – despite the difficulties involved. Organizations which are less aware and relatively inflexible will find they are reacting to situations they do not fully understand. Their results are likely to prove disappointing.

Important changes to the **corporate** strategy may be visionary or the outcome of an analytical planning system. As we saw in Chapter 6 the implementation of these strategies must be planned, but the organization should be ready to amend and change these plans as they learn in a changing environment. The same principles can be applied to competitive strategies and sources of competitive advantage.

At the same time external events – such as requests from customers or poor performance by competitors – can open new windows of opportunity. Vigilant organizations, whose managers are willing and able to act upon these opportunities, will change certain functional strategies. These low-level changes can, of course, impact upon competitive and corporate strategies. On occasions individual managers may be empowered to act without involving a superior or their colleagues in a lengthy decision process; on other occasions it will be either necessary or prudent for them to discuss their ideas and the implications in some detail.

Whatever the appropriate internal process, the essential issue is that changes take place quickly and expeditiously in order that opportunities are seized ahead of competitors. Managers are encouraged to be creative and search continuously for new ways of adding value, either by differentiation or cost reduction. The assumption is that these changes will initially be limited, experimental and low risk. If they succeed their impact can grow and spread.

Limited and low-level changes, designed to bring short-term success, may not always be in the long-term interest of the organization. A subsidiary of a large corporation, anxious to meet its annual budget – a constraint imposed by head office – may cut overtime or make a few employees redundant. Costs are reduced, but morale may also be affected detrimentally. Profits are maintained, but employees may now fear for their jobs. This will not be an appropriate climate for initiative and innovation. We shall see later how this emerges as a threat to Special Components.

We can summarize the strategic challenge as follows:

The environment is	dynamic and competitive
The future is	uncertain
Structures styles and approaches } must be	flexible and adaptive, implying some decentralization
Managers need, to some extent, empowering	
Strategies consequently emerge with learning	

THE DYNAMIC, COMPETITIVE ENVIRONMENT

Causes generate effects. Actions lead to outcomes. On occasions companies may attempt to seize the competitive initiative and introduce an innovatory change. An action by one competitor which affects the relative success of rivals provokes responses. One action can therefore provoke several reactions, depending upon the extent of the impact and the general nature of competition. Each reaction in turn further affects the other rival competitors in the industry. New responses will again follow. What we have in many markets and industries is a form of competitive chaos a competitive business environment which is permanently fluid and unpredictable.

This dynamism is illustrated in Chart 7.1. It is important to differentiate between two sets of similar, but nevertheless different, decisions. First, some actions are innovatory and represent one competitor acting upon a perceived opportunity ahead of its rivals; other actions constitute reactions to these competitive initiatives. Sec-

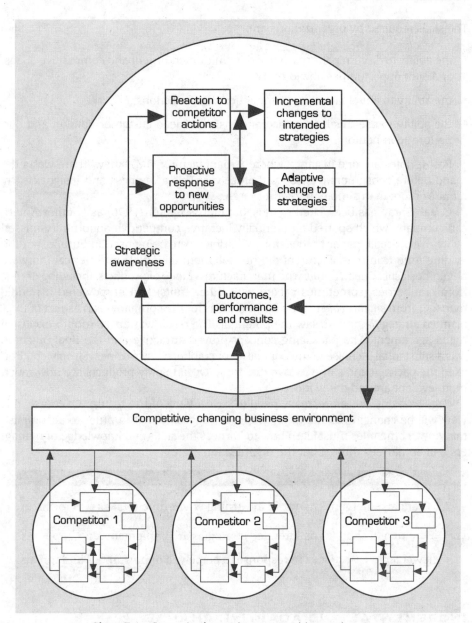

Chart 7.1   Strategic change in a competitive environment

ond, some decisions imply incremental change to existing, intended strategies; on different occasions companies are adapting their strategies (adaptive change) as they see new opportunities which they can seize early, or possible future threats which they are seeking to avoid. The process is about learning and flexibility.

The skills required by organizations are:

- the ability to discern patterns in this dynamic environment and competitive chaos, and spot opportunities ahead of their rivals;

- the ability to anticipate competitor actions and reactions;

- the ability to use this intelligence and insight to lead customer opinion and outperform competitors.

Post-It notes are one instance where a manufacturer, 3M, 'knew' there was a demand before consumers realized it themselves. This awareness and insight clearly requires more than simple market research.

Ocean Spray has been cited by Rosabeth Moss Kanter (1990) as another American company which spotted a potentially lucrative competitive opportunity missed by its rivals. Small 'paper bottles' for soft drinks were being used in Europe, but the leading American manufacturers did not see them taking off in America and were not enthusiastic. Ocean Spray, who manufacture a range of products, including drinks, from cranberries (sometimes mixed with other fruits) had empowered a middle manager from *engineering* to look for new ideas for the company – an aspect of their planned strategy – and he saw the potential. The result was an 18-month exclusive rights agreement. The packaging concept proved attractive and the final outcome was a substantial increase in the popularity of cranberry juice drinks. Simply children liked the package and came to love the drink. Ocean Spray products are now much more evident around the world.

Organizations, therefore, really need to have a view of the future. Of course, this view will be changing all the time! The case suggested that in order to accomplish this view, companies must learn how to harness the skills and knowledge of managers and employees throughout the organization.

Key Point

7.1 Gradual, emergent change in a learning environment takes two forms:

- incremental changes as intended strategies are implemented;

- new, adaptive strategies in response to perceived opportunities and threats.

INCREMENTAL AND ADAPTIVE CHANGE

The conceptual difference between the terms incremental and adaptive change was explained in the previous section. Because the outcomes tend to be the same – ongoing changes to strategies, normally in the form of limited-risk step changes – this section does not separate the terms.

Strategic change is now being seen as an everyday event, not a dramatic, visionary leap forward and not simply part of an annual planning exercise. The annual planning review, however, remains important and complementary. It provides an ideal opportunity to review and evaluate the current situation and the benefits accruing from recent adaptive and incremental changes. In addition incremental changes are invariably part of the implementation process for visionary strategies, which, by their very nature, are conceived in a vague rather than a detailed format.

Organizations are making decisions and changes as part of an orchestrated movement towards long-term objectives and the mission. The direction is clear; there is a consistency of purpose. The detail needs to be worked out with learning in an ever-changing environment. The approach often features trial-and-error experimentation around a common core of products, services and strategies. Ideas generate low-risk trials involving only limited change; the outcomes are evaluated to provide fresh ideas for further trials. If a trial proves successful, the experiment can be built on and further changes introduced. Tentative commitments become firm commitments. If it is unsuccessful, it can be abandoned and the previous strategy brought back. Over time the core of products, services and strategies will change, but the process is gradual and *evolutionary*.

Adaptive and incremental change is particularly important for managing competitive and functional strategies effectively. Corporate strategies can be changed adaptively if a new opportunity arises 'out of the blue' or if the organization plans, say, to look for acquisition opportunities but is unable to predict when suitable targets will be available at the 'right' price. Box 7.1, Hanson, illustrates this point. In the same way, if a large company receives an unexpected but attractive offer for one of its businesses, and is tempted to divest it, this will imply an adaptive change to the corporate strategy.

 HANSON

Hanson is an acquisitive international conglomerate named after its founder, Lord James Hanson. The strategy, known as '*Hansonizing*', is based on three essential principles:

* the key objective is to maximize shareholder value;

* many companies do not do this and are therefore run badly;

* such companies are good buys because their assets can be made to create more value for shareholders. This is usually accomplished by reducing central overheads and then systematically looking for new competitive opportuntities and operating efficiencies.

These principles can be applied successfully in any industry, and Hanson has diversified into a number of unrelated areas including construction, bricks, cement, textiles, tobacco, animal foods and meat processing, pulp, coal, gold and chemicals. In the main entry is via acquisition, and Hanson has purchased a string of companies, mostly in the UK and America, over a period of 25 years. A number of the take-overs have been hostile.

Hanson has not always stayed in the industry, but deliberately divested companies and business units when appropriate for its strategy. Following an acquisition any businesses within a conglomerate which do not fit the basic Hanson strategy will be divested at the earliest suitable opportunity.

In the main businesses in competitive or high technology industries, and ones which require investment, are either avoided or sold, and mature, slow growth companies retained. Cyclical businesses are also attractive targets for Hanson. In the early 1990s some 90% of Hanson's profits were from mature industries. Despite the lack of growth potential in these businesses the Hanson restructuring strategies have generated a high and consistent growth in group profits.

Earnings per share are maximized when business units achieve the highest possible sustainable return on capital employed. Earnings per share can be improved by increasing returns from existing capital or by reducing capital and maintaining earnings. The latter theme encapsulates divestments.

Although it does not always happen it could be argued that in an organization such as this, which is not primarily concerned with staying in particular industries, business units should be sold when their earnings cannot be increased further and should be replaced by others with greater potential.

Shareholders who support such organizations expect the increased returns to be generated quickly, and consequently Hanson is not thought to be interested in companies which cannot be improved within three to four years.

Although earnings per share can be improved by investing and using debt financing rather than equity, Hanson are basically risk averse and seek to constrain their gearing.

Business units are decentralized and given strict targets to achieve, but all capital investments are carefully scrutinized at Board level. Within these financial constraints the businesses can freely *adapt* their competitive and functional strategies.

There is a very clear *vision* behind the corporate strategy and it has hardly changed in the company's lifetime. Hanson centrally *plans* to acquire suitable companies when they might be available at a price which will allow them to quickly add value and improve returns. To this end Hanson perpetually 'tracks' a large number of companies, waiting for the right moment to strike. Because this must be partially uncertain there is a clear element of *adapting* to circumstances. Hanson will, however, plan to be ready by ensuring that acquisition capital is available. The willingness to sell businesses if an attractive offer is received also implies emergent change ■

Box 7.2 lists a number of examples of emergent changes at the competitive and functional levels.

7 2 ADAPTIVE AND INCREMENTAL CHANGE

When Marks & Spencer launch new and different product lines, as they have furniture and books, for example, they use initial trials in carefully selected outlets as a deliberate learning exercise. The strategy emerges as it is improved incrementally.

The managers of Waterstone's bookshops enjoy considerable delegated authority, which is unusual in the major retail chains. If a manager spots a local opportunity for, say, a special and different promotional event, he or she may experiment. If the trial is successful it is likely to be repeated. Moreover, if it is copied by other branches – the spreading of good practice – it may become an important aspect of the company's competitive strategy.

An international charity such as Oxfam (The Oxford Committee for Famine Relief) will plan to be flexible so that it can respond to an unexpected event; a local authority will have outline contingency plans for dealing with an emergency. When the event occurs the strategy will be situation-specific and emergent.

Oxfam really pioneered the high-street charity shop but this was not a planned strategy. Oxfam was offered an empty shop premises in Oxford for storing materials which had been collected for overseas aid, and the idea sprung from this. The strategy has since been developed systematically. There are now shops in most towns, and many of them sell Third World trade goods as well as second-hand clothes and other items which have been donated. New shops are staffed entirely by volunteers, but when turnover reaches a particular trigger level of approximately £2000 per week a professional manager is employed by Oxfam. This often has the effect of changing the culture significantly.

Rolls Royce competes with major rivals like Pratt and Whitney to have its engines specified when large airlines order new aircraft from, say, Boeing or Airbus Industrie. The final competitive strategy will be based on several issues, including price, payment details, delivery schedules, the exact performance specification and maintenenace arrangements. These will change and emerge during protracted negotiations.

Customer complaints or demands for particular product or service features can create strategic change. The following example is hypothetical. Customers complain that labelling on packages is not sufficiently informative. Clearly larger packs could contain much more information than smaller ones. The company might conclude that in addition special promotions could be marketed more effectively if packaging could be more flexible and changed at relatively short notice. New, flexible packaging, therefore, could add more value for customers and improve the company's perceived differentiation and competitive advantage. However extra costs are implied and the company is reluctant to increase prices. The operations staff investigate the problem further and track down a printer who can offer the service flexibility without any increase

> in costs. Determined to capitalize on the opportunity the company establishes a mutually beneficial strategic alliance with its supplier. In this example, functional (packaging), competitive and corporate (the strategic alliance) strategies have all changed and emerged with learning ■

The underpinning issues are:

- a continual search for new opportunities, supported by an ability to respond positively when one is spotted;

- the recognition that potentially damaging actions by competitors have to be dealt with; and

- an appreciation that continuous improvement, innovation and adding new value is a critically important source of competitive advantage.

This is not a search for a best or ideal *solution*; rather it is a process of gradual and continual improvement. Success requires (1) the ability to scan the environment continuously, (2) the ability to capture and share important signals and information and (3) the **empowerment** of employees so that they are able to act quickly. This is more likely to happen if the organization becomes a learning organization, capable of sharing knowledge and best practice, and acting upon it.

Key Point

7.2 If an organization is to deal effectively with an environment which delivers shocks and surprises it needs sound communication and control systems. People and information are therefore critically important strategic resources.

This ability to share is critically important, and it involves **people** and **information**. One of the underlying sources of success for Japanese companies is their ability to bring employees together to share information, ask questions and discuss problems. People, functions and businesses then support each other and internal synergies can be fostered and captured. Moreover, unexpected and good ideas can bubble out of the discussions. Quite simply, employees throughout the organization have invaluable and often up-to-date information and they constitute key variables for the effective delivery of outputs and service to customers. Their experience, expertise and knowledge must be harnessed.

The case was used to introduce the themes and significance of empowerment and learning organizations, which we look at in the next two sections of this chapter. The heart of the argument is that information must reach those employees and managers who need it, and who have the delegated authority to act upon it and change strategies and processes – within specified parameters and the organization's policy framework. As we have seen, strategies may also be changed by a visionary strategic leader and through the strategic planning system. In just the same way the key *internal processes* which underpin the creation and delivery of products, services and customer satisfaction will on occasions need rethinking and a radical overhaul. This is known as *business process re-engineering* and we consider it in the last section of the chapter.

EMPOWERMENT

Empowerment means freeing employees from instructions and controls and allowing them to take decisions themselves. It is clearly linked to total quality management which implies constant improvement to strategies and processes which add value for customers. To achieve this employees should be contributing to the best of their ability. Proponents argue that rules stifle innovation and that future success relies not on past results but on the continuing ability to manage change pressures. Managers must be free to make appropriate changes in a decentralized structure.

There are three main **objectives of empowerment**:

1. To make organizations more responsive to external pressures.

2. To 'de-layer' organizations in order to make them more cost-effective. British Airways, for example, now has five layers of management between the chief executive and the front line who interface with customers. It used to be nine.

    Managers become responsible for more employees who they are expected to *coach and support* rather than direct.

3. To create employee networks featuring teamworking, collaboration and horizontal communications. This implies changes in the ways decisions are made.

It is neither feasible nor appropriate to decentralize all decisions, and therefore the important empowerment questions are why, how and when. The leading retailers, for example, benefited from increasing centralization throughout the 1980s. Information technology has enabled cost savings and efficiencies from centrally controlled buying, store and shelf layouts, stocking policies and reordering. In the 1990s there is little support for changing this in any marked way and delegating these decisions to store level. Consequently it is head office buying and marketing staff who are empowered to adjust product ranges and decide on particular promotions.

The centralized retailers still need strategies for dealing with special local demand patterns, local price competition, and new competitors entering the market or sudden opportunities in particular towns, and this presents a major challenge. The relative success of individual stores will depend on the quality of service they provide to their customers as well as the range and availability of products; and it is in this area that there is considerable scope for empowering branch staff.

As empowerment is increased it is important that employees are adequately informed and knowledgeable, that they are motivated to exercise power, and that they are rewarded for successful outcomes. In flatter organization structures there are fewer opportunities for promotion.

There are **three basic empowerment options**:

1. Employees can be encouraged to contribute ideas. We saw in Chapter 4 (Box 4.2) how several important new product ideas for McDonald's have come from individual franchisees. In reality this may represent only token empowerment, but it is still important. It is as far as many organizations are willing to go.

2. Employees work in teams which share and manage their own work, but within clearly defined policies and limits. This should increase both efficiency and job satisfaction.

3. More extensive decentralization where individuals are much freer to change certain parameters and strategies. Evaluating outcomes is seen as the important control mechanism rather than rules and guidelines. This requires strong leadership, a clear mission and effective communications. Information must flow openly upwards and sideways as well as down. In many organizations there is a tendency for 'bad news' to be selectively hidden, with perhaps two thirds not flowing up to the next layer. Many potential threats are thereby not shared within the company. This would be unacceptable in an empowered organization.

Box 7.3 describes structural changes which have resulted in greater empowerment at IBM.

---

7 3 RESTRUCTURING AND EMPOWERMENT AT IBM

When IBM became the world's largest computer company it had followed a strategy of vertical integration, manufacturing both hardware (including semiconductors, disc drives and assembled computers) and software around the world. IBM had adopted a bureaucratic, centralized structure. Real power lay in the hands of a small élite; the remaining employees have been described as 'a well-drilled army of blue-suited, white-shirted technocrats', rigidly controlled from the centre.

Competition intensified during the 1980s and early 1990s, especially in the worldwide recessions. IBM lost sales and profits as prices tumbled. The structure appeared to be slow and overweight. In the past, with less competition, IBM had been able to offer complete installed systems with a clear pricing structure. In the 1980s it was increasingly possible for customers to obtain a customized package of hardware, software and support services sourced from more than one manufacturer. The 'parts' of the total system could be readily integrated. The overall package, therefore, had to be seen as flexible with a corresponding price flexibility. The final deal would emerge from negotiations, which required more decentralization. IBM decided that 95% of costs should be determined locally, with just 5% central overheads. This implied radical structural change.

In the early 1990s IBM was split into 13 independent – but still interdependent – companies worldwide. In 1993 the developments were accompanied by a change of strategic leadership.

STRUCTURAL CHANGES IN THE UK

The UK home sales operation was further split into a federation of 30 separate businesses. There are three types of sales business incorporated in this breakdown:

- vertical businesses – such as the banking and retailing *industries*; the relevant IBM business focusing on one of these industries is free to buy hardware and software from within IBM (worldwide) or its competitors when piecing together an appropriate package;

- product sectors – mainframes, personal computers etc. It is perfectly feasible in the structure for these businesses also to negotiate directly with a bank or retail customer; internal competition!;

- computing services – consultancy and maintenance.

The sizes of the 30 businesses range from 50 to over 500 employees. Each has the power to fix prices and establish its own cost structure. In the past business managers were accountable for revenue and a share of corporate costs; responsibility for dealing with customer dissatisfaction was frequently 'delegated upwards' to the centre. Now the businesses are totally responsible for customer service and satisfaction. Ownership and accountability has been delegated to people who historically 'took orders'.

Businesses are assessed against five criteria:

- Customer satisfaction } based on opinion surveys
- Employee morale
- Profits
- Market share
- Cash generation

There are no regular monthly reviews as such. The centre intervenes only when the business 'goes off the rails'.

These changes reflect a general programme of staff reduction and delayering. Far more employees now come into direct contact with customers. The UK headquarters has been downsized from 2500 to 100 people as the emphasis has switched to the businesses. Service units such as finance, personnel and distribution are now independent and they must compete with outside specialists for internal business.

The successful implementation of all these changes is seen as a difficult 'uphill' process. A major change of culture is implied to establish the required trust and teamwork – 'the leopard must change its spots'.

NOTE

Cultural change is developed in Chapter 8. The changing role of corporate head offices is discussed in Chapter 9.

REFERENCE

Cane, A. (1993) The shake-up of Big Blue's Army, *Financial Times*, 7 July ■

For many organizations empowerment implies that the core organization strategies are decided centrally, with individual managers delegated a discretionary layer around the core:

It is crucial, first, to find the right balance between the core and discretionary elements, and second, to ensure that managers support and own the core strategy.

THE DECIDING FACTORS

- The competitive strategies and the relative importance of close linkages with customers in order to differentiate and provide high levels of service. When this becomes essential empowerment may imply a conceptually 'inverted pyramid' structure. The structure exists to support front-line managers:

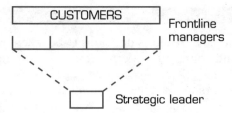

The strategic leader still co-ordinates and controls the organization's efforts, but he or she allows individual managers the freedom to exercise initiative and introduce changes. The extent of the changes implied here should not be under-estimated. While theoretically very attractive, this is challenging and difficult to implement.

- Successful empowerment therefore means putting the 'right' people in place and ensuring they are able to do their job – which they understand and own. In this way they feel important.

- The extent to which the environment is turbulent and decisions are varied rather than routine.

- The expectations and preferences of managers and employees, and their ability and willingness to accept responsibility. Not everyone wants accountability and high visibility. If empowerment is mishandled it is possible that work will be simply pushed down a shorter hierarchy as managers seek to avoid responsibility.

Successful empowerment requires direction – key result areas and objectives must be understood. In addition it is important to ensure that there is constant monitoring and feedback of outcomes. Empowerment requires information to be *shared* throughout the organization, thereby assisting other managers and employees, and enabling them to *learn* more effectively. Where people are free to make limited changes it is still essential for the strategic leader to retain effective control. This requires an information system which can successfully monitor and synthesize the changes. Employees also need the necessary resources and appropriate skills, which frequently implies training. The appropriate style of management is *coaching* – offering help without taking away responsibility. Moreover it is important to link monitoring systems with rewards and sanctions. Finally empowerment must be taken seriously and not simply limited to non-essential decisions. Empowerment implies risk-taking, and any mistakes, while not overlooked, must be handled carefully. It is no easy option.

Empowerment is a powerful motivator as long as it does not suddenly stop when the really important and interesting decisions have to be taken (Jeremy Soper, ex Retail Sales Director, W H Smith).

Key Point

7.3 Empowering employees allows decisions to be taken by people who are closest to events and sources of information. However responsibility also implies accountability.

True empowerment requires changes to both structures and styles of management. Organizations will become flatter, with fewer layers in the hierarchy.

THE LEARNING ORGANIZATION

The basic arguments:

- In a decade when quality, technology and product/service variety are all becoming widely available at relatively low cost, speed of change is essential for sustained competitive advantage.

- If an organization, therefore, fails to keep up with, or ahead of, the rate of change in its environment it will either by destroyed by stronger competitors, or lapse into sudden death or slow decline. The ideal is to be marginally ahead of competitors – opening up too wide a gap might unsettle customers.

- An organization can only adapt if it is first able to learn, and this learning must be cross-functional as well as specialist.

- Learning is continuous; there is no end point where there is nothing left to learn.

Hence a learning organization

> *encourages continuous learning and knowledge generation at all levels, has processes which can move knowledge around the organization easily to where it is needed, and can translate that knowledge quickly into changes in the way the organization acts, both internally and externally* (Senge, 1991).

Strategically important information, together with lessons and best practice, will thus be spread around; and ideally this learning will also be protected from competitors. We saw in the case study that the information flows must be internal, linking functions and businesses effectively, and external, integrating the company with its suppliers and customers. Information about competitors is also essential; benchmarking competitors was introduced in Chapter 3.

THE ESSENTIAL REQUIREMENTS

- Systemic thinking to foster effective internal and external architecture. Systemic thinking is concerned with the *emergent properties* or outcomes from the internal and external processes and interactions, which should generate synergy and mutual benefits.

Ideally decision-makers will be able to use the perspective of the whole organization; and there will be significant environmental awareness and internal co-operation. Departments will treat each other as important internal customers and suppliers.

For many organizations the systemic perspective will be widened to incorporate collaboration and strategic alliances with other organizations in the added value chain.

- Management development and personal growth – to enable effective empowerment and leadership throughout the organization, and in turn allow managers to respond to perceived environmental changes and opportunities.

- A shared vision and clarity about both core competencies and key success factors. Changes should be consistent through strategic and operational levels.

- Appropriate values and corporate culture – to fully exploit core competencies and satisfy key success factors. Kotter and Heskett (1992) argue that the appropriate culture is one which is capable of constant adaptation as the needs of customers, shareholders and employees change. Culture is explained in Chapter 8.

- A commitment to customer service, quality and continuous improvement.

- Team learning within the organization through problem sharing and discussion; information must be communicated freely and widely.

Key Point

7.4 In a learning organization best practices are shared widely. Employees and managers appreciate and take account of the needs and expectations of their colleagues as well as those of their suppliers and customers. Internally departments, functions and employees enjoy supportive supplier-customer relationships.

BUSINESS PROCESS RE-ENGINEERING

To be successful organizations must add value for their customers and other stakeholders in some distinctive way. Hanson (Box 7.1) **as an organization** adds value for its shareholders by exploiting the assets of its subsidiary businesses efficiently. Hanson's head office adds value for the subsidiary companies by acting as a banker. Each individual business is expected to add value for customers through its competitive positioning and the overall service it offers. Chart 7.2 shows that the process of adding value encapsulates four themes:

- strategic diversity and competitive positioning;
- structure;
- core competencies;
- strategic capabilities.

When these are all changed simultaneously we use the term **strategic regeneration**.

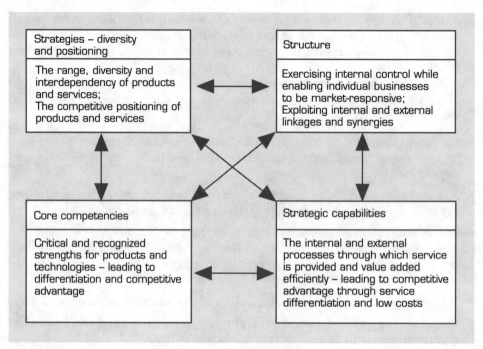

Chart 7.2 Adding strategic value

Strategic capabilities are the means and processes through which value is added, as distinct from the products and services themselves and their competitive positioning. When managers are delegated responsibility for changing and improving the ways in which tasks are carried out it is these **processes** which are being changed incrementally and adapted – illustrated in the top half of Chart 7.3.

Typical processes include:

- supply chain management – to fulfil orders;

- developing new products and services;

- providing service to customers;

- managing people – including, for example, developing people;

- managing finances – especially the cash flow.

Successful innovation in these internal processes can:

- lead to greater efficiency;

- improve quality and service;

- create or enhance differentiation; and thus

- **add value for customers.**

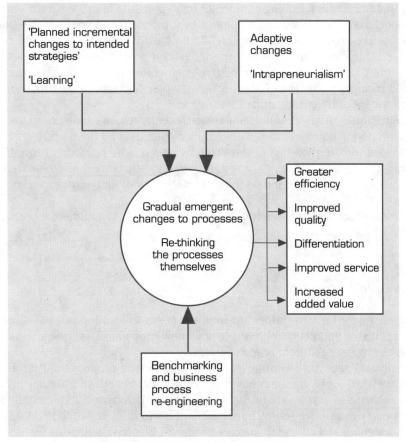

Chart 7.3   Changing business processes

Key Point

7.5 Companies add value for customers in a variety of ways. The actual products, services and strategies can themselves be a source of added value. Equally important are the *processes* through which the products and services are created and supplied.

Products and services will be re-designed and improved in a competitive environment. Processes can also be changed both to save costs (improved efficiency) and improve the overall level of customer service (differentiation).

Sometimes this gradual change may not be enough in a competitive environment. The existing processes – and their outcomes – may simply be inadequate or even unacceptable. Consequently a more radical review is necessary if the organization is to become or remain a leading competitor in an industry. Managers must systematically benchmark and evaluate competitor best practice, and consider the extent to which the processes need redesigning. This objective appraisal, and the changes which result from it, can take the form of *business process re-engineering* – the bottom half of Chart 7.3. Business process re-engineering is really another example of planned change, but it is included in this chapter because of its close links with empowerment and learning organizations.[1]

US Air, British Airways' American partner, recently reviewed the process by which aeroplanes flying domestic routes are emptied, cleaned and the passengers and luggage loaded for the next flight. The outcome was a time reduction from 45 to 25 minutes for selected flights. As a result operating efficiencies are increased – the planes are in the air longer and on the ground less – without passengers being inconvenienced.

Business process re-engineering, illustrated in Chart 7.4, requires the organization to consider two questions:

- How do we do things?

- How could we do them better?

The result might be straightforward improvements to existing processes, or more dramatic, discontinuous change with wholly new procedures as the organization attempts to engineer different outcomes.

Initially it is necessary for managers to define a **value proposition** (Hammer and Champy, 1993). Superior customer service, manufacturing efficiency, innovative products and services – or a mix of these – are possible examples. Once defined this competitively distinctive stance must be created and then implemented by examining, re-designing and changing the core processes involved, which, as we have seen, represent critical strategic capabilities for the organization.

Organizations must determine the weaknesses and drawbacks in existing processes. Delays and operational bottlenecks, for example, represent inefficiency, but they frequently exist and are taken for granted because managers have found ways of working with – or around – them.

The processes in question will normally relate to the way decisions are made inside the organization (involving *people* aspects) and the movement of *information*. Ideally the organization would be able to use accurate cost information for products, services and processes, but this is unlikely. Systems such as activity-based costing are helpful, but difficulties remain with, for example, properly attributing overheads. As a result, there is still an element of judgment, however rigorous the analysis might be.

---

[1] The word engineering is being used here in its widest context. We sometimes use the expression 'engineer a meeting', for example. Some companies practise re-engineering but avoid the title as it is sometimes associated with down-sizing and redundancy.

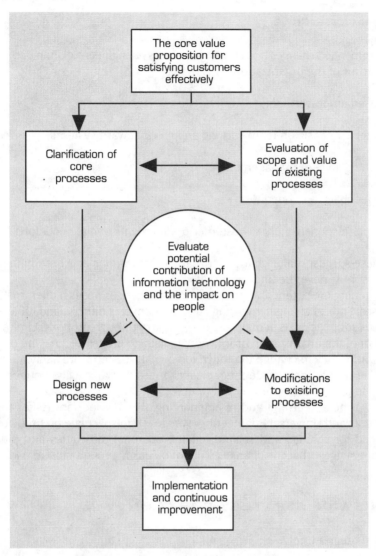

Chart 7.4 Business process re-engineering

It is highly likely that radical process re-engineering will require the reduction or breaking down of functional and individual job boundaries as the new processes do not have to coincide with the existing departmental structure. People and departments will now be expected to be more supportive of each other and *share information and best practices*. These linkages and the greater flexibility in turn imply *empowerment and learning.*

THE CHALLENGES

The recommended changes from business process re-engineering often imply a change in the **culture** of the organization. This may be:

- increased empowerment;

- a greater emphasis on teamworking and group reward systems;

- a coaching style of management;

- more feedback and openness;

- a sharper responsiveness to customer requirements and expectations.

Again these suggest major change for many organizations and the implementation difficulties must never be under-estimated.

Determining the extent and the nature of the changes poses a dilemma for many businesses. Radical change, involving cultural change, is difficult and, unless there is an obvious strategic crisis, it may take time to carry through properly. Limited change to just part of the organization or individual, discrete processes, may be inadequate. If organizations try to change too much too quickly, systems are likely to collapse. If they 'tinker' rather than tackle the radical changes that are really required, systems are likely to drift back to the way they were.

Empowerment, learning and re-engineering are all important issues for Special Components and Universal Engineering. We are left to speculate on first, how urgent is the need for change, and second, on the potential difficulties and pitfalls. The indications suggest that the changes will not be easily brought about.

A REVIEW OF STRATEGY CREATION

Planned strategies imply:

$$\text{Analysis} \longrightarrow \text{Choice} \longrightarrow \text{Implementation}$$

The **visionary** approach suggests more limited formal analysis and a more intuitive selection. Underpinning this is the insight and market 'feel' of a visionary leader who is willing to take risks to back his or her judgment. The power and value of this insight must not be under-estimated. Extending our analogy of a football match, some spectators simply 'follow the ball' while others, able to take a wider perspective, focus on the positioning and movement of the players who are 'off the ball'. They see a different match. We might summarize this as follows:

These two approaches are essentially forward looking in nature. Emergent strategies involve more reflection on events which have just occurred:

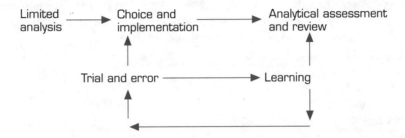

All of these modes of strategy creation are in evidence in some form or another in most organizations at the same time. While individual managers will recognize and appreciate the *existence* of each mode they are likely to disagree on *relative significances*. This results from their personal perspective and position inside the organization. David Marshall, for example, would almost certainly see things differently from a head office analyst. This point will be considered further in the next chapter when we also look at the impact of powerful external stakeholders on strategic choice.

THE VISIT TO GERMANY

David flew to Germany on the following morning. Tony had promised to meet him again and discuss the realities of managing strategic change in greater detail. Tony had also emphasized that organization culture is a critical issue. Major discontinuous changes cannot be implemented without evaluating their potential impact on the existing culture and values, and possibly seeking changes. All the time the culture is a major determinant of the organization's ability to manage adaptive and incremental changes effectively.

David knew that he needed to reach an acceptable agreement with both Ed Grey and Dieter Wild concerning future strategies for the new component. The Americans were currently willing to accept cost over-runs in order to satisfy their customer, Special Components in the UK was reluctant to do this and they had under-estimated the production problems. As a result they had upset both their customer and a leading sub-contractor. Different values and different organization cultures.

It was necessary for the British and American companies to work together more closely in the future, share their knowledge and speed up the learning process. Best practices must be clarified and shared. In addition, Special Components must establish closer links with its German customer. David knew he had to learn more about Dieter Wild's expectations and requirements if Special Components was to add more value for him, improve the level of service and win future business – and then these expectations would have to be met. He already knew that some changes to the corporate culture would be required, but he hoped they would be minimal and feasible.

POINTS FOR REFLECTION

- Exactly how important is it for your organization to be flexible and adaptive?

- Can you identify specific examples of adaptive and incremental change?

- How important and realistic is empowerment in your organization? Are you empowered – and suitably rewarded?

- Would you classify your company as a learning organization? What suggestions do you have for improving organizational learning?

- What are the critical processes in your organization? For any that you are familiar with ... how might they be improved? Are these simply your observations or the result of benchmarking or evaluation?

REFERENCES AND FURTHER READING

Byham, W. C. and Cox, J. (1988) *Zapp! The Lightning of Empowerment*, Century Business. An ideal practical introduction to empowerment.

Garratt, B. (1990) *Creating a Learning Organization*, Director Books. Again a useful practical and introductory book.

Hammer, M. and Champy, J. (1993) *Re-engineering the Corporation*, Harper Business. A comprehensive summary.

Kanter, R. M. (1990) *Strategic Alliances and New Ventures*, Harvard Business School video series.

Kotter, J. P. and Heskett, J. L. (1992) *Corporate Culture and Performance*, Free Press.

Prahalad, C. K. and Hamel, G. (1991) Corporate imagination and expeditionary marketing, *Harvard Business Review*, July–August.

Senge, P. (1991) *The Fifth Discipline: The Art and Practice of the Learning Organization*, Doubleday. (European edition by Century Business, 1992.)

Stacey, R. D. (1993) *Strategic Management and Organisational Dynamics*, Pitman. A valuable text on the dynamics of competition.

A SUMMARY OF THE STRATEGIC LESSONS

In a dynamic and competitive environment the future is uncertain. Structures and styles of management must be flexible and adaptive. This implies decentralization and empowerment. Strategies then emerge with learning.

The environment for many organizations represents a form of competitive chaos. Changes are constant as companies act and react in response to their competitors. Vigilance and awareness are essential.

A distinction can be made between incremental strategic change – the attempt to improve intended strategies as they are implemented – and adaptive changes, where companies seek to respond quickly to perceived opportunities and threats. The outcomes are broadly similar – emergent, gradual change.

In this change process, people and information become critically important strategic resources.

Emergent change requires employees to be empowered. They must be given more responsibility and accountability. It can sometimes prove difficult for some employees to accept this. A new coaching style of management is required, and an effective information system is essential for co-ordinating the changes taking place in a decentralized organization.

The ability of an organization to manage emergent change is enhanced if best practices can be determined and shared, and employees can understand the implications of their decisions for other parts of the organization, suppliers, customers and other important stakeholders. An organization can accomplish this and manage its competitive environment more effectively if it becomes a systemic learning organization. Attractive conceptually, this is difficult to achieve.

Sometimes the internal processes which add value for customers need to be carefully evaluated and changed. The extent of the changes may be limited or substantial. Business process re-engineering provides a framework for this.

Strategic changes require analysis, choice and implementation. These are all present in the visionary, planning and adaptive/incremental modes of strategy creation, but they are manifested in different ways.

8   POWER, POLITICS AND CULTURE

In this chapter we look behind the visionary, planning and adaptive/incremental modes of strategy creation and explore the reasons for their selection and preference. We examine how the culture of the organization and the possession and utilization of power and influence are important determinants.

CUSTOMER EXPECTATIONS

Dieter Wild was very friendly when David and Ed Grey arrived at the German plant. He accepted their assurances – David was able to provide him with positive results from Roger Ellis' new tests – and stressed he was far more concerned with the future than the past.

The three men discussed the increasing closeness and interdependency between Universal Engineering and the car manufacturer. Dieter used the expression 'shared destiny'. Although Universal supplied bearings to several European car manufacturers, including direct rivals to Dieter's company, the German company was the leading vehicle customer for Universal's electrical products. Dieter explained that he could buy components from all round the world but he preferred to deal with only a limited number of suppliers from whom he demanded:

- a wide range of component products, where this was appropriate;
- fast, reliable service;
- consistent high quality; and
- the 'right prices' for the mutual benefit of both partners.

He was currently exploring the potential for Universal's electrical division to supply him with fully assembled dashboards for a number of different models. Universal already manufacture *parts* for dashboards but they do not produce the facias, which they would have to buy in from another supplier. Dieter explained that dashboards are critical components. If they rattle, and many of them do, customers are really annoyed. They are fiddly items to fit; the plastic mouldings must be produced to very tight tolerances. The secret lies in the quality of the dies from which they are pressed.

THE DEMANDS ON SPECIAL COMPONENTS

It was clear to both David and Ed that the supply chain is becoming increasingly complex and, for many companies, critically important for strategic success. Special Components UK and US needed to form a *network* which also incorporated Dieter Wild and Clark Precision Engineering. There would be additional networks within Universal Engineering with whom they would need to co-operate. Value creation through design, production, marketing and service would be critical. David agreed when Dieter suggested they also needed to create a community of employee stakeholders who are committed to the company, the customer, quality and continuous improvement. Tony Anderson had given him essentially the same message.

David decided he would organize a follow-up meeting with Susan Scott and Roger Ellis and his team to address these issues. It would be difficult to forge an effective team but it was essential to try. Managers in Special Components were set in their ways; at times their thinking was rigid and inflexible. Because some of them had been in post for several years they had established strong power bases and were politically manipulative.

David also thought that their arrangement that Roger Ellis would deal with suppliers and sub-contractors, and Susan Scott and himself would liaise with customers, might be improved. There could be real benefits from regular contacts between Roger and Dieter.

DIFFERENT CULTURES AND VALUES

David and Ed pledged to work more closely with each other and aim to provide a more consistent service in Germany and America. Dieter was satisfied they were committed and the discussions turned to more general aspects of culture and values in their organizations.

Dieter argued that his company was 'typically German'. He believed they were successful because they had developed a strong, technically-skilled workforce who produced very reliable cars and took great pride in their work. He acknowledged they were less innovative than their main Japanese competitors. His company valued its *partnerships* with both suppliers and distributors and saw itself as very much 'European'.

Ed commented favourably about the success of the company's plant and cars in America. Ed thought that many American organizations have less of an international perspective than the typical Japanese and the leading European corporations. David felt that this is also true of Britain. Ed also suggested that American companies tend to be strong on customer service but relatively weak with supplier relationships, while their Japanese rivals are very strong on supplier networks and not as closely linked to their customers. Distribution systems in Japan are complex and multi-layered; companies often rely on their ability to innovate and develop new products to satisfy their customers.

David mused that the short-term financial orientation of many UK businesses means they have not forged close links with either their suppliers or distributors in the past, but the need is now clearly recognized. The increasing need for supply chain networks, involving improvement in both *internal and external architecture*, will place demands on organizational cultures everywhere in the world.

POWER, POLITICS AND CULTURE

In looking *behind* the visionary, planning and adaptive/incremental modes of strategy creation, examining why they are selected and preferred by different organizations, this chapter explores in greater detail how the feelings and actions of people inside organizations affect strategy. People create and implement change, and they are affected by changes happening elsewhere in the organization.

Any group of people who live and work together for any length of time form and share certain beliefs about what is right and proper. They establish behaviour patterns based on their beliefs, and their actions often become matters of habit which they follow unconsciously and routinely. These beliefs and ways of behaving constitute the organization's **culture** (definition 1).

The formation of, and any changes to, the culture of an organization is dependent upon the leadership and example of particular individuals, and their ability to control or influence situations. This is itself dependent upon a person's ability to obtain and use **power** (definition 2).

Definition 1

Culture is reflected in the way people in an organization perform tasks, set objectives and administer resources to achieve them. It affects the way that they make decisions, think, feel and act in response to opportunities and threats.

Culture also influences the selection of people for particular jobs, which in turn affects the way that tasks are carried out and decisions are made. Culture is so fundamental that it affects behaviour unconsciously. Managers do things in particular ways because it is expected behaviour.

The culture of an organization is therefore related to the people, their behaviour and the operation of the structure. It is encapsulated in beliefs, customs and values and manifested in a number of symbolic ways.

Definition 2

Power is related to the potential or ability to do something or make something happen, and it flows from the relationships and interactions between people which build up over time. Power is sometimes reflected in force; on other occasions it takes the form of influence and persuasion.

Organizational politics is the process by which individuals and groups utilize power and influence to obtain results. Politics can be legitimate and positive; equally it can be used negatively and illigitimately by individuals pursuing personal objectives against the best interests of the organization.

Culture and power affect the choice, incidence and application of the modes of strategy creation discussed in the previous three chapters. The preferred mode will reflect the values and preferences of the strategic leader and the organization. It must, though, be appropriate for the organization's strategic needs, which are, of course, affected by competition.

We saw earlier that culture and values determine the ability of an organization to create and sustain a match between their resources and the environment – E-V-R Congruence. The case generalized on how organizations in particular countries have developed different cultural traits. As industries and markets have become increasingly international, many organizations have come under pressure to change their cultures in order to be effective competitors and sustain E-V-R congruence.

In addition the culture, political activity and the use of power and influence inside the organization affect the outcomes from the decision processes which underpin the adaptive/incremental mode. We are concerned with the way an organization reacts to a particular opportunity or threat; affected organizations will not all behave in the same way. As we shall see later, powerful external stakeholders can sometimes dictate the strategy of an organization.

Moreover, culture and power are such strong forces that any intended changes must take account of them. If they are overlooked, implementation may not happen. The UK government, for example, recently sought to introduce extensive testing in schools at several different ages. Teachers and their unions were opposed and successfully mobilized parent support. The government partially backed down and reduced the extent of the testing.

Quite simply, as we saw in Chapter 1 (Chart 1.5), culture is at the heart of all strategy creation and implementation. Organizations are seeking to respond to perceived strategic issues. Resources must be deployed and committed, but successful change also requires the 'right' attitude, approach and commitment from people. This *mind set*, which might, for example, reflect a strong customer and service focus, could imply further empowerment and consequently cultural change.

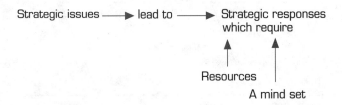

Strong cultures are an important strategic asset. Internalized beliefs can motivate people to exceptional levels of performance. An effective strategic leader will understand and mould the culture in order that a vision can be pursued and intended strategies implemented.

Large organizations formed by a series of acquisitions will frequently exhibit different cultures in the various divisions or businesses. In many international businesses this is inevitable. The challenge for corporate headquarters is to ensure that certain critically important values are reflected in all branches of the corporation and cultural differences do not inhibit *internal architecture* and synergy.

Key Point

8.1 The culture of an organization permits, supports or inhibits strategic change.

It influences every decision concerning which strategies to follow.

Without an appreciation of the cultural implications strategies are difficult to implement.

The culture can be best understood by considering three things:

- manifestations, including values and behaviours;

- people and communications; and

- power.

CULTURE

CULTURAL DETERMINANTS

The points discussed in this section are illustrated in Chart 8.1; Box 8.1 applies the ideas to Our Price, the music and video subsidiary of W H Smith.

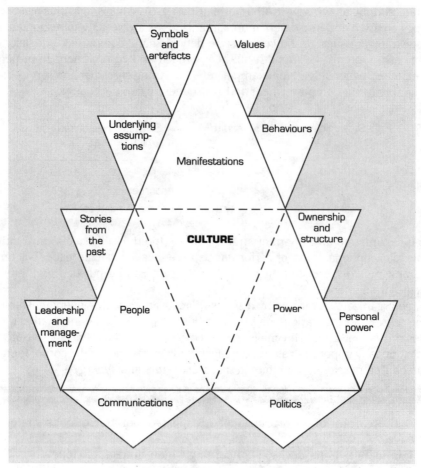

Chart 8.1 Determinants of culture

8 1 OUR PRICE

Our Price, part of W H Smith, is a leading specialist retailer of music and video products, including computer games – markets where the majority of competing *products* are identical. At the end of the 1980s, following years of growth, this market had flattened out. Our Price was acknowledged to be a company which provided excellent service but its stores were seen as 'dull, drab, boring and intimidating'.

W H Smith was determined to 're-position the brand' to revitalize it while ensuring it was easily distinguishable from its major competitors, especially the informal Virgin Megastores and the mainstream W H Smith stores, which are more formal and traditional. It was thought necessary to change the ways in which products are displayed and sold, media and in-store promotions, aspects of the service, and, especially, staff attitudes and behaviour.

New vision and values were defined 'to build an attitude and way of behaving in all that we do in the business that will support ... the re-positioning of the brand'.

THE OUR PRICE VISION

- The first place everybody thinks of for music.
- The place its customers keep coming back to.
- The place where the involvement and fulfilment of its people creates commercial success.

THE REQUIRED VALUES

To pursue the vision effectively Our Price would need:

- to 'delight' its customers, who need to feel satisfied even if they leave the store without purchasing;
- to empower its people;
- to drive itself forward and embrace change ...

while recognizing the need to be commercially successful.

CHANGES

There has subsequently been a number of changes to the physical manifestations at Our Price, namely:

- new store interiors, which are less cluttered and less confusing and feature new service counters;
- new rackings, displays and header cards – with different colour schemes for each section;
- a new logo;
- new advertising and promotion campaigns;
- new window displays;
- revisions to the stocks;
- distinctive polo shirts for the staff, which are thought to be casual rather than a uniform.

> **NEW VALUES**
>
> In-company training has focused on customer service, personal accountability, decision-making and coaching skills – we saw in Chapter 7 that this implies offering help without taking away responsibility.
>
> The aim has been to *cascade* the new values down and through the whole organization. 'Every manager or supervisor is required to take responsibility for involving those who report directly to them in order to gain their commitment.' The opportunity for people to contribute to decision-making (from the bottom up) has been built in.
>
> (*Readers might usefully visit an Our Price store and evaluate the relative success of these attempts to change the culture and values.*) ■

Cultural determinants can be grouped into three areas:

1. MANIFESTATIONS

These include **symbols and artefacts** such as expensive, city-centre head offices, high technology plant and equipment, the products themselves, advertising, brand names and the dress codes followed by employees. Some companies, for example, will encourage smart casual wear, rather than formal dress, to encourage an informal working environment. **Values** constitute ideas and convictions about 'what ought to be', which, with experience and learning, become **underlying assumptions**, or beliefs and established practices. One belief accepted by employees within a bank might be that all lending must be secure. A football team could be committed to always playing attractive, open football. A university might be expected to have clear beliefs about the relative importance of research and teaching, but this is likely to be an issue where employees 'agree to disagree' leading to a fragmented culture. Examples of **behaviours** are speedy new product development, long working hours, formal management meetings and regular informal meetings or contacts with colleagues, suppliers and customers.

2. PEOPLE

This will include **stories of *past* successes and heroes, and the *present* strategic leadership and styles of management**, which includes *innovation*.

Linked to this is *communication*, an essential aspect of culture. The organization might be seen as open or closed, formal or informal. Ideally employees from different parts of the business, and at different levels in the hierarchy, will feel willing and able to talk openly with each other, sharing problems, ideas and learning. 'Doors should be left open.' Employees should also be trusted and empowered to the appropriate degree. Good communications can 'stop nasty surprises'. It is helpful if employees know how well competitors are performing, where they are particularly strong, so they can commit themselves to high levels of achievement in order to out-perform their rivals.

Communication is clearly essential for creating effective *internal and external architecture*.

Hampden-Turner (1990) argues that culture is *based on communication and learning*. The strategic leader's vision for the organization must be communicated and understood; events and changes affecting the organization also need to be communicated widely. Managers should be encouraged to seek out new opportunities by learning about new technology and customer expectations, and to innovate. The organization should help them to share their experiences and their learning.

Box 8.2 describes how the culture of British Airways has been changed during its transition from a nationalized to a profitable, privatized business. A commitment from the strategic leader provided the foundation for the changes.

3. *POWER*

Power is reflected in the **ownership** of the business. It may be a family company with strong, concentrated power. A small group of institutional shareholders could control the business, in which case it is conceivable that short-term financial targets will dictate strategies. **Structural issues** include the extent to which the organization is centralized or decentralized, the role and contribution of corporate headquarters, and control and reward systems. These issues are the subject of Chapter 9. **Personal power and politics** are discussed later in this chapter.

 BRITISH AIRWAYS

Prior to privatization British Airways was fragmented. Leadership was, to some considerable extent, 'military', with strict rules and procedures, and top-down communications. Cabin staff were essentially powerless and insufficiently customer oriented. Customer attitudes and reactions were not fed back into the organization, and BA was seen as less friendly than many of its rivals.

When Colin Marshall (now Sir Colin) became Chief Executive in 1983 he set 'giving the best service' as a key objective. He argued that this involved:

- appreciating what the market wants;
- being able to respond quickly to changes in customer demand and expectations by
- having an appropriate organization structure; and
- being adequately resourced.

These were to be achieved by ensuring that employees throughout BA were committed to providing a high level of customer service and that managers were equally aware of the needs and expectations of employees. Marshall sought to change the culture of BA to one of service orientation by:

- issuing a new mission statement reflecting the revised objectives and values;

- a management training programme entitled 'Managing People First', designed to 'substantially enhance the participant's personal performance as a manager of others' by concentrating on developing a sense of urgency, vision, motivation, trust and a willingness to take responsibility;

- improving both performance appraisal and a linked reward system;

- customer service training for all employees who dealt directly with customers – entitled 'Putting People First';

- establishing 'Customer First' teams where groups of staff meet regularly to discuss their learning.

Front-line staff have been given more authority to use initiative, on the assumption they will behave more warmly to passengers. Positive and negative responses (complaints) are now fed through formalized channels, aided by increased use of information technology. Staff became more professional, and the organization more effective and more profitable.

New, revised service campaigns – 'Winning for Customers' and 'Managing Winners' – have been introduced in the 1990s, after the Gulf War caused a slump in air travel and airline profits ■

CULTURE AND STRATEGY CREATION

The essential cultural characteristics will dictate the *preferred* mode of strategy creation in an organization. All the modes are likely to be present to some degree. Miles and Snow (1978) developed a typology of organizations based on values and objectives, and in Table 8.1 this has been linked to the visionary, planning and adaptive/incremental modes. Defenders, prospectors and analysers are all seen as positive organizations; reactors must adopt one of the other dominant styles or they will suffer long-term decline.

The culture will influence the ability of a strategic visionary to 'sell' his or her ideas to other members of the organization and gain their support and commitment to change. The planning mode is most suitable in a reasonably stable and predictable environment, but a reliance on it in a more unstable situation can lead to missed opportunities. It is an ideal mode for a conservative, risk-averse, slow-to-change organization.

Where environmental opportunities and threats arise continuously in a situation of competitive chaos an organization must be able to deal with them if it is to survive. It is the culture, with its amalgam of attitudes, values, perceptions and experiences, which determines the outcomes and relative success. The structure must facilitate

Table 8.1 Organizations' values and strategies

Type	Characteristics	Strategy formation	Examples
Defenders	Conservative beliefs Low-risk strategies Secure markets Concentration on narrow segments Considerable expertise in narrow areas of specialism Preference for well-tried resolutions to problems Little search for anything really 'new' Attention given to improving efficiency of present operations	Emphasis on planning	GEC
Prospectors	Innovative Looking to break new ground High-risk strategies Search for new opportunities Can create change and uncertainty, forcing a response from competitors More attention given to market changes than to improving internal efficiency	Visionary mode	Amstrad Sony
Analysers	Two aspects: stable and changing Stable: formal structures and search for efficiencies Changing: competitors monitored and strategies amended as promising ideas seen (followers)	Planning mode Incremental mode	Marks & Spencer
Reactors	Characterized by an ability to respond effectively to change pressures Adjustments are therefore forced on the firm in order to avert crises	Adaptive mode	IBM

awareness, sharing and learning and people must be willing and able to act. People 'learn by doing' and they must be able to learn from mistakes. The reward system is critical here. Managers and employees should be praised and rewarded for exercising initiative and taking risks which prove successful; failures should not be sanctioned too harshly – as long as they are not repeated!

Key Point

8.2 The culture of an organization can be changed, but the process requires time and dedication. Effective leadership is essential, and resistance is almost inevitable.

CHANGING CULTURE

Ideally the culture and strategies being pursued will complement each other, and, again ideally, the organization will be flexible and adaptable to change when it is appropriate. But these ideals will not always be achieved.

The culture of an organization can be changed, but it may not be easy. Strong leadership and vision is always required to champion the change process. If an organization is in real difficulty, and the threat to its survival is clearly recognized, behaviour can be changed through fear and necessity. However, people may not feel comfortable and committed to the changes they accept. Behaviour may change, but not attitudes and beliefs. When an organization is basically successful the process of change again needs careful management – changing attitudes and beliefs does not itself guarantee a change of behaviour.

The potential for changing the culture is affected by:

1. the strength and history of the existing culture;
2. how well the culture is understood;
3. the personality and beliefs of the strategic leader; and
4. the extent of the strategic need.

Lewin (1947) contends that there are three important stages in the process of change: unfreezing existing behaviour, changing attitudes and behaviour, and refreezing the new behaviour as accepted common practice.

The first steps in changing culture are recognizing and diagnosing the existing culture, highlighting any weaknesses and stressing the magnitude of the need to change.

One way of changing behaviour would be the establishment of internal groups to study and benchmark competitors and set new performance standards. This would lead to wider discussion throughout the organization, supported by skills training – possibly including communication, motivation and financial awareness skills. People must become committed to the changes, which requires persistence by those who are championing the change and an emphasis on the significance and the desired outcomes.

Unless the changes become established and part of the culture, there will be a steady drift back to the previous pattern. While critical aspects of the culture should remain rock-solid and generate strategic consistency, this must not mean the organization becomes resistant to change without some major upheaval. Competitive pressures require organizations to be vigilant, aware and constantly change-oriented, not change resistant.

Resistance to change should always be expected. People may simply be afraid because they do not understand all the reasons behind the proposed changes; they may mistrust colleagues or management because of previous experiences; communications may be poor; motivation and commitment may be missing; internal architecture may be weak, causing internal conflict and hostility; and the organization may simply not be good at sharing best practice and learning.

The following example of successful change in an engineering company utilizes the seven key aspects of culture devised by Pümpin (1987):

Aspects of culture	Change from	Change to
The extent to which the organization is market-oriented, giving customers high priority	Low	High
The relationship between management and staff, manifested, for example, through communications and participation systems	Closed	Open
The extent to which people are target oriented and committed to achieving agreed levels of performance	Poor	Committed
Attitudes towards innovation	Isolated	Need understood (further progress required)
Attitudes towards costs and cost reduction	Accepted with resignation	Accepted
The commitment and loyalty to the organization felt, and shown by, staff	High, as a means of survival	Less loyal but more committed as fortunes improve
The impact of, and reaction to, technology and technological change and development, including information technology.	Cautious	Improving

Key Point

8.3 The ways in which people obtain, preserve, defend, pass on and relinquish power are important aspects of the culture.

The use of power and influence by both internal and external stakeholders – known as *organizational politics* – impacts on every decision, and consequently affects both strategic choice and strategy implementation.

POWER, POLITICS AND STRATEGY

Strategies are frequently the outcome of bargaining, negotiation and accommodation between different interest groups, or stakeholders, both inside and outside the organization. In this respect strategy *creation* is not the product of logical analysis or personal vision – although bargaining and accommodation are invariably required when any new strategies are implemented. Change is implied, and fears and resistance must be overcome.

Table 8.2 Power levers: how managers obtain and use power

Reward power is the ability to influence the rewards given to others. These can be tangible (money) or intangible (status). Owner managers enjoy considerable reward power, managers in larger public-sector organizations very little. For reward power to be useful, the rewards being offered must be important to the potential recipients

Coercive power is power based upon the threat of punishment for non-compliance, and the ability to impose the punishment. The source can be the person's role or position in the organization, or physical attributes and personality.

Legitimate power is synonymous with authority, and relates to an individual manager's position within the structure of the organization. It is an entitlement from the role a person occupies. The effective use of legitimate power is dependent upon three things: access to relevant information; access to other people and communication networks inside the organization; and approaches to setting priorities – this determines what is asked of others.

Personal power depends upon individual characteristics (personality) and physical characteristics. Charm, charisma and flair are terms used to describe people with personality-based power. Physical attributes such as height, size, weight and strength also affect personal power.

Expert power is held by a person with specialist knowledge or skills in a particular field. It is particularly useful for tackling complex problem areas. It is possible for people to be attributed expert power through reputation rather than proven ability.

Information power is the ability to access and use information to defend a stance or viewpoint – or to question an alternative view held by someone else – and is important as it can affect strategic choices.

Connection power results from personal and professional access to key people inside and outside the organization, who themselves can influence what happens. This relates particularly to information power.

The impact of individual managers, employees and external stakeholders upon strategy creation and implementation is affected by their ability to acquire and use power and influence to affect negotiation and bargaining situations. Some powerful managers will seek to dictate strategies and policies; others will rely on their ability to persuade. Decisions can be the outcome of honest debate and argument; equally they can result from the manipulation of a situation by a politically astute manager.

The critical power issues concern how it is obtained, how it is preserved, how it is defended, how it is passed on and how it is relinquished. Table 8.2 lists the main sources of power. The relative significance of any power is affected by its scarcity and the ease with which it can be replaced. An exceptionally skilful footballer, who would be difficult to replace if he were to leave, can easily become a powerful force in a team and influence the style of play. If a restaurant is dependent upon its chef he or she will also be in a strong position to, say, dictate menus.

Different stakeholders will not seek to influence every decision in the same way or to the same extent; their use of power and influence will reflect the significance of the issue for them personally.

Politics is concerned with the way people use power to influence situations and affect decisions. All managers are therefore political. Where power and influence are used in an appropriate way, to bring about outcomes which are clearly in the best interests of the organization as a whole, together with its suppliers and customers, we can use the term *positive political activity*. Sometimes, though, situations are structured, and people manipulated, to meet the personal objectives of individual managers, functions, divisions or business units at the expense of other parts of the organization. These incidences reflect the *negative side of politics*.

Lukes (1974) identified three further important sources of power:

* the ability to prevent a decision, or not make one;

* the ability to control the issues on which decisions are to be made; and

* the ability to ensure that certain issues are kept off agendas.

From these we can see how power might be used by individuals to inhibit changes which may be in the long-term interests of the organization.

POWERFUL EXTERNAL STAKEHOLDERS

On occasions organizations and strategic leaders are simply not free to set the objectives and select the strategies they would wish to prioritize. Some strategies are followed by all competitors in an industry because they are the norm and customers demand them. Distribution channels, for example, might be dictated by customer expectations. Individuality is always possible, but it is likely to be high risk.

In other situations organizations are *constrained* by identifiable, powerful external stakeholders:

* The recently privatized gas, electricity, water and telecommunications companies are subject to control by independent **regulators**, who, for example, can impose price formulae which restrict their strategic freedom.

* Legislation can force companies to follow particular strategies – or prevent them from doing certain things.

   Box 8.3 looks at strategic changes by leading European drug manufacturers in response to changes in government policies.

   Many organizations benefit in some way from government funding and subsidies, but these opportunities can become threats if policies are changed. In the UK in recent years a number of theatres, opera houses and museums have seen the real value of their grants cut – strategic changes have been forced on them. Air France is just one relatively unprofitable European airline to have received government subsidies throughout the 1980s and into the 1990s. European regulations require this funding to be reduced and the airline's survival will depend upon its ability to implement painful strategic changes.

* Powerful customers may change their specifications or requirements, and interested suppliers will have to accept the changes or lose the business.

8.3 THE EUROPEAN DRUGS INDUSTRY

The total spend on prescription drugs rose throughout Western Europe in the 1980s and early 1990s. Between 1989 and 1992 it grew by nearly 50% in real terms. Almost all of the cost is borne by the public purse. The main reasons for the growth are ageing populations and medical advances. However, in the economic recession, governments have become less and less willing to meet an ever-increasing bill; and in 1993 drug spending was deliberately curbed. The pharmaceutical companies have been forced to respond, and they have reacted in a number of ways:

- Workforces have been reduced and sites closed. Hoechst and Bayer (German), Glaxo, Fisons and Wellcome (British) and Ciba (Swiss) have all followed this strategy.

- New marketing strategies have been developed, actively promoting to doctors and hospitals those drugs that governments are still willing to pay for. This applies particularly to drugs which are differentiated, protected by patent and not subject to intense competition.

- Research and development has been redirected to focus on:

  1. programmes which could lead to innovative and high-revenue drugs; the development of 'me-too' brands, which must be sold with lower margins in more competitive markets, is now seen as only low priority;

  2. *generic* (unbranded) drugs where patents have expired. Margins are low but generic drugs are popular with governments.

- European companies are forging alliances with American companies to obtain their greater expertise in cost management and in the research and development of generic products.

- Industry restructuring and acquisitions:

  - Roche of Switzerland has bought the US company Syntex (in 1994);

  - SmithKline Beecham (Anglo-American) and Merck (US) have both acquired leading American drugs wholesalers – again in 1994 ■

Key Point

8.4 Powerful external stakeholders can be in a position to constrain organizations and effectively dictate the strategies they follow.

In the main case study, the insistence by Universal Engineering head office that Special Components produce the new component for the German car manufacturer is an example of a powerful stakeholder dictating the strategy of a business unit. Similarly, Dieter Wild's preference for buying complete dashboards from Universal Engineering, requiring the electricals division to buy in components not manufactured within the group, is an example of a strong and important buyer putting pressure on their supplier.

STRATEGY CREATION

We are now in a position to summarize the complex process of strategy creation in organizations. Chart 8.2, which is an updated version of Chart 4.5, highlights that strategic management is far more than the creation of intended strategies. We really need to understand how the actual strategies pursued are decided upon.

The **strategic leader** is primarily responsible for the mission of the organization, together with a suitable structure and communications network. **Visionary strategies** will reflect the mission and the ideas of the strategic leader; the structure and management systems will together determine the formally **planned strategies**. Together these comprise the intended strategies.

Some intended strategies will later be discarded. They will either prove to be inappropriate – because of changes in customer demand or competitor activity – or incapable of implementation. Those that are implemented successfully are likely to

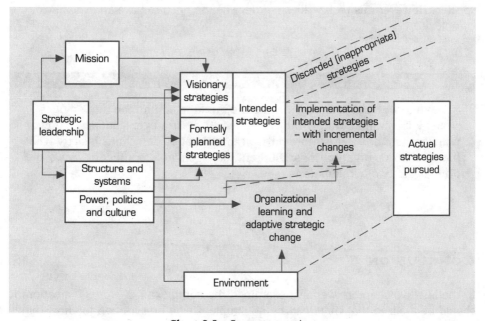

Chart 8.2   Strategy creation

be **changed incrementally** as part of an organizational learning process. New **adaptive strategies** will be added in response to environmental opportunities and, again, learning.

The ability of the organization to learn and to adapt and incrementally change strategies is dependent upon **politics, power and culture**. Strategies reflect experiences inside political-cultural structures. The powerful external stakeholder is encapsulated in the line joining the environment with the planning mode of strategy creation.

DIFFERENT PERSPECTIVES

While we can generalize and summarize the process of strategy creation in Chart 8.2, the reality of what happens inside organizations is very complex. It is fair to conclude that the chart does explain the process and that all the modes are likely to be present to some extent in an organization at any time. The difficulty lies in understanding the relative significance and contribution of each mode. Managers in different parts of a large organization, say in different business units with their own distinct cultures, or at different levels in the hierarchy, will not see the organization from the same perspective, and their explanations of the strategy processes will inevitably differ. Managers in corporate head offices deal with different stakeholders from those who work closely with the individual businesses in the corporation. This will again influence their perspective and explanation.

As a result it is truly difficult to understand exactly what happens inside organizations and how strategies are actually created. Explanations are situation-specific. However this reality does not devalue the need to have an overview of the complexity.

Key Point

8.5 While we can readily appreciate the thinking behind the three modes of strategy creation, and how they are affected by strategic leadership, power, politics and culture, it is more difficult to accurately determine exactly what happens inside organizations. Different managers hold conflicting views and offer a variety of explanations.

CONCLUSION

In the last five chapters we have examined the complexity of strategy creation. It should be realized that there can be no simple, single prescription for **how** things should be done. There is no ideal mode of strategy creation. The real issues concern

(1) whether what actually happens brings effective results and (2) how the process might be improved. Everything depends upon the processes inside the organization structure. Consequently it is now appropriate to examine structural and control issues in greater detail.

POINTS FOR REFLECTION

- How would you describe the main features of your organization's culture? Is is a strong, well-established culture? Is it essentially appropriate or inappropriate for your environment and circumstances? Is there a positive attitude towards change?

- What are your personal power bases? How do you use your power bases to influence and manage other people?

- Are organizational politics rife? Is the activity leading to mainly positive or negative outcomes? If negative ... what do you feel should be done in an attempt to change the situation?

- Do any powerful external stakeholders impact upon your organization? How?

REFERENCES AND FURTHER READING

Deal, T. and Kennedy, A. (1982) *Corporate Cultures: The Rites and Rituals of Corporate Life*, Addison Wesley.

French, J. R. P. and Raven, B. (1959) The bases of social power. In *Studies in Social Power* (ed. D. Cartwright), University of Michigan Press. A useful introduction to sources of personal power.

Hampden-Turner, C. (1990) *Corporate Culture – From Vicious to Virtuous Circles*, Economist Books.

Handy, C. (1978) *Gods of Management*, Souvenir Press – provides an interesting explanation of different organization cultures.

Lewin, K. (1947) Frontiers in group dynamics: concept, method and reality in social science, *Human Relations*, **1**.

Lukes, S (1974) *Power: A Radical View*, Macmillan.

Miles, R. E. and Snow, C. C. (1978) *Organization Strategy, Structure and Process*, McGraw-Hill.

Pümpin, C (1987) *The Essence of Corporate Strategy*, Gower.

A SUMMARY OF THE STRATEGIC LESSONS

In this chapter we have looked *behind* the visionary, planning and adaptive/ incremental modes of strategy creation in a search for explanations concerning their selection and preference. We have concluded that power, politics and culture are major determinants.

Culture defines how things happen inside organizations, the decisions people take and the actions they follow. Behaviour is often affected unconsciously as people simply accept 'this is the way things are done' in this organization.

Both strategic choice and strategy implementation are affected.

The culture can be best understood by considering its manifestations, including values and behaviours, people and communications and power.

Cultural change is difficult and takes time. Effective leadership from a champion of change is a fundamental requirement. People are invariably resistant to change.

The selection and implementation of strategies reflects internal and external power and influence. We need to understand how people acquire and use power to drive decision-making.

The term *organizational politics* describes this use of power and influence. Used in the best interests of the organization, politics is positive – and an important skill for every manager. It is also necessary to appreciate that some politically astute managers will seek to manipulate situations and decisions for their own personal benefit rather than the long-term needs of the organization.

Powerful external stakeholders, such as governments and major customers, can constrain organizations and impose strategies on them.

We finished the chapter by concluding that it is realistic to suggest that all modes of strategy creation can be found in an organization at any time, driven by strategic leadership, culture and power. It is, however, far less realistic to believe we can explain exactly what happens in any particular firm. Managers in different parts of the organization will have different perspectives and opinions.

STRATEGY IMPLEMENTATION AND STRATEGIC CONTROL

In this chapter we look at how the structure of an organization affects strategy creation and implementation. We examine alternative structural forms, the style of corporate management and the role and contribution of corporate head offices.

To be effective organizations must achieve congruency between strategy, structure and the style of managing the organization.

BOB LANGLEY'S NEW CHALLENGE

David Marshall was satisfied with the outcome of his visit to Germany. As long as Special Components – and Roger Ellis's team in particular – remained vigilant, the worst of their problems with the new component appeared to be behind them. This did not mean there was no room for improvement; nor did it imply that the internal linkages and architecture were good enough. David still intended to try and mould his sales and production colleagues into a more effective, integrated team.

David went to report back to Bob Langley but he found the managing director was pre-occupied. Once David assured him that the new component was no longer a major *problem*, Bob began to talk about his new challenge. He had been invited to join a company-wide committee which was charged with reviewing the role of Universal Engineering's head office. In the previous year the cost of maintaining the current head office structure amounted to 1 % of Universal's turnover, representing over 10 % of pre-tax profits. The committee had been asked to produce recommendations on the size, scope and operations of corporate headquarters, with the objective of reducing this financial burden without any detrimental effect to the business.

Bob wanted to discuss his initial ideas with David, who had previously worked in head office and had an insight into its role and culture. Bob saw this as an opportunity for the divisions to challenge the power bases at head office; David mused that restructuring implied further change.

CORPORATE HEAD OFFICE

It is essential that head office is seen to be adding value to the whole organization, and fulfilling a purpose that cannot be accomplished more effectively within the individual businesses. Its role must fit:

- Universal's corporate strategy, and the ways in which changes to strategies are to be created;
- the diversity and geographic location of the constituent businesses;
- the structure of the organization – which could, of course, be changed;
- the chief executive's preferred style for controlling the various businesses and activities, and how centralized he wants things to be.

He is known to believe the current centralized structure is unable to deliver an adequate international focus for the three diverse businesses. With competitors around the world a global focus is essential.

CENTRALIZE OR DECENTRALIZE?

Bob's divisional general manager, together with the other two divisional heads, has also made it clear that he feels Universal is too centralized. The ability of the various companies to compete effectively is inhibited; change decisions are too slow and there is inadequate innovation. People away from head office are in a better position to think tactically and pragmatically. A number of activities currently located at head office might usefully be decentralized to the individual businesses.

There is, however, no question that the strategic leader must be able to drive the *corporate* strategic changes because the three businesses are inter-linked.Co-operation and occasional sacrifices are necessary to create synergy. This co-ordination is better directed from the centre rather than by delegating too much independence and assuming the businesses will freely help each other. Internal politics are rife, and some vested power interests might mean a decentralized Universal Engineering was even less committed to innovation and change.

Drawing on his conversations with Tony Anderson and Dieter Wild, David suggested that future internal *processes* and *attitudes* should not be overlooked in the review. Having worked in the head office planning department David feels there is a tendency for head office staff to feel elitist and detached from the businesses. They do not see themselves as suppliers of a service, with the businesses comprising their customers. Bob commented that one other option being considered was outsourcing. Which current head office functions might be better bought-in from external specialists rather than just decentralized? The supplier–customer attitude would then be even more critical.

STRATEGY IMPLEMENTATION AND STRATEGIC CONTROL

To be successful an intended strategy must be implemented. Chart 9.1 shows how strategy implementation requires the deployment and control of the organization's strategic resources to carry out action plans and hopefully achieve target milestones.

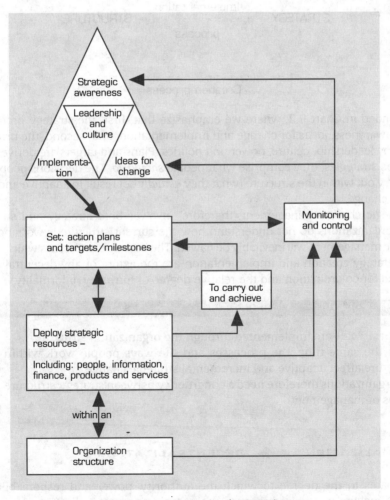

Chart 9.1   Strategy implementation

These strategic resources include finance, technology, people, information, and products, services and their distribution. This is accomplished through the design of the organization (the structure) and the processes encapsulated within the structure. These are the themes of this chapter. It is also essential that progress is monitored and changes introduced when they are necessary.

The structure must, therefore, be capable of implementing strategies, and it can be described as the *means* by which an organization seeks to achieve its strategic objectives. However, we also saw in Chapter 8 that the structural processes are a reflection of culture, power and political activity, and that where people are empowered in a decentralized organization, it is these processes which determine the actual adaptive/incremental strategies pursued. Consequently the structure must be capable of both formulating and implementing strategy.

A simple circular relationship:

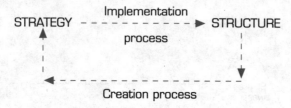

is expanded in Chart 9.2, where we emphasize that, first, the strategy process involves awareness, ideas for change and implementation, and, second, the process is driven by leadership, culture, power and politics. Plans and targets are derived from intended strategies; they comprise what people *should do*. The decisions people take and carry out within the structure (what they *actually do*) result in adaptive and incremental change.

Strategic change management, therefore, involves both strategy and structure, and if organizations do not understand how the current structure is working, their strategic management will inevitably be flawed. The key structural issues which impact upon strategy creation and implementation are the extent of any decentralization, the need for co-ordination and the relative degree of formality–informality.

Key Point

9.1 Strategies are implemented through the organization structure.

At the same time, the processes and the ways people work within the structure affect adaptive and incremental strategic change.

Organizations therefore need a congruency between strategy, structure and styles of management.

CENTRALIZATION ⟷ DECENTRALIZATION

This relates to the degree to which the authority, power and responsibility for decision-making is devolved through the organization. Centralization is where all

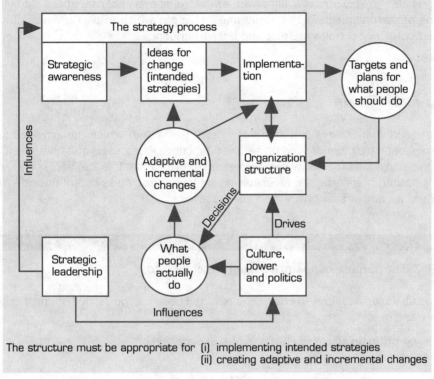

The structure must be appropriate for (i) implementing intended strategies
(ii) creating adaptive and incremental changes

Chart 9.2 Strategy ⟶ structure; structure ⟶ strategy

major strategic decisions are taken at head office by the strategic leader or a group of senior strategists. Strictly enforced policies and procedures constrain the freedom of managers responsible for divisions and business units to change competitive and functional strategies without reference back to head office. As more and more responsibility for strategic change is delegated, the organization becomes increasingly **decentralized**.

Centralization brings consistency and control; unfortunately centralized organizations may be slow to change in a dynamic environment, and ambitious, entrepreneurial managers may feel constrained and demotivated.

> *The holistic planner overlooks the fact that it is easy to centralize power, but impossible to centralize all that knowledge ... necessary for the wise yielding of that centralized power ... (so) the greater the gain in power, the greater will be the loss of knowledge* (Sir Karl Popper).

Decentralization allows for competitive and functional strategies to be changed more quickly by managers who are in close touch with the competitive environment and who will also be responsible for implementing any changes. In addition, it can improve motivation. However, information networks must ensure the whole organization is able to stay strategically aware or control is inevitably sacrificed. Individual parts of the organization can easily make changes which impact unfavourably on other parts, neglecting synergies and interdependencies.

CO-ORDINATION

Organization structures and charts represent the way in which the activities to be carried out have been divided up between functions, businesses and divisions. Clear delineation allows for clarity of purpose and prioritization. It is also necessary for the organization to incorporate mechanisms for integrating these contributions – *internal architecture* – if synergies are to be achieved.

> ### Key Point
>
> 9.2 The purpose of an organization structure is to:
>
> - divide up activities to ensure the required tasks can be carried out properly; and
>
> - co-ordinate all these efforts to obtain synergies.

FORMALITY ←→ INFORMALITY

Restrictive policies, procedures and reporting systems represent formality. More informality is required if managers and other employees are to use their initiative, innovate change and share their knowledge and learning. Decentralization and informality both imply **empowerment**

FOUR STRUCTURAL TYPES

Small firms often have a powerful central figure who relies on informal communications to lead the business entrepreneurially. A more formal structure is required when the size and complexity grows.

Centralized, formal organizations tend to be bureaucratic and slow to change, but efficient in stable circumstances. Historically much of the public sector has adopted this model, but has seen a relaxation on both dimensions in recent years as the environment has become much less certain.

Decentralized, formal organizations are typically large businesses which have been divided up into divisions and business units. Some power is devolved to allow *adap-*

tive and incremental change, with formal communications systems and performance measures used for co-ordination. Universal Engineering is an example, although it is clearly still centralized in respect of major changes. Informal communications will operate alongside the formal channels – without these, co-operation would prove impossible.

Decentralized, informal 'organizations' are often seen in the form of temporary project groups and task teams existing inside a more formal structure. The individual businesses within Richard Branson's Virgin Group, though, operate with both decentralization and informal communications – but within a framework of centralized **corporate** strategy creation.

Quite simply, in a centralized organization, **planned activities and intended strategies** – which may, of course, be out-of-date – are controlled. Decentralization means the **dynamic external links** are controlled more effectively. The situation is often unstable as companies attempt to find an appropriate balance, and trade-off growth with stability.

We saw above that as small companies succeed they switch from formal to informal communications to enable further growth. Centralization maintains control. Companies later tend to decentralize when they want to continue growing and need to be able to implement changes quickly. Any loss of control, and especially if the organization's financial performance deteriorates, will lead to a desire to restore stability and a temptation to re-centralize decision-making. Eventually decentralization will again be used to fuel renewed growth.

Key Point

9.3 The centralization-decentralization debate involves two trade-offs: one between control (efficiency) and speed and flexibility (effectiveness in a dynamic environment), and the second between control and growth.

Decentralization can empower and motivate managers, but their individual efforts must be co-ordinated.

Morgan (1993) uses the analogy of a spider plant, with a number of small, growing offshoots, to examine linkages in complex, multi-activity organizations. As the plant grows the offshoots can be retained with a permanent link back to the mother plant, or they can be severed and given independence. Without independence, their growth will be limited; with freedom they can easily grow larger than the mother plant, which is now likely to produce more new offshoots. Organizations can be similarly 'severed' through extensive decentralization and large numbers of relatively independent divisions, business units and profit centres enjoying a degree of independence and autonomy. It is also possible for non-core businesses to be sold off, but with links retained. In Chapter 5 the case study described Clark Precision Equipment as a management buy-out from a manufacturer of earthmoving equipment to whom it is still an important specialist supplier.

The lines of communication which need addressing – and establishing as either tight controlling feeders or less formal linkages – are:

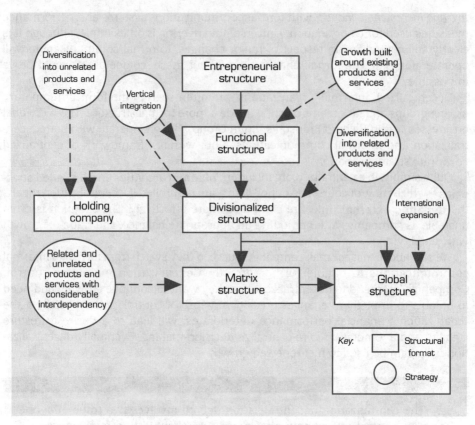

Chart 9.3 Growth strategies and related structural formats

- values, purpose and objectives;
- information flows;
- resources and dependencies;
- accountability;
- rewards.

Where growing organizations are put together for financial rather than synergistic reasons we can expect tight controls and a strong focus on resource efficiency. Where synergies and interdependency are critical, performance measurement needs to be more creative. Similarly where people work in teams and depend on each other it is important to ensure the reward systems reflect this.

Although we often use diagrammatic charts to illustrate the structure of an organization, it is important to recognize that charts are static and unable to explain the processes and interactions which determine how the structure actually works.

In the following sections we look at how these issues impact on:

- the type of structure adopted;
- the style of strategic control; and
- the contribution of head offices.

STRUCTURAL ALTERNATIVES

Organization structures are unique to individual firms, but they are likely to relate to one of the forms discussed in this section. The six alternative forms are illustrated in Chart 9.3 where they are shown in a hierarchy and linked to growth strategies. As organizations grow, and new strategies are developed, it is normal for an organization to adopt or change its structure in some logical way.

Key Point

9.4 Although it is crucial to look beyond a passive structure chart and examine internal processes, we can identify six discrete forms. These can be related to appropriate strategies and stages of growth.

THE ENTREPRENEURIAL STRUCTURE

This is a typical small organization structure built like a web around the owner/manager, who retains control of all important decisions. It is heavily centralized and features informal channels of communication, and in some respects it is not really a 'structure' at all. While ever the organization remains small it is very flexible, but it is inappropriate beyond a certain size if only one person is deciding all major issues.

THE FUNCTIONAL STRUCTURE

A functional structure is appropriate when businesses have outgrown the entrepreneurial structure but remain focused on a limited range of clearly related products and services. Given this qualification it can work for both small/medium and much larger organizations. The business is built around functional activities – production, marketing, sales, personnel, finance, research and development and information management are all examples – each of which is headed by a manager with some delegated authority. Special Components (as a business unit) operates with a functional structure inside a divisionalized organization. Success is very dependent upon the ability of the managers to work as a team.

THE DIVISIONALIZED STRUCTURE

When the number and diversity of the products and services increases, the simple functional structure is inadequate. Individual products and services cannot be championed and prioritized effectively. Consequently the organization will normally be split into a number of divisions, based on products, geography or both. Each division will have a general manager/managing director, and may be further sub-divided into individual business units which are all profit centres. This is the case in Universal Engineering. Power and authority is increasingly decentralized, but if the divisions are interdependent the need for organized linkages cannot be ignored. Divisionalization and decentralization are not synonymous terms, but they often accompany each other. It is not essential that they do.

Changes to the overall corporate strategy normally remain the responsibility of head office, but divisional heads may be free to alter their own portfolio of activities. Competitive and functional strategic change will be devolved – either within formalized policies and controls, or with some considerable autonomy given to the respective divisions and businesses.

THE HOLDING COMPANY STRUCTURE

This is ideal for a diverse, multi-product organization where the businesses involved are independent of each other, rather than interdependent. It is especially appropriate where the underlying corporate strategy concerns **restructuring** – buying, rationalizing and then selling businesses when there are no longer any opportunities for adding further value.

Each business is run as an individual company, but controlled by tight financial management. Budgets – which must be achieved – and regular formal reporting are essential features. Head office will retain responsibility for, say, buying and selling businesses, and the overall corporate portfolio, delegating the strategic responsibility for each business to its own managers. Subsidiaries are more likely to benefit from low-cost head office financing than they are from links with other businesses in the holding company.

THE MATRIX STRUCTURE

Matrix structures are an attempt to combine the benefits of decentralization (motivation of identifiable management teams; closeness to markets; speedy decision-making and implementation) with those of co-ordination (achieving economies and synergies across the business units, territories and products). This structural form is, however, complex and difficult to implement; managers often have dual reporting relationships. A typical example would be an organization comprising divisions based on product groups, and responsible for co-ordinating the production and marketing of a number of products manufactured in several plants, alongside geographic divisions responsible for co-ordinating the sales, marketing and distribution of all the corporation's products, regardless of where they are produced, within their territorial area. Box 9.1 explains the matrix structure adopted by ABB (Asea Brown Boveri).

Managers in divisionalized organizations may be members of ad hoc project teams, which cut across several businesses or divisions and are charged with carrying out a specific task, at the same time as they continue in their normal roles. This overlay represents a temporary form of the matrix structure.

 ABB (ASEA BROWN BOVERI)

ABB was formed in 1988 when the Swedish company Asea merged with Brown Boveri of Switzerland to create a global electrical engineering giant. ABB has since acquired a series of smaller businesses. The chief executive is Percy Barnevik, and he sees a challenge in maintaining drive and dynamism while digesting large acquisitions. He is committed to a matrix structure and his aim is to make ABB the global low-cost competitor.

ABB has been divided up into 1300 identifiable companies and 5000 profit centres. These are aggregated into eight business segments and 59 business areas. The eight segments are:

- power plants, itself further sub-divided into

  - gas turbine plants;

  - utility steam plants;

  - industrial steam plants;

  - hydro power plants;

  - nuclear power plants;

  - power plant controls;

- power transmission;

- power distribution;

- electrical equipment;

- transportation;

- environmental controls;

- financial services;

- other activities.

The segments are responsible for organizing manufacture around the world and for product development. Horizontally ABB is divided up into a mix of countries and regions. There is a 12-member executive board representing products, regions and corporate operations, and a slim head office in Zurich. It is not seen as essential that the divisional headquarters for the eight business segments are located in Zurich.

'ABB is a multi-national without a national identity.'

Financial reporting and evaluation is on a monthly basis.

The basic structure, therefore, is based on small units (of 50 people each on average) supported by good communications and information technology. Although ABB comprises distinct businesses, both technology and products are exchanged. Every employee has a country manager and a business sector manager. Dual responsibilities such as this are often key issues in matrix structures which fail. However Barnevik insists that ABB's version is 'loose and decentralized' and that it is easily recognized that the two bosses are rarely of equal status.

Barnevik believes that if a large company is to manage internal communications effectively it must develop a *horizontal integration process*. The role of middle managers – in a flatter structure – concerns coaching and technology and skill transfer. Strategic leadership is about creating purpose and challenging the status quo; it is not simply, as historically it was, to allocate corporate resources and resolve internal conflicts.

Barnevik has also commented that the biggest problem has been 'motivating middle and lower level managers and entrenching corporate values – particularly a customer and quality focus'. He believes that his executives should see the business as their number one priority and assumes that highfliers will spend up to 30 hours a week (in addition to their regular tasks) travelling, attending conferences and evening seminars and lectures ■

THE GLOBAL STRUCTURE

The challenge for large, diverse, international businesses lies in:

* exercising control and containing structural costs through decentralization while

* remaining sensitive to varying customer tastes and expectations in different geographic markets and

* innovating and transferring learning internationally (Bartlett and Ghoshal, 1989).

Production may be in selected locations to achieve scale economies; equally it may be dispersed and closer to the markets where the products are sold. Marketing and sales efforts can be handled for the whole world from a central location; again they can be localized and dispersed. If the organization is divisionalized, and it almost certainly will be, all the divisional head offices can be located in one single corporate headquarters or spread around the world. When they are dispersed the activities of each business are likely to be markedly different, with only limited interdependency.

Clearly the organization needs a global mission and core values, such as consistent quality worldwide, and Bartlett and Ghoshal (1992) recommend that regardless of the structural format, *integration* is co-ordinated centrally at the top of the corporation, with individual businesses and countries given clear sets of expectations. This would appear to suggest that it is probably unimportant whether *production* is essentially centralized or decentralized. The real issue concerns the location of 'future focus' activities such as research and development and product design and development and whether these are centralized or decentralized. The normal tendency will be centralization.

We have seen how the basic structure can relate to the corporate strategy. It is now important to consider how strategic change is managed within the structure. The relationship between head office and the individual businesses and divisions in a large complex organization is critically important. This is reflected in the size, scope and role of the corporate headquarters, and the way in which the centre seeks to control strategy creation. Control is vital, but it should not be achieved by over-elaborate reporting, which slows down strategic change, or by expensively duplicating activities at head office and in the divisions and businesses.

STYLES OF CORPORATE MANAGEMENT

Goold and Campbell (1988) and Goold, Campbell and Luchs (1993) have researched in depth how head offices advise, control and add value to their constituent businesses. They categorize three distinct styles (described below), and conclude that all the styles can work successfully – the secret lies in adopting the style which is appropriate for the range and diversity of the businesses in the group. The culture and the preferred approach of the strategic leader are, of course, also important influences.

Key Point

9.5 We can identify three distinct styles of managing an organization and the changes to its strategies.

The style should be appropriate for the particular portfolio of businesses and activities.

The first of these three, financial control, is ideal for an organization comprising independent, unrelated businesses in a holding company structure.

FINANCIAL CONTROL

An ideal approach for a holding company where the businesses are seen as independent and unrelated. Hanson (Box 7.1) provides an excellent example.

- Strategy creation is heavily decentralized to business unit managers. Within their agreed financial targets they are free to develop and change their competitive and functional strategies.

- Budgets and targets – and their achievement – are critically important control mechanisms.

- Head office monitors financial returns closely and regularly, intervening when targets are missed.

- Head office also acts as a corporate investment banker for investment capital.

- Achievement is rewarded, and units are encouraged to put forward and chase ambitious targets. Under-performing managers are likely to be removed.

- The head office *adds value* by acquiring and improving under-performing businesses; if additional value cannot be added it may well sell-off businesses.

Growth is more likely to be by acquisition than organic investment, with many financial control companies taking a short-term view of each business and being reluctant to invest in speculative research and the development of longer term strategies.

Key Point

9.6 **Strategic planning** represents centralized control and is most appropriate when there is a limited range of core businesses.

STRATEGIC PLANNING

This tends to be adopted in organizations which focus on only a few, and preferably related, core businesses. Examples include Cadbury Schweppes, United Biscuits and BP. Historically it has been the favoured approach for most public-sector organizations.

- Strategic plans are developed jointly by head office and the business units, with head office retaining the final say. Strategic planning is centralized.

- Day-to-day operations only are wholly decentralized.

- Head office sets priorities and co-ordinates strategies throughout the organization, possibly initiating cross-business strategies.

A long-term perspective is realistic, and the search for opportunities for linkages and sharing resources and best practice can be prioritized. This normally requires central control. Individually the businesses would tend to operate more independently; organization-wide synergies may involve sacrifices by individual businesses.

Goold and Campbell conclude there are co-ordination problems if this approach is used in truly diversified organizations.

- Budgets are again used for measuring performance.

- The tight central control can become bureaucratic and demotivate managers, who may not feel **ownership** of their strategies.

Other dangers are, one, thinking may become too focused at the centre, with the potential contributions of divisional managers under-utilized, and two, the organization may be slow to change in response to competitive pressures. Value can be added successfully if corporate managers stay aware and expert in the core businesses and if the competitive environment allows this style to work.

Key Point

9.7 **Strategic control** is a search for the benefits of decentralization and co-ordination with a diverse but interdependent portfolio.

STRATEGIC CONTROL

Financial planning and strategic planning are appropriate for particular types of organization, but both styles, while having very positive advantages, also feature drawbacks. The strategic control style is an attempt to obtain the major benefits of the other two styles for organizations which are clearly diversified but with linkages and interdependencies. Value is added by balancing strategic and financial controls.

- Strategy creation involves decentralization to the business units, although head office still controls the overall **corporate** strategy.

- The role of head office is to review divisional and business plans, and approve strategic objectives and financial targets, accepting they may need to be changed in a competitive environment.

- Strategy creation and budgetary control can be separated, allowing for more creative performance measurement.
  Sometimes competitive pressures and misjudgments mean strategies have to be changed, and hoped-for financial targets may be missed. A strategic control style can recognize this and deal with the implications.

- Head office does, however, monitor and control financial performance and success against strategic milestones and objectives.

Although decentralization is a feature, head office still requires considerable detail about the various businesses if it is to ensure the synergy potential is achieved and very short-term thinking is avoided. Political activity will be prevalent as individual businesses compete with each other for scarce corporate resources.

Two leading organizations which utilized this style – ICI and Courtaulds – concluded they were over-diversified. There were numerous businesses and some were clearly inter-linked. At the same time these 'clusters' had little in common and featured different strategic needs and cultures. Because of these differences, and the inevitable complexity, corporate headquarters could not add value with a single entity. Both companies split into two distinct parts to enable a stronger focus on core competencies and strategic capabilities.

THE ROLE AND CONTRIBUTION OF CORPORATE HEADQUARTERS

There are two fundamental purposes of corporate headquarters:

- serving the global legal and financial needs of the business; and

- supporting strategy-making.

Many head offices have historically provided a more extensive range of services to their constituent businesses, including, for example:

- marketing;

- management development and personnel;

- property management;

- centralized research and development;

- corporate public relations;

- industrial relations.

There is a clear need for head offices to add value to the corporation and not simply 'spend the money earned by the businesses'.

The recent trend has been for organizations to slim down the size and scope of head offices, and some centres have seen the bulk of their previous activities devolved to the individual businesses. Only corporate strategy, financial reporting and control and secretarial/legal services are centralized. Some head offices retain a responsibility for *policies* but not the activities.

Key Point

9.8 The centralization–decentralization debate is also reflected in the size, role and contribution of corporate head offices.

In recent years there has been a tendency for large companies to reduce the numbers of people and activities in their head offices.

It is vital that head offices are seen to add value to the business and not impose an unacceptable cost burden.

Summarizing points made earlier, large centralized head offices where all the key business heads are located in one place – Unilever is an example – can control the corporation *efficiently*, but strategies can easily become top-down and slow to change. Decentralized organizations such as ABB (Box 9.1) push profit responsibility down to the businesses and empower managers. The head office provides more of a support role with few discrete functions. The challenge is one of co-ordination.

In considering how head offices can best add value to the business as a whole, three issues must be addressed:

- how to control and co-ordinate the constituent businesses;
- how to advise the strategic leader and keep him or her strategically aware;
- which activities should be
  1. provided from head office – for which a fee should be levied;
  2. devolved to the individual businesses;
  3. bought-in from outside specialists?

Chart 9.4 summarizes the structural form and the role of head office for a selection of companies featured in this book.

ORGANIZATIONS IN THE LATE 1990S

Handy (1994) contends that in order for companies to remain competitive internationally they must re-think their basic structures. 'Fewer people, paid very well, producing far more value.' Companies will be smaller, focused and closely networked to their suppliers and customers. More activities and components will be bought-in from specialists than is the case at the moment – *external architecture*. Internally they will also comprise networks, with the 'centre' (as distinct from a traditional head office) doing only what the parts cannot do themselves. The real power will switch from the top of the organization to the businesses, and consequently a co-ordinating mission and purpose will be essential.

Supported by sophisticated information technology and systems, people will become the most important strategic resource, and, because their expertise and intelligence is an intangible asset, largely unquantifiable, it will become harder to value the **real** assets of a business. Consequently the appropriate measures of performance

		Role of corporate head office			
		Bare minimum – legal, secretarial requirements plus corporate finance	Corporate strategies	Strategies plus various support systems	Centralized service provision
S T R U C T U R E	Holding company		Hanson		
	Divisionalized – largely independent	ABB	General Electric		
	Largely interdependent	IBM (1990s) ◄─────		IBM (1980s)	
	Integrated/ functional				British Airways

Company references: Hanson: Box 7.1; General Electric: Boxes 5.1 and 10.3; IBM: Box 7.3; ABB: Box 9.1; British Airways: Boxes 2.1, 6.1 and 8.2.

Source: developed from a diagram produced by Mercer Management Consulting

Chart 9.4   Structural forms and head office roles

must be carefully evaluated; and reward systems will have to be derived which motivate and keep those managers who are potentially the most mobile. They will not all be at the most senior levels.

Handy's argument implies major changes to strategies, structures and styles of management. Where these are simultaneous – **strategic regeneration** – the changes are dramatic, painful and often difficult to carry through. This is the subject of our final chapter.

A CHANGE OF STYLE?

After his discussion with Bob Langley David thought more about Universal Engineering. The Group really needs a strategic control style of corporate management. Its businesses are related, but they are still diverse. They have different key success factors and require different competencies and abilities. Their cultures are not identical. In reality, however, Universal Engineering is closer to strategic planning.

In practice Universal's head office does not concern itself with the on-going strategic problems and **strategic issues** faced by all the individual businesses. Their focus is on the group's *major* products. In the case of the new component, Special Components had simply been instructed to develop it. They had made mistakes, but their possible production difficulties had never been discussed.

The general style of management through the Special Products division to Bob Langley is 'don't give me problems; give me solutions'. Bob Langley frequently adopts this approach as well.

Because the emerging strategic issues are not really shared outside the individual businesses, budget targets tend to be the main form of strategic control. Once targets are agreed between Bob Langley and head office, there is tremendous pressure to achieve them. Moreover, because Special Components is perceived as a peripheral small business within Universal Engineering, it is typically given high achievement targets 'to justify its existence'.

David wondered how much this might change if there was more decentralization. In the meantime, he must not allow himself to be distracted by Bob Langley's new project. As long as he checked developments with the new component problem he could now concentrate on Benson's, always assuming, of course, no fresh crises arose.

POINTS FOR REFLECTION

- How would you categorize the structure of your organization? Is it 'right' for your circumstances and strategies? What changes, if any, would you recommend?
- To what extent is your organization decentralized? Is it more formal or informal?
- If your company is part of a larger group,
  - how would you describe the style of corporate control?
  - what is the role and function of corporate headquarters?
- Attempt to think or look ahead five years ... how different do you think your organization will be and feel? How do you personally feel about the changes you foresee? How will they affect you? How might you affect them?

REFERENCES AND FURTHER READING

Bartlett, C. and Ghoshal, S. (1989) *Managing Across Borders: The Transnational Solution*, Harvard Business School Press.

Bartlett, C. and Ghoshal, S. (1992) What is a global manager?, *Harvard Business Review*, September–October.

Goold, M. and Campbell, A. (1988) *Strategies and Styles*, Blackwell.

Goold, M., Campbell, A. and Luchs, K. (1993) Strategies and styles revisited: strategic planning and financial control, *Long Range Planning*, **26**(5).

Goold, M., Campbell, A. and Luchs, K. (1993) Strategies and styles revisited: strategic control – is it tenable?, *Long Range Planning*, **26**(6).

Greiner, L. E. (1972) Evolution and revolution as organizations grow, *Harvard Business Review*, July–August. Provides real insight into how structures change when strategies develop.

Handy, C. (1994) *The Empty Raincoat*, Hutchinson.

Mintzberg, H. (1993) *Structure in Fives: Designing Effective Organizations*, Prentice-Hall. Gives a different perspective on structural forms.

Morgan, G. (1993) *Imaginization*, Sage.

A SUMMARY OF THE STRATEGIC LESSONS

Strategic management comprises analysis, choice and implementation. Strategies are implemented through the organization structure. However, as we have seen in earlier chapters, the structural processes are the determinants of adaptive and incremental changes. As a result there is a circular relationship between strategy and structure.

Effective control is achieved when strategy and structure are matched and are also congruent with the style of corporate management. At the end of the chapter we highlighted that simultaneous change to these three, what we have earlier termed *strategic regeneration*, is difficult, but sometimes necessary for organizations.

Structures are designed to, first, split up and separate the key activities and tasks which the organization must carry out, and second, integrate and co-ordinate efforts to achieve synergies. In relation to this, organizations must decide how much responsibility should be centralized and how much can be effectively decentralized and devolved to divisions and business units.

Centralization yields control. Decentralization may be required for growth and flexibility. It is also more likely to motivate managers.

Organizations are likely to conform, either closely or loosely, to one of six identifiable structural forms: the entrepreneurial structure, the functional structure, the divisionalized corporation, the holding company, the matrix structure or the global organization.

Head office will look to exercise both strategic and financial control over the business. When the organization is multi-product or multi-service, and possibly diversified, control is likely to be exercised in one of three ways.

Financial control is ideal for an organization which comprises independent, unrelated businesses in a holding company structure.

Strategic planning reflects centralization. It is most appropriate when there is a limited range of possibly related core businesses.

Strategic control is most likely to be found when there is a diverse group of businesses which are related in some way.

Corporations also need to address the size, role and contribution of their corporate headquarters, which should be seen to be adding value to the whole business. In recent years the general trend has been for head offices to be slimmed down and for more and more activities to be re-deployed to the individual businesses.

10 STRATEGIC SUCCESS AND CHANGE

In this concluding chapter we pull together the main themes of strategic management and effective strategic performance. We look at the challenges facing organizations if they are to deal successfully with change pressures in a modern competitive environment. Strategies, structures and styles of leadership and management may all have to change.

We emphasize again how strategy is a complex subject, full of dilemmas yet based on straightforward underlying principles.

THE CHALLENGE OF IMPLEMENTATION

Bob Langley had delegated interim control of the new subsidiary to two experienced Benson managers, and after his return from Germany, David Marshall worked closely with them. By mid-October, a month after the initial presentation at Benson's by David and Bob, the team of three had prepared a set of proposals for the future. A meeting with Bob Langley was set up.

Prior to the presentation David had also arranged another evening out with Tony Anderson. Bob joined them.

Although the actual details of the merger between Special Components and Benson Engineering were not discussed, strategy implementation and change were major topics of conversation. The consultant remarked that seemingly good strategic ideas frequently fail to be implemented effectively. Having a sound, visionary idea does not in itself guarantee success. For one thing, the person with the idea will not always be the best tactician for managing the implementation. In addition, a committed *team* is essential. Successful change needs planning, championing and persistence. Quite often a good idea is taken up initially with great enthusiasm, but the results and benefits are slow to arrive; when this happens it is all too easy to lose confidence and abandon the change.

MERGING TWO COMPANIES

Tony warned Bob and David that mergers and acquisitions generally have a high failure rate, especially if a hostile take-over is involved. Expectations may be over-optimistic because too high a price has been paid. David reassured his companions that the Benson managers were committed and enthusiastic; they welcomed their new challenge.

Tony was not easily convinced; the managers had after all chosen to stay with the declining Benson's. He cautioned:

- Anticipated synergies may be illusory. It is easier to gain synergy from production and operations than it is from marketing.

- The real weaknesses of an acquired company are normally unknown at the time of purchase.

- There are cultural and managerial problems when two companies are fused and run as one business.

- Quite often the key skills and competencies which should be transferred to the new business are not readily available. Because they are critically important they are already likely to be fully committed.

- The most valuable managers should be spotted and retained.

Tony concluded that successful implementation and change requires the right people with the right motivation. Individual managers in central jobs may be the major barrier to effective change; they should go if they remain hostile. Sharing and co-operation are essential; managers must work together as a team.

STRATEGIC CHANGE IN THE 1990S

Returning to issues they had discussed at Heathrow, Tony summarized what he believed to be the major strategic changes taking place in the 1990s:

- Innovative and high quality products and services are becoming increasingly important if a company is to **add value** and obtain any **competitive advantage** over its rivals.

- **Collaborations** with customers, suppliers and other organizations are becoming more popular and more significant.

- The business environment is increasingly unpredictable and competitive. Organizations need a range of strategic skills and competencies.

Effective strategic leaders, able to deal with these challenges and pressures, will succeed because they learn how to:

- trust other managers, delegate responsibility to them, encourage them to take limited risks and live with their periodic mistakes and misjudgments;

- form and nurture alliances and networks, both internally and externally;

- change – *continually and consultatively* – and persuade others to follow. Ideally these changes will be planned to some degree and controlled; the organization must not become wholly reactive. Tony showed them a comment from John Welch, Chief Executive of General Electric in America:

Managing success is a tough job. There's a very fine line between self-confidence and arrogance. Success often breeds both, along with reluctance to change. The bureaucracy builds up. The people start to believe they're invulnerable. Before they know it, the world changes and they've got to react.

Effective organizations, in Tony's opinion, will have:

1. *The right strategy* This may require portfolio rationalization to focus on related products and services and on **core competencies** Organizations might be split into parts; new alliances and joint ventures may be formed.

    It also implies **competitive advantage** for individual products and services, again based on competencies and **strategic capabilities**

2. *The right structure* Decentralization, empowerment and effective communications – to spot opportunities and threats and to spread best practices – are likely to be essential. The proper development and reward of managers and other employees is essential for achieving this.

3. *The right style* Leadership and culture are crucial here. Organizations must be able to deal quickly with challenges and opportunities and relate to – and satisfy – all their major stakeholders. Companies can also benefit if they behave ethically and socially responsibly.

After Tony had left the restaurant, David and Bob discussed once more the extent of the changes which were really required at both Special Components and Universal Engineering if the conglomerate was to survive and prosper in the mid/late 1990s. Were the businesses fundamentally sound, but still capable of improvement with gradual and continual changes; or was **strategic regeneration** – simultaneous and major changes to strategies, structures and styles of management – going to be necessary?

Much would depend on their customers and on changes in certain markets. The turbulent motor vehicle industry was especially significant for Universal Engineering as a whole. The American automobile industry was growing in the early 1990s, having fought back strongly against their Japanese competitors, who in turn were less buoyant than they had been in the 1980s. Europe was still characterized by overcapacity. The ambitious and fast-growing Korean manufacturers appeared to pose the next major threat.

STRATEGIC SUCCESS AND CHANGE

The E-V-R Congruence framework (environment-values-resources) was introduced in Chapter 2 (Chart 2.1) to explain that effective strategic management requires an organization to **manage** the matching of its resources with its environment, when both E and R are subject to change pressures. Throughout the book we have discussed those strategic skills and competencies which are most likely to be needed for creating and maintaining an effective E and R match. We have also looked sequentially at how strategies can be created, evaluated and changed with these needs in mind. In this chapter we will attempt to draw these themes together and consider the strategic demands on organizations in modern business environments. We look at the challenges they face if they are to survive and prosper. We recap on how straightforward ideas underpin strategic management but argue that managing strategies and strategic change is complex. Organizations and managers must deal with key strategic dilemmas in an environment of change.

There is no single recipe for creating long-term strategic success. We have seen that 'what works today' is unlikely to remain appropriate for a changing future, a principle which can apply to strategies, organization structures and approaches to managing circumstances and change. The case at the beginning of this chapter indicated that effective organizations ideally need, at any time, the right strategy, the right structure and the right style.

Key Point

10.1   Organizations which aim to be successful during the turbulent and competitive 1990s must address five critical issues:

- adding value;

- core competencies and capabilities;

- architecture, linkages and synergy;

- competitive advantage and innovation;

- the possible need to be strategically regenerative.

We have argued that there are a number of important ideas which underpin this ideal and which will contribute towards its achievement. These are:

- the ability to **add value** – and innovatively create new values – for customers in ways which separate the organization from its competitors; linked directly to this is:

- the ability to create and sustain **competitive advantage** through cost leadership, differentiation and speed of change;

- **core competencies and strategic capabilities**: the ability to exploit the organization's most critical resources to create and add value and, in turn, generate competitive advantage; *synergies* should be sought and resources, including people, should be stretched to higher levels of achievement; people must be able to learn and willing to change;

- Internal and external **architecture and linkages**: to enjoy the benefits of synergy, organizations must be able to create and sustain internal cohesion – people must adopt supportive, teamworking behaviours, learning and sharing best practices. Further benefits are possible if the organization can ally itself more closely with the other organizations in its supply chain, particularly its suppliers and distributors, to create a 'continuous value stream'. Effective communications networks, trust and sharing are at the heart of this.

In summary, strategic success requires the organization to develop and retain a wide range of competencies which enable it to out-perform its competitors and deal with the pressures of increasingly dynamic and turbulent business environments.

Individual chapters in the book have explored the strategic management process and explored the various ways in which strategies are created, managed and changed in organizations. From this approach we can conclude that strategic success requires:

1. strong and possibly visionary *leadership* to ensure (a) the organization has a clear direction, (b) supported by appropriate, feasible and desirable strategies and (c) it

is able, if necessary, to cope with the demands of discontinuous change pressures – dynamic pressures which force organizations to re-think their corporate strategies, structures and their culture and style of management;

2. a robust *planning* system to translate the corporate direction and strategy into more specific objectives and milestones for individual businesses and managers, to monitor progress and to reward performance appropriately; together with

3. the ability to *change* competitive and functional strategies in line with the demands of the competitive environment for each business. To achieve this the organization must harness the skills, knowledge and commitment of people throughout the organization and at all levels in the hierarchy.

The theme of strategic change is central to all our arguments concerning strategic success. Chart 10.1 takes the concept of E-V-R Congruence and restates the idea from the perspective of effective change management. The **environment** provides opportunities for organizations to benefit from innovation and continuous improvement;

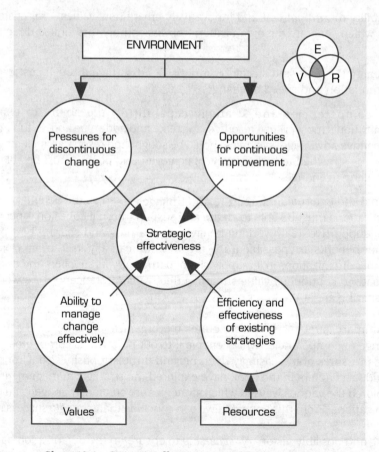

Chart 10.1   Strategic effectiveness and E-V-R Congruence

on other occasions the environment will encourage more dramatic, discontinuous change. This pressure can take the form of a threat (major environmental disturbance) or an opportunity (an ability to 'see' the future ahead of competitors). The relative strength of the organization's **resources** is reflected in the success of existing strategies; **values** dictate the ability of the organization to manage change effectively. Strategic effectiveness demands congruency.

STRATEGIC LEARNING

The relationship between an organization and its environment is based on a perpetual circular relationship:

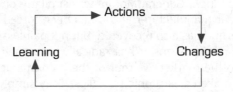

An organization will **learn** about the need to change from its observations and interpretation of events in the environment, often events created by the actions of other companies. As a result, managers decide upon the **actions** they should take; and they implement the necessary **changes**. These changes affect other organizations (competitors, suppliers, customers) in what we have termed an environment of competitive chaos. In turn, they react, and our organization is again able to **learn** about the impact and outcome of its decisions.

There is an important double-loop matching process. The organization is attempting to match its strategies with a changing environment; at the same time, it is attempting to shape and manage its environment in order to best exploit its strategic abilities and resources.

Internal and external architecture, which we have stressed throughout the book, are central to an organization's attempts to manage its environment. Externally, mutual trust and interdependencies must be built and nurtured with suppliers, distributors and customers; internally, alliances constitute an attempt to generate synergies and maximize the returns from resources. We have also discussed how powerful stakeholders – employees, suppliers and customers, for example – can, like competitors, spring surprises. There is, therefore, always the likelihood of corporate, structural or architectural chaos in addition to competitive chaos. No strategy or alliance should be seen as safe, certain and perpetual. The future of the fifteen year alliance between Rover and Honda, and still very important for both partners, was placed in turmoil when British Aerospace sold Rover to BMW in 1994. In the same way, key employees can resign, important suppliers might go out of business and major customers can change their requirements.

A fast reaction and an ability to deal with change pressures – ideally changing a threat into an opportunity – will always be required alongside proactive endeavours to shape and manage the environment.

STRATEGIC CHALLENGES

We saw earlier in the book (Box 7.3) how IBM was forced to make major strategic and structural changes. The world's leading computer company had allowed its competitors to seize the initiative. Reflecting the extent of the changes at IBM, in April 1994 the company agreed to sell the microprocessor chips at the heart of its latest mainframe computers to its leading competitor, Hitachi of Japan. IBM argued that its long-term interests would be better served by licensing its technology and exercising stronger control over the supply chain than by protracted, and, if history was to be repeated, bitter, competition. General Motors was similarly once recognized as the world's number one car manufacturer. It too has been forced on the defensive by Japanese competition, and has also recovered, but not painlessly. GM has new models and new working practices and it has radically shortened the time it takes to bring new products to the market. Neither of these companies had poor strategic leaders; they did not make catastrophic mistakes. They simply continued with the strategies that had once made them successful for a little too long. They failed to appreciate the significance of changing *at the right time*. Successful organizations must be willing to make changes while they are still successful and before major painful change becomes imperative for survival.

Key Point

10.2 Timing is essential. 'Winning' companies change proactively when they are still successful.

Effective strategic change management implies balancing the expectations of shareholders and customers with the pressures placed by competitors. Trade-offs may be required.

A CORPORATE JUGGLING ACT

The secret appears to lie in an organization structure and culture which welcomes change rather than fights it, and in understanding priorities and strategic needs. This implies a corporate juggling act, whereby the organization must succeed in dealing with three potentially conflicting influences:

- The performance requirements of **shareholders**, which, if met satisfactorily, will tend to be relatively stable and consistent. The problem occurs when their needs and expectations are not met. The survival of the business can be under threat; shareholders may be willing to sell out. They will certainly look for changes to strategies, and possibly of strategic leadership.

- The needs and expectations of **customers**, who are also targeted by

- **competitors**, who, like the organization, should be looking for new ways of adding value and creating competitive advantage.

When shareholders impose short-term financial performance demands, more speculative investments, aimed at securing long-term competitive advantage, may have to be constrained. Equally, while competitor benchmarking is essential (Chapter 3), focusing too much on what competitors are doing, and might do, can lead to defensive strategies, or a reluctance to act until competitors have been seen to be doing something similar. It is original and innovatory ideas which develop new market opportunities.

Equally it will not always be helpful to simply carry out or rely on market research into customer expectations. We are sometimes looking for radically new ideas for imaginative and different products and services which will create needs that are not recognized at the moment. Much of the innovative drive must come from within, although ideas might be obtained from a variety of external as well as internal sources. These forces are illustrated in Chart 10.2.

Strategy authors disagree on whether the essential **long-term purpose** of organizations is concerned with maximizing the returns for shareholders (the philosophy of Hanson – Box 7.1) or with meeting the needs and expectations of a range of stakeholders.

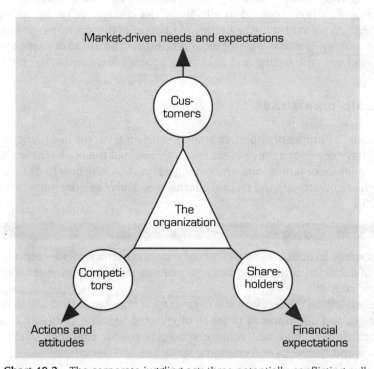

Chart 10.2   The corporate juggling act: three potentially conflicting pulls

Two things are clear:

1. shareholder expectations **must** be met, both in the short and long term;

2. this cannot be achieved without satisfying customers, which in turn needs co-operation and support from suppliers and distributors and from people inside the organization.

Neither of these can be achieved without some regard for competition.

Many would also contend that shareholder expectations *should* not be achieved at the expense of unethical or socially irresponsible behaviour.

This notion of a corporate juggling act can be used to compare and contrast the Hanson philosophy with that of Richard Branson and Virgin, a privately-owned company. Lord Hanson has said 'it is the central tenet of my faith that the shareholder is king. My aim is to advance the shareholders' interest by increasing earnings per share.' Virgin became a publicly quoted company in 1986, but Branson bought it back in 1988, arguing he felt uncomfortable with the pressures and expectations of institutional investors. Branson is renowned for being innovative and committed to customer service.

Both organizations are extremely successful. Both strategic leaders exercise centralized control over major corporate strategic changes, and both organizations are substantially decentralized. Managers in the businesses are empowered to improve competitive and functional strategies. Hanson adopts the financial control style – business unit managers operate with clear financial targets. Virgin is a more informal organization. While Hanson and Virgin have different corporate philosophies, values and cultures, they both succeed in effectively matching their resources with their environment. As we said at the beginning of Chapter 1, there is no single best way of managing strategy. The challenge for organizations is to be aware of change pressures and opportunities, and willing and able to act appropriately and at the right time.

STRATEGIC DILEMMAS

We introduced a number of important strategic challenges at the beginning of Chapter 1, and we have developed the relevant issues throughout the book. These challenges pose dilemmas for organizations, and managers must choose how to deal with them. There are no right answers and no best alternatives. The major dilemmas are restated in Table 10.1.

Key Point

10.3 Strategy in action – the process of strategic management – represents a series of decisions concerning strategy creation, strategy implementation and strategic change.

These decisions reflect how the organization chooses to deal with strategic challenges and dilemmas in order to innovate, add value, create and sustain competitive advantage and achieve synergies by, for example, establishing alliances and networks and changing strategies and structures.

Table 10.1 Strategic challenges and dilemmas

The strategic environment

- Recognizing that the past and the future may not be related directly. Continuous improvement and gradual, emergent change – while essential – may be inadequate. Discontinuous strategic change could be necessary.

Corporate objectives and strategies

- Balancing the expectations of shareholders (sometimes focused on short-term financial success) with the longer term needs of customers, while paying constant attention to competition – the corporate juggling act.
- Whether the corporate should be **diversified**, and whether this should be related (marketing or technology) or unrelated, or **focused** on either core competencies or specific products. Within this, the extent of **vertical integration** and how best to manage the whole supply chain.
- The geographic scope: from global to single continent or country. Linked to this: how to structure the organization to achieve both global presence (where relevant) and local identity in different national cultures.
- The timing of investments to stimulate growth. The dilemma of needing to invest in a recession (when current revenues do not justify spending) to be ready for expansion at the right time.
- When investing, finding the right balance between spending levels and understanding. Speculative investment in the long-term is risky because spending precedes understanding; avoiding such risks, and spending only when there is understanding, may imply inadequate investment for building a future for the organization.

Competitive strategies

- Should the products and services be targeted at the mass market or selected niches?
- Balancing the potential from differentiation (adding value for customers with special features) with the price advantages which can result from low costs – thus adding value in a different way.
- Realizing that competition will continue to come from existing rivals but also from newcomers to the industry – newcomers with fresh competitive ideas.

Structural

- Centralization (for control) versus decentralization and empowerment (which yields greater flexibility and the ability to change more quickly).
- The need to encourage businesses in a corporation to compete for scarce resources, and thus avoid slackness and complacency, while encouraging them to co-operate and achieve internal synergies.
- Related to this, co-ordinating the various activities while being able to separate them sufficiently that the corporation can discern how profitable each discrete product and business is.
- Deploying people in the most appropriate places in the organization. One could argue that people should be flexible and the strongest managers readily moved out of moribund businesses into the best growth opportunities.

Values

- The need to be both proactive and reactive simultaneously – staying up with existing competitors while looking to change the rules of competition.
- The need to act quickly in response to opportunities and threats, but not at the expense of either control or product and service quality.
- The need for large organizations to think and act like small ones.

(This is not meant to be a comprehensive list of all the challenges and dilemmas organizations might face.)

STRATEGIC CHANGE

THE CHALLENGE OF STRATEGIC CHANGE

Effective change management requires the following:

- A clear perception of need, or dissatisfaction with the existing status quo. A recognition that current strategies, however successful they might be at the moment, will be inadequate for achieving future objectives and expectations.

  Sometimes the need for change will be obvious. Reduced profits, falling market share, operating problems. On other occasions nothing will seem to be fundamentally wrong – at the moment. The challenge is one of timing, and, as we said earlier, changing while the organization is still successful. In the latter case, persuading people of the need to change will clearly be more difficult. Open communications is essential; people must be given both information and reasons.

- A way forward – a vision of a better future, a new direction or a perceived opportunity. Implicit are a clear and shared mission and environmental awareness.

- The capability to change. The necessary resources and strategies which are capable of implementation. This requires clear targets or definable 'winning posts' and suitable rewards for success.

- Commitment – change needs managing. There should be a commitment to both the continual improvement of existing strategies and to genuinely new directions. Change is ongoing.

  In this race ... you run the first four laps as fast as you can – and then you gradually increase the speed (William Weiss, CEO, Ameritech).

Key Point

10.4 As well as the ability to manage a programme of change, it is also useful for a company to develop a culture which is responsive to continuous change pressures.

Strategic change can be categorized in six levels, each level exhibiting different degrees of difficulty and complexity.

MANAGING CHANGE AND A CULTURE OF CHANGE

In Chapter 8 we looked at a number of important issues involved in attempting to change the culture of an organization. Change can be required and implemented at several levels, namely:

1. the corporate culture;
2. the organizational mission;
3. corporate strategies;
4. organization structures, systems and processes;
5. competitive strategies; and
6. operational tasks and functional strategies.

While the complexity and difficulty of the challenge increases as we ascend this hierarchy of six levels, the basic principles we discussed are relevant for every occasion.

The **management of a change programme** requires, first, that existing behaviours are *unfrozen*. People must be convinced about the need for change. Behaviours must be *changed* to a better way; and, last, these new ways must be *refrozen* and seen as normal. Championing and persistence are essential. Kurt Lewin, who introduced this description of the change process, also emphasized the importance of *force field analysis* (Lewin, 1951).

Key Point

10.5 Force field analysis is a useful framework for analysing resistance to change.

Change pressures are constant, especially at the competitive and functional strategy levels. Customers provide new opportunities and active competitors constitute an ever-present threat, for example. As we have already seen, markets represent a form of *competitive chaos*. These are our pressures – or forces – for change. The survival and economic prosperity of the business demands that they are dealt with.

People driving the changes will encounter *resistance* in the form of countervailing pressures or forces. Crucially the reasons for the resistance are more concerned with the social implications than with the economic logic, highlighting the importance of effective management if desirable or necessary changes are to be implemented successfully. People often feel threatened by change and by the unknown; they are concerned about the possibility of losing their jobs or status. They worry about whether they will be able to cope with the new pressures the change will place on them. People have often become both comfortable with, and expert at, the existing ways. It is not unnatural that they should feel personally threatened. They are really being asked to question their existing beliefs.

Ideally the organization will seek to develop a culture where people do not feel threatened when they are constantly asked to question and challenge existing behaviours and acknowledged ways of doing things – and change them. **A culture which sees innovation and change as normal** A culture that is ideal for dealing with the competitive chaos which characterizes many industries and markets. This cannot happen without strong strategic leadership which fosters, encourages and rewards intrapreneurial and innovative contributions from managers and other employees throughout the organization.

A culture such as this will frequently be based around a working atmosphere of creativity and fun; people must enjoy doing things differently and originally, actively looking for new competitive opportunities, instead of simply copying others.

A change culture is highly desirable for many organizations but very difficult to achieve

EMPOWERMENT AND CHANGE

To sustain such a culture of change, employees must be empowered, but, as we saw in Chapter 7, not everyone is comfortable with added responsibilities and accountability. They are risk-averse, and again, resistance can be expected. It would seem inevitable that change-focused organizations will be happy to see such people leave, for, while they stay they constitute barriers to change. They actively seek to prevent changes which may be essential for the future of the business. Unfortunately many of these people are likely to be very experienced and knowledgeable; their underlying expertise is valuable. Their expertise might also be useful – at least temporarily – to a competitor, and for this reason there may be a reluctance to release them.

Empowerment cannot succeed without an appropriate reward system to support it. Financial rewards will remain important, but they are not the complete answer. People must not be rewarded simply because they are holding down a particular job or position; part of their pay must be based on their measured contribution. Outstanding performers must be rewarded for their continuing efforts, and, of course, as organizations are increasingly 'flattened', with fewer layers in the hierarchy, a series of promotions no longer provides the answer.

Organizations can benefit from developing people, building their abilities and self-confidence and then providing them with greater stimulation and challenge. Success will yield the opportunity to take on more responsibility. Initially the organization motivates them but they become increasingly self-motivated. Part of their reward package is their enhanced reputation in a successful business, together with increased informal power and influence. They develop the ability to foster and champion innovation and change – strategic changes which they *own*.

A motivation–self-motivation loop is illustrated below:

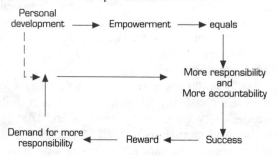

Continued personal development and training will be required to sustain the loop.

10.6 Strategic change in the turbulent 1990s often requires empowerment, which must be linked to an appropriate reward system.

Motivation ⟶ Contribution ⟶ Reward

⟶ Renewed self-motivation

Box 10.1 describes the very successful and innovatory American company Rubbermaid. While this organization will not be instantly recognizable to most readers, it has been deliberately chosen because the types of everyday product it manufactures are ubiquitous worldwide.

 RUBBERMAID

In the 1994 Fortune rankings, Rubbermaid was deemed to be America's **most admired company**. This award is based on a range of performance measures and indicators, not simply financial measures. It is both subjective and objective – managers in a number of industries are asked to evaluate other companies in their own industry.

IBM, dominant in computers for many years, was America's most admired company every year from 1982 to 1985. As we have seen IBM has been faced with the need to regenerate strategically, highlighting just how transient success can sometimes be.

Rubbermaid, based in Ohio, manufactures over 5000 different household goods, including plastic buckets, sandwich boxes, dustpans, mops and washing up brushes. All low-technology products in an industry with few entry barriers and competition from low labour cost countries.

BEHIND THE SUCCESS

* Rubbermaid introduces new products at the rate of more than one a day.
* Competition is fierce – Rubbermaid recognizes innovation to be a 'do-or-die affair'.
* The company is very strongly customer focused. Its buckets are designed to hold their shape (and not spill their contents) when completely full; laundry baskets are hip-contoured for easier carrying; food storage boxes have extra wide protrusions for easy opening.
* In addition to constant product improvements there are genuine new product ideas. Rubbermaid pioneered a step-stool with an incorporated tool box, for example.

This idea sprung from the drive to develop products for smaller households. 'The company looks for opportunities in every trend, be it fashion-led, sociological, demographic or global.'

- Rubbermaid has 20 business teams, each dedicated to a product line, and comprising people from marketing, manufacturing, finance, R & D and sales. Each team has responsibility for product developments and profitability – emphasizing the search for product improvements to improve profitability.

- Ideas are sought from 'everywhere'. Certainly employees and suppliers. One supplier provided a new type of plastic for easier-to-use ice cube trays – the cubes come out more readily; and because of the material's flexibility, the trays last longer.

  Ideas in one product area are frequently plagiarized and adapted for other products. Best practices are being shared.

- There is no formal product testing. Instead, and because speed is essential, the company uses specialist critiquing.

We don't want to be copied. It's not that much riskier to just roll it out. Plus it puts pressure on us to do it right first time.

- Rubbermaid has a target of 33 % of revenue from products introduced in the last 5 years.

- Poorly performing products are dropped almost as quickly as new ones are introduced. Constant renewal.

Innovation is ingrained in the culture. That is the one thing that is not going to change.

REFERENCE

Farnham, A. (1994) America's most admired company, *Fortune*, 7 February ■

A culture of innovation and gradual but continuous change will impact mainly on competitive and functional strategies – the lowest two levels of the hierarchy featured above. Clearly they also support corporate strategic changes which may themselves be emergent in nature or the outcome of either a visionary or a planning mode of strategy creation.

In the last section of the chapter we look further at the potential impact of *discontinuous change* pressures on organizations.

DISCONTINUOUS CHANGE AND STRATEGIC REGENERATION

We have seen how powerful environmental issues such as deregulation, globalization, lower trade barriers and economic recessions have combined in the 1990s to place enormous change pressures on companies. The individual significance of these issues will vary from year to year, but, in aggregate terms, the outcome is an increasingly turbulent and uncertain business environment for most organizations, private and public sector, manufacturing and service, large and small, profit-seeking and not-for-profit.

Companies have responded. Many have sought to manage their assets and strategic resources more efficiently and effectively – again levels (5) and (6), the lowest two levels of the change hierarchy. Some have restructured; others have radically changed their processes through business process re-engineering. This implies level (4) change. The need for innovation has been accepted.

However, continuous improvement to an organizations's *competitive* capabilities, essential as it is, will not always be sufficient to meet these pressures. Tom Peters argues that for some companies the challenge is 'not just about a *programme* of change ... strategies and structures need to change perpetually'. Peter Drucker (1993) agrees and contends that 'every organization must prepare to abandon everything it does'. Both authors are implying wholesale corporate renewal or reinvention, which we have earlier termed **strategic regeneration.**

Successful regeneration requires both an external and an internal focus. Externally organizations must search for new product, new service and new market opportunities, working with suppliers, distributors and customers to redefine markets and industries. Internally structures, management styles and cultures must be capable of creating and delivering these products and services. Innovation is dependent upon processes and people. **Strategic awareness, information management and change are critically important if the organization is to out-perform its competitors.**

The summary box, Box 10.2, describes how Rosabeth Moss Kanter (1990) sees the competitively successful organization in the 1990s.

Achieving this position may require *simultaneous* changes to corporate strategies and perspectives, organization structures and styles of management. In order to implement strategic regeneration, Goss, Pascale and Athos (1993) insist that companies must be able to change their *context* – 'the underlying assumptions and invisible premises on which their decisions and actions are based'. Their 'inner nature or being' must be altered. Managers must learn how to think strategically, and be open to new paradigms and perspectives. The requirement is that they change 'what the company is' and not simply the things it does. Companies are being challenged with changing levels (1), (2), (3) and (4) of the change hierarchy simultaneously, a huge and complex task for any organization.

10 2 COMPETITIVENESS IN THE 1990s

Competitive success lies in the **capability** to change and to accomplish key tasks by using resources more efficiently and more effectively. Organizations must be innovative and, at the same time, control their costs. Sustainable competitive advantage, however, does not come from either low costs, or differentiation, or innovation alone. It needs the **whole organization** to be *focused, fast, flexible and friendly* (Kanter, 1990).

Being **focused** requires investment in core skills and competencies, together with a search for new opportunities for applying the skills. Intrapreneurship should be fostered to constantly improve the skills; and managers throughout the organization should be strategically aware and innovative. They should own the organization's mission, which, by necessity, must be communicated widely and understood.

Fast companies move at the right time, and are not caught out by competitors. New ideas and opportunities from the environment will be seized first. Ideally they will be innovating constantly to open up and sustain a competitive gap, because gradual improvements are likely to be more popular with customers than are radical changes. But 'instant success takes time' – the organization culture must be appropriate.

Flexibility concerns the search for continual improvement. The implication is a 'learning organization' where ideas are shared and collaboration between functions and divisions generates internal synergy. This, in turn, suggests that performance and effectiveness measures – and rewards – concentrate on outcomes.

Internal synergy can be achieved with cross-functional teams and special projects, and by moving people around the organization in order to spread the best practices. It is important that internal constraints (imposed by other functions and divisions) and which restrain performance are highlighted and confronted. To be effective this requires a clear and shared vision and purpose for the organization, decentralization and empowerment.

Friendly organizations are closely linked to their suppliers and customers to generate synergy through the added value chain. Such external collaboration may be in the form of strategic alliances.

REFERENCE

Kanter, R. M. (1990) Honouring the business experts, *Economist* conference, London, March ■

High-street banks, for example, have been forced to adopt a new paradigm. They have recognized that they are not simply a home for secure savings and current accounts, but diversified financial services institutions. The changes – visible to all of us who are bank customers – have clearly involved strategies, structure and culture, and they have proved painful. Jobs have changed dramatically and there are fewer of them.

Incremental change at the competitive and functional level, trying harder and searching for improvements, must appear to offer an easier, less painful route. The fundamental question is: alone, is it enough to meet the strategic demands of the contemporary business environment?

Some of the international companies featured in this book have clearly attempted to tackle these important challenges. British Airways realized in the 1980s that, contrary to much popular opinion at the time, airline customers are willing to pay extra for service. The challenge lies in defining that service and differentiating successfully. BA has consequently changed its strategies, structure and culture and become one of the most profitable airlines in the world.

General Electric of the US is another example. The regeneration philosophy and programme at GE is described in Box 10.3.

---

10 3 STRATEGIC REGENERATION AT GENERAL ELECTRIC

John F. (Jack) Welch became Chief Executive Officer at General Electric (GE) in 1981. His structural vision was summarized earlier, in Box 5.1. This caselet describes 'one of the most far reaching programmes of innovation in business history'.

The programme involves three stages:

(1)	Awakening	the realization of the need for change
(2)	Envisioning	establishing a new vision and harnessing resources
(3)	Re-architecting	the design and construction of a new organization.

- Although Welch is the identified strategic leader, several committed senior managers worked together to drive through the cultural changes.

- GE has been restructured, and clear progress has been made ... but the process of change continues. The implementation of the programme is not yet complete.

GE IN THE EARLY 1980s – THE NEED FOR CHANGE

The company had sound assets, reflected in a strong balance sheet, but it was seen as bureaucratic and heavily focused on America. It was not 'technologically advanced' and it clearly needed a more international perspective.

Specific problems were diagnosed:

- Revenue growth was slow. GE's core business (electrical equipment) was particularly slow.
- As a result, expensive investments were creating cash flow problems.
- Poor productivity was causing low profit margins.
- Innovation was limited.
- Decision-making was slow.
- Negative internal politics was rife.

AWAKENING

Welch realized his first challenge was to determine which managers offered the greatest potential as 'transformational leaders', agents of discontinuous change.

He then sought to clarify and articulate the extent of the need for change, focusing on the above weaknesses. Resistance took three forms:

- Technical   a reliance on existing bureaucratic systems and a fear of the unknown; a distrust of international expansion
- Political   a desire to protect existing power bases, especially where the strategic value of the particular business was declining
- Cultural   an unwillingness to accept competitive weaknesses – over-confidence from past successes.

CHANGES

- Welch forced people to benchmark competitors' performance standards and achievements, rather than rely only on internal measures and budgets.
- He also took control of external corporate communications and
- radically changed GE's approach to management training and development. Rigid rules and procedures about how things should be done were abolished.

ENVISIONING

A new vision was developed gradually during the mid-late 1980s, and it finally became encapsulated in a matrix. Highlights of the new vision are featured in Table 10.2.

Table 10.2 Highlights of GE's corporate vision

	Strategy	*Structure*	*Management style*
Technical	Focus on market (segments) where the company can be no. 1 or no. 2	Decentralized Foster the sharing of best practices	Different reward systems for different businesses, dependent on needs
	Prioritize high growth industries	Pull down internal boundaries	Continuous training and development
Political	Foster internal and external alliances to harness synergy potential	Flatter, open structure to remove power bases Cross-function and cross-business development teams Empowerment to the lowest levels of management	Flexible reward systems '360 degree evaluations' from superiors, peers and subordinates
Cultural	Speedy change to strategies Intrapreneurial innovative incremental and adaptive change (as a result of) Learning from upward, downward and lateral communications	Corporate values but individual business cultures and styles	Track attitudes and values Commitment to customers and quality – and out-performing competitors

Welch saw the technical, political and cultural systems as three strands of a rope which must be changed and re-aligned together.

RE-ARCHITECTING

At the heart of the vision is an 'organization without boundaries' and with an emphasis on internal and external linkages and architecture. Information must flow freely. People must be in a position – and willing – to act quickly. 'A large organization with the speed, flexibility and self-confidence of a small one.'

A number of boundaries had to be removed as part of the implementation process:

1. Vertical/hierarchical. Management layers were removed. Welch introduced performance incentives for many more managers and employees; in the past GE had focused on only senior executives.

2. Horizontal/internal walls. Cross-functional project teams were created.

3. External. There was a new emphasis on the whole supply or added value chain; alliances were forged with suppliers; customer satisfaction levels were tracked.

Removing these boundaries clearly required radical changes to the ways in which people worked together, made decisions and carried out tasks. Welch believed the changes must be inspired from the top and that any senior managers who resisted the new style 'would have to go'.

SOURCE

Adapted from Tichy, N. M. (1993) Revolutionize your company, *Fortune*, 13 December ■

The changes at BA have proved successful, but they are not yet complete. The alliances described in Box 6.1, in particular the strategic investment in US Air, have yet to become as profitable as the core business. General Electric has successfully reduced waste and improved efficiencies and competitive strategies. The first step of basically maintaining output levels while reducing assets (thus improving return on capital employed) has been achieved; the future challenge lies in regenerating the company and creating new growth from the reduced size. This subtle change of emphasis requires new values. The culture becomes one of challenging at the frontiers of technology and competition – discontinuous changes to create new futures ahead of competitors. It is different from a culture of benchmarking, productivity gains, process re-engineering and continuous improvement.

Hamel (1994) contends strategic regeneration needs vision and perseverance. Companies must invest resources in an attempt to set the new 'competitive high ground' first by changing the key success factors. This inevitably implies time and risk, and it must be a managed and understood process. Speculative investment in the long-term must be risky because *spending precedes understanding*; companies are heading into unknown territory. However, companies which choose to avoid the risk, and rely instead on monitoring and copying competitors (such that *understanding precedes spending*) may be caught out.

10.7 Strategic regeneration implies simultaneous changes to strategies, structures and styles of management.

It is obviously a major challenge for any organization, but for some it is important for survival. Continuous, gradual, emergent change may be inadequate for the discontinuous change pressures they face.

THE FUTURE

Three days later Bob Langley reviewed the presentation at Benson's. He remembered Tony Anderson's words of caution about the implementation of acquisitions, but he was impressed with the ideas from David Marshall and the two Benson managers – Mike Jordan (production) and Simon Green (sales). He thought that both Simon and Mike seemed to be bright, knowledgeable, positive, energetic and willing to embrace the changes that were required. All the right qualities for the 1990s. Additionally they had both been courageous enough to argue with Bob Langley when he disagreed with them!

Bob mused that it was going to be easier to carry through the necessary strategic and structural changes at Benson Engineering than it was at Special Components, where the need for substantial changes had become increasingly apparent in the last few weeks.

CHANGING FORTUNES

Special Components had agreed their strategic performance targets and annual budget with Universal Engineering head office early in September. The new targets built on the company's recent record of success. However, they were below target after just one month.

Increased competitor activity in a static market was putting pressure on their prices; sales targets were still being achieved, but the financial returns on these sales, and in turn their profitability, was disappointing. It had all happened very quickly. Bob, David and Susan Scott in sales had all failed to anticipate the compound effect of a single competitor starting to offer much bigger discounts. Other rivals had followed – too quickly and without thinking it through properly, in Bob's opinion.

Two new products were close to the launch stage. Bob knew they were genuinely differentiated from those they would replace, and provisional customer trials confirmed they were perceived to be offering extra value. The extent and value of any competitive lead was unknown.

Special Components' competitor intelligence was not very good in this respect. The new products might help restore the company's fortunes; on the other hand they might simply prevent Special Components falling backwards in the competitive race. In this case something *really* new and different would be needed. Bob's divisional general manager was already commenting that if profits continued to fall, Special Components would have to find further cost reductions. Management-level redundancies could not be ruled out.

Benson Engineering, meanwhile, was ahead of target. Simon Green had contacted all their major customers and obtained a variety of commitments – as long as they improved and maintained their quality and service. By actively involving supervisors and production operatives, Mike Jordan was already proving that substantial improvements were realistic. The changes at Benson's had been partially facilitated by a number of the longest serving employees accepting an early retirement package. Some of their skills would be missed, but at the same time, several of them were seen as change-resistant. Simon and Mike had also been working closely with David to produce a number of ideas for possible new products and markets.

Bob knew from past experience, though, that cutting back and rationalizing an organization in difficulty is more straightforward than rebuilding the smaller company. The initial successes achieved by Simon and Mike made Bob feel optimistic, but he realized he must not become complacent about Benson's – the biggest challenges lay ahead.

STRUCTURAL CHANGES

Susan Scott, the sales manager at Special Components, was leaving. She was going to Special Components in America to work with Ed Grey and broaden her experience. Bob knew this provided him with an excellent restructuring opportunity. He would not replace her.

Special Components and Benson Engineering had to learn to think and behave as a single company. Their products were complementary and could easily be produced alongside each other on a single site. Special Components was the larger of the two sites, but at the moment the plant is fully occupied. An extension is possible if Universal Engineering agrees to the investment. Keeping the companies separate, though, is not necessarily a disadvantage, at least for the moment. Their technologies and investment needs are different; and the problems of fusing two culturally different workforces are postponed.

Finance and personnel had already been integrated; sales and marketing could also be pulled together quite easily. This would have to be followed up by improved communications between the two sites to encourage sharing and teamworking. Bob decided to put Simon Green in charge of sales for both companies – and move him over to Special Components. David Marshall would be responsible for all marketing and new product development. Bob decided to promote Mike Jordan to a new post as site manager for Benson's, in charge of all activity in the plant. Mike would report directly to Bob, and he would run Benson's with a flat organization structure. There would be no other middle or senior managers working on the site.

Bob realized that there was likely to be concern about additional changes at Special Components, especially in production, where there was clearly some complacency and a real fear of the unknown. But the change pressures could not be resisted. Bob was worried that Roger Ellis would actively fight the need to cut costs further, improve efficiency and provide an all-round better service to their customers. He is very set in his ways – and, to be fair to him, he is already seen as an efficient manager. If Bob's fear turned out to be true, Roger would unfortunately have to go, possibly providing an opportunity to fully integrate the operations of the two companies.

Bob remembered that David Marshall had been attempting to streamline their overseas distribution network when he inadvertently upset one of their agents. This project was currently on hold. David would have to pick it up again; there was a real opportunity to save costs and improve returns in this critical area.

BOB LANGLEY'S DILEMMA

From his discussions with David Marshall, and particularly with Tony Anderson, Bob Langley knew what he had to do. Strategic and structural changes were needed, and he was reasonably confident about the way forward. However speed was essential, and Special Components may not be able to change quickly enough. Critically his own style of management would have to change. He would have to provide clear, and ideally inspirational, leadership – and deliver the results head office demanded. If he failed, he too would almost certainly become a casualty. Moreover he would have to achieve this with fewer managers and employees. His new management team would need to trust and support each other; negative political activity must be curtailed. Personally he needed to develop a more open style of management. He knew he was not seen as a good sharer; instead, his managers tended to see him as a boss who 'played things close to his chest', telling them only what he felt they needed to know.

The more Bob Langley thought about the scale of the challenge, the more he began to doubt his own abilities. Did he really have the courage, energy and judgment that was required? Could he encourage the management team to achieve and sustain the high levels of competitive performance that would be required? Was he still the right strategy maker to lead Special Components?

The choice, motivation and direction of management is crucial. Leaders should not be slow constantly to encourage change. They should see all problems as solvable and all questions as answerable (Lord Hanson, Chairman, Hanson plc).

ANOTHER CHANGE PRESSURE

As Bob reflected on the future he needed to create, David Marshall and Roger Ellis arrived with some startling news.

A small chemical company adjacent to Clark Precision Engineering had caught fire overnight. The flames spread quickly and Tom Clark's factory had been destroyed. There were no casualties, but there would be no sub-contract machining work for several months. For the immediate future, Special Components in America could probably increase production and ship to Europe – but it would be expensive. Beyond this what should they do? And who was going to ring Dieter Wild?

POINTS FOR REFLECTION

- Returning to the first Reflection Point in Chapter 1, can you add any more important strategic challenges facing your organization? How well do you believe your organization deals with strategic dilemmas and challenges?

- How well do you think your organization succeeds in juggling shareholders, customers and competitors?

- Evaluate the effectiveness of the way in which you managed an identifiable strategic change.

- How significant – current and future – are any discontinuous change pressures for your organization? Would you see the organization as strategically regenerative?

- Having thought about strategic management in some depth, what are you, as a strategy maker, going to do differently in the future?

REFERENCES AND FURTHER READING

Drucker, P.F. (1993) *Managing in Turbulent Times*, Butterworth Heinemann.
Goss, T., Pascale, R. and Athos, A. (1993) The reinvention roller coaster: risking the present for a powerful future, *Harvard Business Review*, November–December.

Hamel, G. (1994) *Competing for the Future*, *Economist* Conference, London (June).

Hampden-Turner, C. (1990) *Charting the Corporate Mind: From Dilemma to Strategy*, Blackwell. A valuable discussion of strategic dilemmas.

Kanter, R. M. (1983) *The Change Masters*, and Kanter, R. M. (1989) *When Giants Learn to Dance*, both published by Simon & Schuster, are excellent texts on the challenges of change in modern business environments.

Kanter, R.M. (1990) *Honouring the Business Experts, Economist* conference, London (March).

Lewin, K. (1951) *Field Theory in Social Sciences*, Harper & Row.

Peters, T. (1992) *Liberation Management – Necessary Disorganization for the Nanosecond Nineties*, Macmillan.

A SUMMARY OF THE STRATEGIC LESSONS

In this final chapter we have drawn together the essential themes upon which the whole book has been based. We first highlighted that organizations which aim to be successful in the turbulent and competitive 1990s must address five critical issues: adding value, core competencies and strategic capabilities; architecture, linkages and synergy; competitive advantage and innovation; and possibly strategic regeneration.

We also recapped how strategic success requires leadership, planning and an ability to manage change, together with an ability to manage the various strategic dilemmas faced by the organization.

The timing of change is essential. Companies which enjoy long-term strategic success change proactively while they are still successful. If they wait too long they will be forced on to the defensive.

Not only must companies be able to manage a programme of change, they should look to develop a culture which is responsive to perpetual change pressures.

Strategic change implies a corporate juggling act. The expectations of shareholders and customers must be considered alongside the pressures placed by competitors. Trade-offs may be required.

Strategic change can be categorized in six layers:

- corporate culture;
- organizational mission;
- corporate strategies;
- structure, systems and processes;
- competitive strategies;
- functional strategies.

These six layers can be seen as a hierarchy of complexity. Competitive and functional strategies can be changed far more easily than the corporate culture, for example.

It is useful to examine the forces for and against change. Resistance can always be expected.

A culture of change requires empowerment; this in turn must be linked to an appropriate reward system.

Some organizations are faced with powerful, discontinuous change pressures. Gradual, emergent change will be inadequate. They need to change strategies, structures and styles of management simultaneously. This constitutes a major challenge which few organizations will truly relish.

GLOSSARY

Acquisition The purchase of one company by another, either for cash or equity in the parent. Sometimes the word *takeover* is preferred when the acquisition is hostile, and resisted by the company being bought. Similarly *mergers* are when two companies simply *agree* to come together as one.

Adaptive strategic change Strategies which emerge and develop on an on-going basis as companies learn of new environmental opportunities and threats and adapt (or respond) to competitive pressures.

Adding value Technically the difference between the value of a firm's outputs and its inputs; the additional value is added through the deployment and effort of the organization's resources. Successful organizations will seek to add value to create outputs which are perceived as important by their customers. The *added value or supply chain* is the sequential set of activities from suppliers, through manufacturers and distributors which is required to bring products and services to the marketplace.

Alliance (strategic alliance) An agreement, preferably formalized, with another organization. The alliance might be with an important supplier, with a major distributor, or possibly with a competitor, say for joint research and development.

Architecture A relational network involving either or both external linkages (see strategic alliance) or internal linkages between managers in a company or businesses in a conglomerate. The supply chain is one such network. The main benefits concern information exchanges for the mutual gain of those involved, and synergies (see below) from interdependencies.

Benchmarking A process of comparative evaluation – of products, services and the performances of equipment and personnel. Sometimes companies attempt to benchmark their competitors; on other occasions they will benchmark those organizations which are seen as high performers.

Business process re-engineering The analysis and re-design of workflows and processes within organizations and between them (i.e. along the supply chain).

Competitive advantage The ability of an organization to add more value for its customers than its rivals, and thus attain a position of relative advantage. The challenge is to sustain any advantage once achieved.

Competitive strategy The means by which organizations seek to achieve and sustain competitive advantage. Usually the result of distinctive *functional strategies*. There should be a competitive strategy for every product and service produced by the company.

Core competency Distinctive skill, normally related to a product, service or technology, which can be used to create a competitive advantage. See also *strategic capability*.

Corporate strategy The overall strategy for a diversified or multi-product/multiservice organization. Refers to the overall scope of the business in terms of products, services and geography.

Cost leadership The lowest cost producer in a market – after adjustments for quality differences. An important source of competitive advantage in either a market or a segment of a market. Specifically the cost leader is the company which enjoys a cost advantage over its rivals through the management of its resources, and not because it produces the lowest quality.

Culture The values and norms of an organization, which determine its corporate behaviour and the behaviour of people within the organization.

Decentralization/centralization The extent to which authority, responsibility and accountability is devolved throughout the organization. Centralization should yield tight control; decentralization motivates managers and allows for speedier reactions to environmental change pressures.

Differentiation Products and services are differentiated when customers perceive them to have distinctive properties which set them apart from their competitors.

Directional policy matrix A planning technique used to compare and contrast the relative competitive strengths of a portfolio of products and services produced by an organization. Used to help evaluate their relative worth and investment potential.

Diversification The extent of the differences between the various products and services in a company's portfolio (its range of activities). The products and services may be related through say marketing or technology, or *unrelated*, which normally implies they require different management skills.

Divisionalization A form of organization structure whereby activities are divided and separated on the basis of different products or services, or geographic territories.

Effectiveness The ability of an organization to meet the demands and expectations of its various stakeholders, those individuals or groups with influence over the business. Sometimes known as 'doing the right things'.

Efficiency The sound management of resources to maximize the returns from them. Known as 'doing things right'.

Empowerment Freeing people from a rigid regime of rules, controls and directives and allowing them to take responsibility for their own decisions and actions.

Entrepreneurial/visionary strategies Strategies created by strong, visionary strategic leaders. Their successful implementation relies on an ability to persuade others of their merit.

E-V-R Congruence The effective matching of an organization's resources (R) with the demands of its environment (E). A successful and sustained match has to be managed and frequently requires change; successfully achieving this depends on the organization's culture and values (V).

Financial control The term used to describe the form of control normally found in a holding company structure (see below). Strategy creation is decentralized to independent business units which are required to meet agreed financial targets.

Focus strategy Concentration on one or a limited number of market segments or niches.

Functional strategies The strategies for the various functions carried out by an organization, including marketing, production, financial management, information management, research and development, human resource management. One or more functional strategies will typically be responsible for any distinctive competitive edge the company enjoys.

Governance The location of power and responsibility at the head of an organization.

Holding company A structure where the various businesses are seen as largely independent of each other and managed accordingly.

Horizontal integration The acquisition or merger of firms at the same stage in the supply chain. Such firms may be direct competitors or focus on different market segments.

Incremental strategic change Changes to intended (possibly planned) strategies as they are implemented. Results from on-going learning and from changes in the environment or to forecast assumptions.

Innovation Changes to products, processes and services in an attempt to sharpen their competitiveness – through either cost reduction or improved distinctiveness. Strategically it can apply to any part of a business.

Joint venture A form of strategic alliance where each partner takes a financial stake. This could be a shareholding in the other partner or the establishment of a separate, jointly-owned, business.

Key (or critical) success factors Environmentally based factors which are crucial for competitive success. Simply the things an organization must be able to do well if it is to succeed.

Learning organization One which is capable of harnessing and spreading best practices, and where employees can learn from each other and from other organizations. The secret lies in open and effective communications networks.

Market entry strategies The various means by which an organization might implement its chosen strategies.

Market segment(ation) The use of particular marketing strategies to target identified and defined groups of customers.

Matrix organization A multi-divisional organization which seeks to link the various functional activities across the divisions – to achieve the synergy benefits of interdependency.

Mission statement A summary of the essential aim or purpose of the organization; its essential reason for being in business.

Objective A short-term target or milestone with defined measurable achievements. A desired state and hoped-for level of success.

Organization politics The process by which individuals and groups utilize power and influence to obtain results. Politics can be used legitimately in the best interests of the organization, or illegitimately by people who put their own interests above those of the organization.

Performance measures/indicators Quantifiable measures and subjective indicators of strategic and competitive success.

PEST analysis An analysis of the political, economic, social and technological factors in the external environment of an organization – which can affect its activities and performance.

Planning gap A planning technique which enables organizations to evaluate the potential for, and risk involved in, seeking to attain particular growth targets.

Policies Guidelines relating to decisions and approaches which support organizational efforts to achieve stated objectives. They are basically guides to thoughts (about how things should be done) and actions.

Portfolio planning Techniques for evaluating the appropriate strategies for a range of (possibly diverse) business activities in a single organization. See *directional policy matrix*.

Power The potential or ability to do something or make something happen. Externally it refers to the ability of an organization to influence and affect the actions of its external stakeholders. Internally it concerns the relationships between people.

Quality Strategically quality is concerned with the ability of an organization to 'do things right – first time and every time' for each customer. This includes internal customers (other departments in an organization) as well as external customers. *Total quality management* is the spreading of quality consciousness throughout the whole organization.

Stakeholder Any individual or group capable of affecting (and being affected by) the actions and performance of an organization.

Strategy The means by which organizations achieve (and seek to achieve) their objectives and purpose. There can be a strategy for each product and service, and for the organization as a whole.

Strategic business unit A discrete grouping within an organization with delegated responsibility for strategically managing a product, a service, or a particular group of products or services.

Strategic capability Process skills used to add value and create competitive advantage.

Strategic change Changes which take place over time to the strategies and objectives of the organization. Change can be gradual, emergent and evolutionary, or discontinuous, dramatic and revolutionary.

Strategic control A style of corporate control whereby the organization attempts to enjoy the benefits of delegation and decentralization with a portfolio of activities which, while diverse, is interdependent and capable of yielding synergies from co-operation.

Strategic issues Current and forthcoming developments inside and outside the organization which will impact upon the ability of the organization to pursue its mission and achieve its objectives.

Strategic leader Generic term used to describe those managers who are responsible for changes in the corporate strategy.

Strategic life cycle The notion that strategies (like products and services) have finite lives. After some period of time they will need improving, changing or replacing.

Strategic management The process by which an organization establishes its objectives, formulates actions (strategies) designed to meet these objectives in the desired timescale, implements the actions and assesses progress and results.

Strategic planning *In strategy creation*: the systematic and formal creation of strategies – to be found in many organizations, and capable of making a very significant contribution in large, multi-activity organizations.
As a term used in strategic control: centralized control, most ideal where there is a limited range of core businesses.

Strategic regeneration (or renewal) Major and simultaneous changes to strategies, structures and styles of management.

Stretching resources The creative use of resources to add extra value for customers – through innovation and improved productivity.

SWOT analysis An analysis of an organization's strengths and weaknesses alongside the opportunities and threats present in the external environment.

Synergy The term used for the added value or additional benefits which ideally accrue from the linkage or fusion of two businesses, or from increased co-operation between either different parts of the same organization or between a company and its suppliers, distributors and customers. Internal co-operation may represent linkages between either different divisions or different functions.

Turnaround strategy An attempt to find a new competitive position for a company in difficulty.

Vertical integration Where firms directly enter those parts of the added value chain served by their suppliers or distributors, the term used is vertical integration. To achieve the potential benefits of vertical integration (specifically synergy from co-operation) without acquiring a business which normally requires specialist and different skills firms will look to establish strong alliances and networks.

A SUMMARY OF THE MAJOR TOPICS COVERED IN THE SPECIAL COMPONENTS THEME CASE

CHAPTER 1 (PAGES 1–5)

Bob Langley, the Managing Director of Special Components, informs his managers that a small competitor, Benson Engineering, is being acquired, constituting an unplanned change of corporate strategy for the company. He begins to look ahead at the implementation challenges and seconds his marketing manager, David Marshall, part-time to the project. We also see how the competitor, a once successful family company, has suffered with weak management and ineffective succession.

CHAPTER 2 (PAGES 23–7)

The corporate strategy change is taken further as David Marshall puts together a presentation for the managers at Benson Engineering. Prompted by Bob Langley he enlists the help of a consultant friend, Tony Anderson.

The second major theme in the case study is introduced: there is a quality problem with a new product being supplied to an important customer in Germany. Poor functional strategies have led to a weak competitive strategy and customer dissatisfaction, a second strategic challenge for Marshall.

The chapter also covers:

- environment–values–resources (E–V–R Congruence) as a simple framework for understanding strategy;

- the relationship between corporate head office and subsidiary businesses. Special Components is part of a large conglomerate;

- the **content** of effective strategies for the 1990s. The critical themes of adding value, core competencies and strategic capabilities, architecture and synergy, competitive advantage and strategic regeneration are introduced.

CHAPTER 3 (PAGES 45–7)

An internal meeting of Special Components' managers covers internal architecture and team building, and highlights different and conflicting perspectives and priorities.

CHAPTER 4 (PAGES 65–6)

The analogy of a professional football match is used to explain three important **processes** in strategy formulation and strategic change, namely visionary leadership, planning and emergent (adaptive and incremental) change.

CHAPTER 5 (PAGES 89–91)

David Marshall visits a critically important subcontractor and we see illustrations of effective strategic leadership, core competencies and strategic capabilities, external architecture and supply chain management. A strategic focus strategy, together with the peripheral issue of management buy-outs, is discussed briefly.

CHAPTER 6 (PAGES 111–16 AND 117–18)

A presentation by David Marshall to the Benson managers is used as a vehicle to describe a typical strategic planning framework. The contribution of such systems and their limitations are also considered, together with portfolio analyses for multi-product businesses. Bob Langley concludes the meeting by summarizing the issues involved if the two businesses are to be merged effectively.

CHAPTER 7 (PAGES 131–3)

A second meeting with David's consultant friend Tony Anderson introduces a number of new and important topics:

- empowerment;
- learning and sharing knowledge and best practice, linked to adaptive and incremental strategic change; learning organizations;
- business process re-engineering.

CHAPTER 8 (PAGES 157–9)

David visits their customer in Germany. Adding value issues are reinforced and we look in detail at the relationship between organizations linked in the supply chain.

The discussion also provides an opportunity to introduce the important topic of corporate culture.

The competitive strategy problem is brought to a satisfactory resolution.

CHAPTER 9 (PAGES 177–9)

The case introduces us to aspects of organization structures, alternative styles of corporate control and the role and contribution of corporate head offices. Centralization and decentralization are also featured.

CHAPTER 10 (PAGES 199–202 AND 221–4)

The case is in two parts in this final chapter.

Initially, Tony Anderson draws attention to important general issues in strategy implementation and, more specifically, the potential pitfalls when two businesses are merged. Strategy **content** issues are reviewed and strategic regeneration introduced.

Finally, Bob Langley reflects upon the strategic and structural issues involved in the corporate strategy change. The competitive situation has been changing in a dynamic and turbulent environment; new surprises and problems have emerged. Langley considers the future challenges faced by both himself and Special Components.

INDEX